TO MY FAMILY, MENTORS, AND CREATIVE MINDS THAT MADE THE FOLLOWING WORK POSSIBLE

EZRA PETRONIO
VISUAL & IMAGE THINKING & IMAGE MAKING

Φ

8 FOREWORD by Charlotte Cotton

12 SELECTED WORKS PART I

112 THE CHLOÉ SAGA

136 ON VISUAL THINKING
An interview by Charlotte Cotton

144 BEHIND THE LENS

184 THE JUXTAPOSED

216 SELECTED WORKS PART II

308 SELECTED WORDS

320 SELF SERVICE MAGAZINE

384 ON INDEPENDENT PUBLISHING
A conversation with Jefferson Hack

387 ON IMAGE-MAKING
A conversation with David Sims, Jane How,
and Lana Petrusevych

388 ON THE EARLY DAYS
A conversation with Suzanne Koller

390 INITIATED DIALOGS

404 THE UNEDITED

410 VISUAL BIOGRAPHY

SCAN THE ABOVE QR CODE WHENEVER YOU SEE IT
THROUGHOUT THE BOOK TO ACCESS ADDITIONAL CONTENT.

A Shared Journey.
Great image-making and art direction are about embracing the idea that the finality is the sum of many parts—the perfect juxtaposition and blending of various ingredients and talents. Whether it be an advertising campaign or an overall branding, the end result is always a reflection of true collaborative magic by a unique group of creative and strategic minds.

This book gives you an insight into my aesthetics and creative world as well as the diversity of projects and variety of mediums I have been inspired to develop and accomplish over the years. The inception of this book was very much about my desire of transmission—the values, principles, practices, and mindset of art direction in its truest and original form. It also attempts to encapsulate in a personal and subjectively assembled manner the creative journey I have had the privilege to undertake over the last three decades.

In my case, I have never exercised my various crafts of art direction, publishing, photography, and graphic, typographic, and product design in a solitary manner but always as a shared and collaborative process and journey. Today, my creative partner Lana Petrusevych, with whom I have edited this book, and I continue to engage and challenge our constantly evolving industry and cultural landscape. With Suzanne Koller, my previous partner, I cofounded my first agency, Work in Progress, and Self Service magazine in the early 1990s. My collaborative process has involved the talented and devoted people who have worked for me; the designers, C.E.O.s, and others I have worked for; and the photographers, directors, stylists, models, artists, musicians, and other creative minds I have worked with. When I look back at all these years, what inspires me is the memory of the incredible, collective, soulful spirit of passion and creative drive that I have encountered in the making of the work presented here. When we have the immense chance of working in a creative, artistic, and journalistic industry, when we have the incredible luxury to question and challenge, when we have the possibility to exercise what we do in a more meaningful manner, then it becomes our prerogative to live up to this privilege. It becomes fundamental to rid ourselves of comfort zones, to make mistakes, to find meaning in what we do—continuously challenging ourselves and conventions with the aim of maintaining creative integrity and independence in the face of conformity. When there is nothing to lose, there is often freedom and the ability to create and engage without compromising our integrity or identity. With inspiring resilience, courage, and a touch of rooted defiance, we can hopefully ignite disruption! —Ezra Petronio

FOREWORD BY CHARLOTTE COTTON

Ezra Petronio's astounding capacities as tastemaker, interlocutor, and collaborator in the realms of fashion and image cultures are grounded within an unrepeatable, almost 30-year creative journey. *Visual Thinking & Image-Making* is a unique, dazzling, surprising, and multivalent capturing of the simultaneous creative paths that Petronio has taken since setting in motion the reshaping and reanimation of contemporary culture in Paris in the early 1990s. He has been a continually heralded, keenly observed pathfinder within three creative professions. Firstly, he is an art director and designer who has orchestrated the visual languages of fashion and beauty brands, from overall branding and a silhouette of perfume bottles through to trailblazing 360 ad campaigns. Secondly, Petronio's Polaroid portraits have documented and honored a critical mass of global artists in the fields of film, fashion, art, music, and literature, and made him a preeminent photographic chronicler of artistic culture. Thirdly, Petronio is perhaps most renowned for his roles of editor-in-chief and publisher of the ultimate fashion reference magazine, *Self Service*, which has been, for nearly 30 years, a biannual compendium of the best original ideas of the moment and the prescient cultural actions that move creative industry forward.

Pivoted on the extent and range of Petronio's vision and craft, *Visual Thinking & Image-Making* maps both a personal journey and an epic story of the evolution of the creative industries and image-making arenas since the 1990s. Graphic and product design, typography, creative direction, editorship, photography, film direction, and art direction stand out as the foundational tools for the expansive, image-led creativity that Petronio has practiced. His trajectories have their roots in a pre-desktop-publishing, analog world and crescendo through to the ingenious possibilities he finds in the new digital tools and platforms today. Petronio has created far-reaching and influential digital proposals, made at his agency Content Matters with his creative partner Lana Petrusevych, which provide distinct vantage points onto the cultural and aesthetic landscape of digital space. Petronio's conceptual rigor across the platforms that host advertising as well as editorial and visual communication—including motion graphics, augmented reality, and new degrees of consumer interactivity—is testimony to his understanding of the digital world as a realm of entirely new "canvases" upon which to work, but where he continues to insist on the possibilities to design with intentional specificity.

A fundamental premise and enduring character of Petronio's indelible work are its continued celebration and support of independent experimentation and exploration. One of Petronio's aesthetic signatures is being an interlocutor of culture who designs and orchestrates remarkable situations for visual thinking and image-making. From this basis, his epic creative journey has unfolded. We see this across the board, from the film versions of *Self Service* published during the recent pandemic to the longstanding creative partnerships that Petronio has developed over the course of his creative life. Through his creative collaborations, many of Petronio's remarkable contributions to visual communication have been made. His cohorts within fashion have included virtuoso designers such as Miuccia Prada, Rei Kawakubo, Jil Sander, Phoebe Philo, Karl Lagerfeld, Alessandro Michele, Anthony Vaccarello, and Pieter Mulier, among others. Through their collaborations with Petronio, the exquisite visions of image-makers—including Inez & Vinoodh, Juergen Teller, Glen Luchford, Mert and Marcus, and David Sims—and the unique energies of stylists such as Joe McKenna, Jane How, and Melanie Ward, among others, are given generous and impeccable spaces and contexts, and their capacities to bring their intuition and instinct for the direction of artistic intention are respected and given care. Petronio's Polaroid portraits speak to the even wider circles of creative minds he has encountered and form his curated archive—and a pantheon—of the critical mass of cultural transformers who work and labor and, like Petronio, commit to bringing as much of themselves as they can into everything they do.

Petronio's collaborative practices resist institutionalism or the conventions of outmoded hierarchies and are—deliberately—ways of framing new expressions that provide freedom of experimentation for established and emerging artists alike. This has been continuously

BY CHARLOTTE COTTON

evident in the pages of the outstanding *Self Service* magazine, cofounded by Petronio with Suzanne Koller in Paris in 1994, and first published the following year. In 1992, Koller and Petronio had started their first creative agency, Work in Progress, in the basement of his parents' home, the same year that Olivier Zahm had started *Purple Prose* magazine, and Mathias Augustyniak & Michael Amzalag had started their art and design partnership M/M (Paris). *Self Service* magazine came into being in the context of wider conversations about independent magazine publishing, and as part of the dialog within the constellation of innovative regional and international brilliance that was on the verge of reshaping the tenets of visual thinking, design, and the cultural industry in Paris. This was a determined generation of innovators whose ambition and flare counterpointed the wholesale disinterest of the French mainstream media and the cultural establishment in the new cultural proposals that were so dynamically being pushed out into the world by the radical creators, including Petronio, in 1990s Paris.

Petronio's unique methodology as a magazine editor-in-chief and creative director who creates a context for pioneering and unfiltered creativity is premised on his extraordinary capacity to shine a light on new as well as lasting, unassailable talent. Of equal importance to his modus operandi are the ways in which he articulates and manifests the motivations and beliefs that he shares with his collaborators in each issue of *Self Service*, never shying away from being open about the context of cultural practices, the challenges faced by the creative industries, and the urgency of resisting censorship and control. One of Petronio's earliest taglines was, "Revisiting the past, engaging the present, to create the future." This maxim could be readily applied to this book and its disarmingly positive and galvanizing testimony to an ongoing creative journey and to a belief in the power of ideas to find their visual form. *Visual Thinking & Image-Making* embodies Petronio's unbroken track record of providing ideations and permissions for the future of creativity that spans the still-resonant heritage of the analog past of visual thinking and through audacious digital excellence. In so doing, his remarkable endeavors define a creative space for us all to practice a bright and inclusive future.

YVES SAINT LAURENT SS09 POSTER
OPPOSITE: SAINT LAURENT RIVE DROITE BRAND IDENTITY

COMME DES GARÇONS PARFUMS GRAPHIC DESIGN

ALAÏA
PARIS

HIVER
PRINTEMPS
2023
03.07.2022
20H00

ALAÏA SHOW INVITATION
OPPOSITE: ALAÏA SF22 LOOKBOOK

HIVER PRINTEMPS 2023

ALAÏA
PARIS

NOM: Lana Petrusevych

SIÈGE: E4

ADRESSE: 15 RUE DU FAUBOURG SAINT-HONORÉ
75008 PARIS

DATE & HEURE: 03.07.2022 20H

| L | M | M | J | V | S | D |

CETTE INVITATION STRICTEMENT PERSONNELLE
VOUS SERA DEMANDÉE À L'ENTRÉE.

ALAÏA

LE MASCARA CHANEL
COLLECTION NOIRS OBSCURS

LE MASCARA CHANEL
COLLECTION NOIRS OBSCURS

CHANEL ADVERTISING

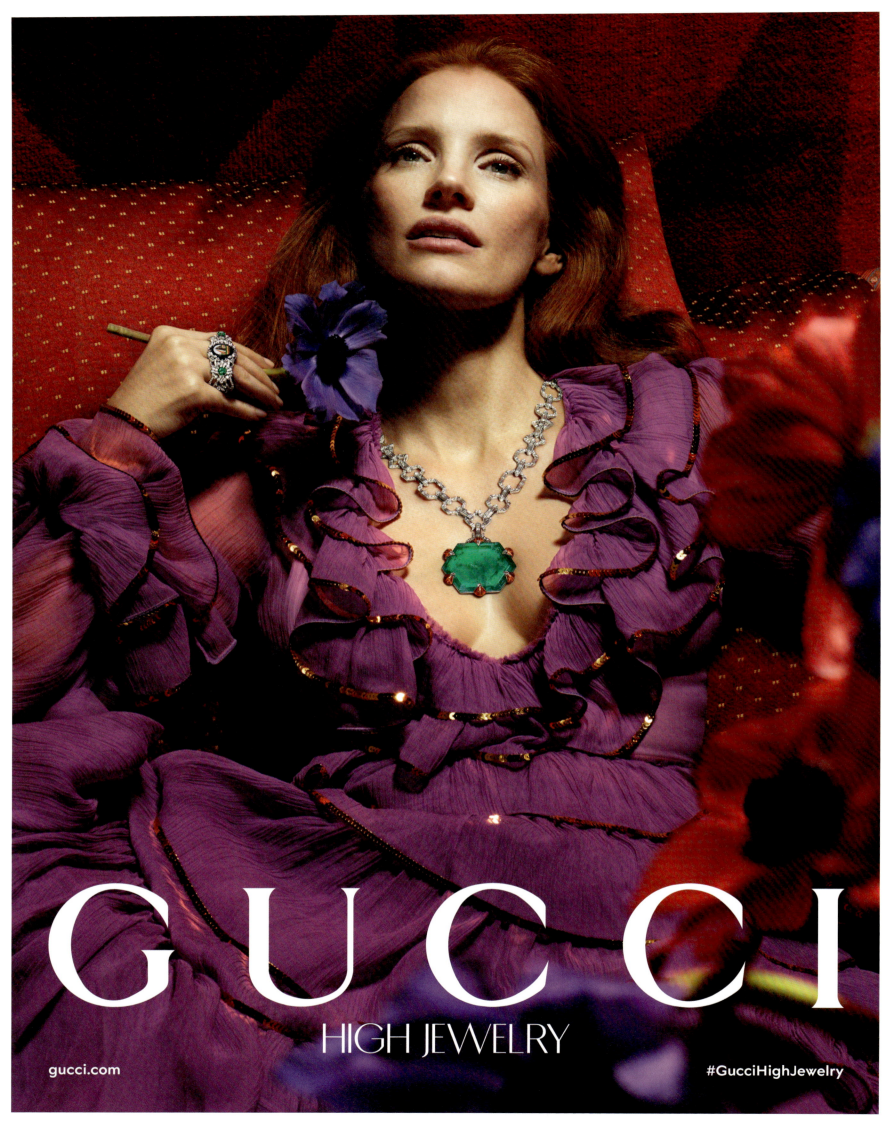

PRADA PARFUMS PRODUCT DESIGN
OPPOSITE: GUCCI ADVERTISING

SAINT LAURENT RIVE DROITE HOT FOIL STAMPING TOOL
OPPOSITE: COMME DES GARÇONS PARFUMS PACKAGING

VICTORIA BECKHAM, BRAND IDENTITY & PRODUCT DESIGN
OPPOSITE: CHLOÉ SS06 ADVERTISING

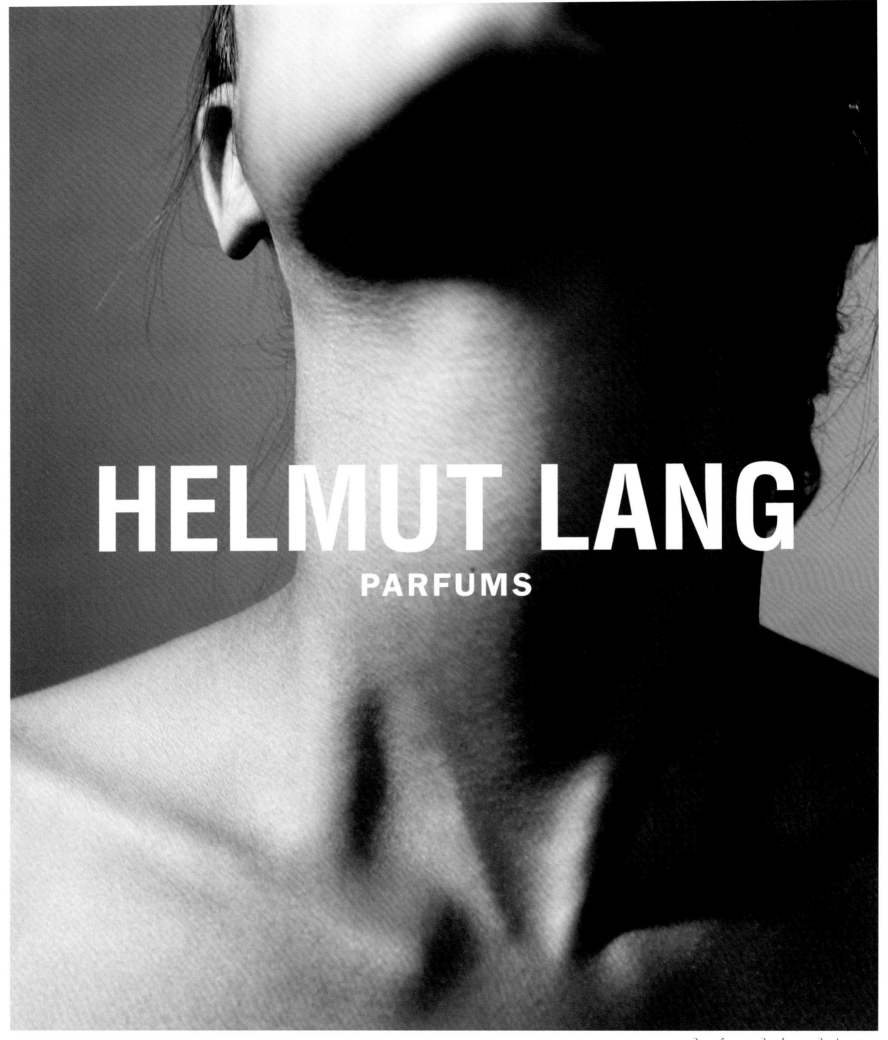

SAINT LAURENT RIVE DROITE LAUNCH CAMPAIGN
OPPOSITE. PRADA PATTERN RESEARCH

EMILIO PUCCI

PRADA
OBVIOUS CLASSICS #1
3X1

Expanding fashion's intersections.
Stripping excessive information.
Experiencing luxury through simplicity.
Recognizing the essential.
Challenging fundamental assumptions.
Embracing esthetic pragmatism.
Asserting one's stylisticfreedom.
Endorsing iconic essentials.

In fashions' current landscape, filled with visual clutter and information overload, it is in understated quality that the very essence of luxury is found. For this reason, we are constructively engaged in implementing new choices of simplicity, attempting to create openings for distinction through the innovation of essentials. These timeless basics are an answer to modernity ; embracing stylistic pragmatism and fundamental understated sophistication while keeping a certain confidence through assured functional intention. The whole is only as good as the sum of it's parts, these basics are solid componants, iconic essentials for building your look.

CHLOÉ PARFUMS ADVERTISING
OPPOSITE: PRADA PACKAGING & COPYWRITING

COMME des GARÇONS SHIRT
FALL-WINTER 2000 COLLECTION

EXHIBITION
25-28 JANUARY 2000

COMME DES GARÇONS S.A. 23 PLACE DU MARCHÉ SAINT-HONORÉ 75001 PARIS
PHONE : (33) 1 47 03 60 80 FAX (33) 1 42 97 56 37

APPOINTMENTS
NEW YORK

COMME DES GARÇONS LTD. 601 WEST 26TH STREET 14TH FLOOR NEW YORK, NY 10001
PHONE (212) 604 0013 FAX (212) 929 1757

PARIS

COMME DES GARÇONS S.A. 16 PLACE VENDÔME 75001 PARIS
PHONE (33) 1 47 03 60 80 FAX (33) 1 42 97 56 37

AGENTS
BENELUX
BRITAIN-EIRE
ITALY
JAPAN
SPAIN-PORTUGAL
©2000

JOSÉ-LOUIS ROMERO
MILES GREEN
NEVENKA DE BEAUCHAMP
COMME DES GARÇONS CO. LTD.
CARLOS A. VARELA

COMME DES GARÇONS S.A.

PHONE (32) 2 479 7408
PHONE (44) 01298 8146 11
PHONE (39) 02 76 01 10 16
PHONE (91) 3 3486 7611
PHONE (34) 91 594 06 51

PRINTED IN FRANCE

FAX (32) 2 479 7408
FAX (44) 01298 8146 11
FAX (39) 02 76 01 10 21
FAX (81) 3 3498 2107
FAX (34) 91 594 09 83

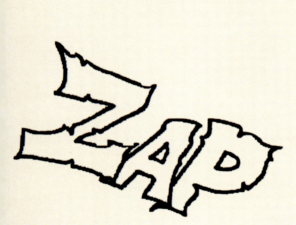

EXHIBITION

4-7 JULY 2000
COMME DES GARÇONS S.A. 16, PLACE VENDOME 75001 PARIS
PHONE : (33) 1 47 03 60 80 FAX (33) 1 42 97 56 37

APPOINTMENTS
NEW YORK

COMME DES GARÇONS LTD. 601 WEST 26TH STREET 14TH FLOOR NEW YORK, NY 10001

EXHIBITION
9 - 13 OCTOBER 2000
15 - 30 OCTOBER 2000
AGENT GERMANY - AUSTRIA
©2000

COMME DES GARÇONS S.A.
A&A S.R.L.
MONICA STAHR
COMME DES GARÇONS S.A.

16, PLACE VENDÔME
VIA BRERA, 8
PRINZREGENTENSTRASSE, 79
PRINTED IN FRANCE

75001 PARIS
20121 MILANO
81675 MUNICH

COMME des GARÇONS
*
COMME des GARÇONS
*

COMME des GARÇON
*
COMME des GARÇONS

www.ysl.com

YVES SAINT LAURENT FW08/09 ADVERTISING
PREVIOUS SPREAD: COMME DES GARÇONS GRAPHIC DESIGN

ysl.com

YVES SAINT LAURENT FW09/10 ADVERTISING

Yves Saint Laurent
Manifesto
F/W 2009-10

vlm_ysl_019-009-02-04a.tif
Photography by Inez van Lamsweerde & Vinoodh Matadin
Shot 1 - Sunday, March 22, 2009

The YSL Manifesto: a global fashion statement directly diffused across borders and demographics. A message in a gesture, amplified to democratize a system of dressing, given rhythmic effect through repetition. Fashion made larger than life, taken off-stage, manifested in the street and at the moment it seems the most incidental, and at once the most profound. The Yves Saint Laurent Fall/Winter 2009-2010 collection: Stefano Pilati's art of understatement. Illusion stripped away from a posture to reveal its heart; a pure, punctuated chic. Black leather and grey flannel as the ingredients of a signature expression of tailoring and technique. A story of classic fashion rewritten, inherited forms recast. This is what happens in the ushering in of a new era.

MANIFESTO FALL/WINTER 2009-10

BLACK SHINY PLONGÉ LEATHER CROSS-BACK JUMPSUIT PAIRED WITH BLACK LEATHER 105MM PLATFORM KNEE-HIGH BOOTS.

BLACK SHINY PLONGÉ LEATHER JUMPSUIT WITH HIDDEN METAL CHAINS AND TEXTURED BLACK SUEDE 105MM PLATFORM PUMPS.

YVES SAINT LAURENT FW09/10 MANIFESTO

JIL SANDER GRAPHIC DESIGN

ALAÏA BRAND IDENTITY
OPPOSITE: SAINT LAURENT RIVE DROITE PRODUCT DESIGN

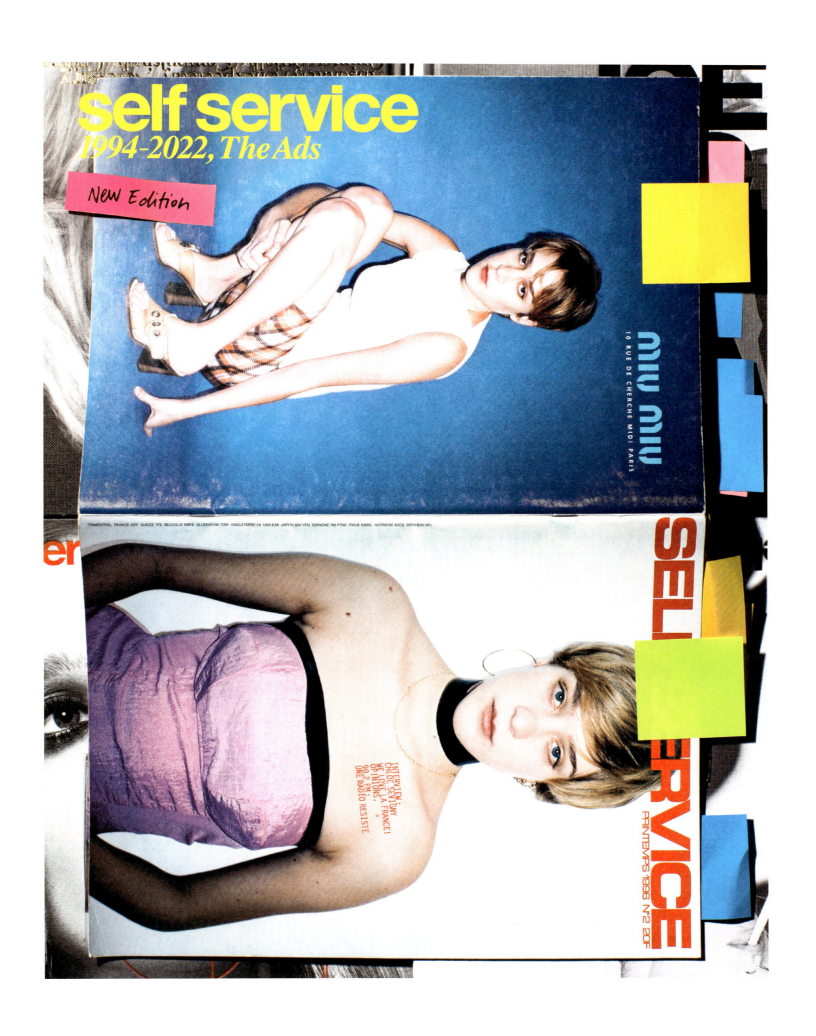

SELF SERVICE BOOK
OPPOSITE: ALAÏA WS23 ADVERTISING

REPOSSI

6, PLACE VENDÔME, PARIS

REPOSSI.COM

REPOSSI SS13 ADVERTISING
OPPOSITE: LA BOUCHE ROUGE BRAND IDENTITY & PRODUCT DESIGN

PRADA PARFUMS PRODUCT & PACKAGING DESIGN

100 OXFORD STREET
LONDON W1A 1AB
WWW.JILSANDER.COM

JIL SANDER

JIL SANDER

CHANEL STILL LIFE PHOTOGRAPHY RESEARCH

WORK IN PROGRESS

ADIDAS SS09 ADVERTISING

HUSSEIN CHALAYAN BRAND IDENTITY
OPPOSITE: **SAINT LAURENT RIVE DROITE** PRODUCT DESIGN

hussein chalayan

C'EST COMME ÇA
SL

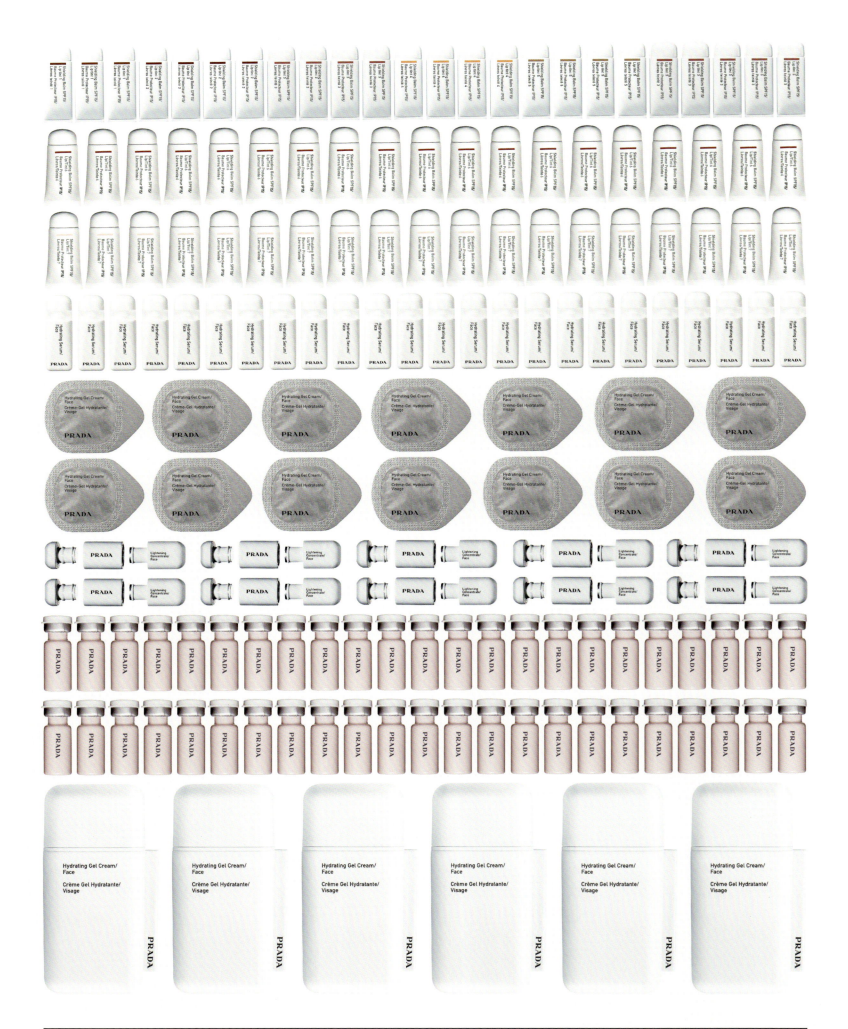

purity, potency and effectiveness in every precious dose.

no unnecessary additives or preservatives. | for sensitive skin.

www.prada.com | Dermatology tested. Ophtalmologist tested. | PRADA

Shielding Balm SPF15/Lip/Tint 3   Baume Protecteur IP15/Lèvres/Teinte 3   Schutzbalsam SPF15/Lippen/Col.3
You'll never know how clean, how clear, how radiant, how positively glowing your skin can look until you try Prada skincare. Prada has formulated a range of products like no others. Prada skincare ingredients are 100% fresh, pure and active. And because every Prada pack is 100% airtight, those ingredients stay fresh, pure and active until the moment you apply them. This freshness makes them extremely effective, giving you visible results But no need.skincare. Prada has formulated a range of products like no others. Prada skincare ingredients are 100% fresh, pure and active. And because every Prada pack is 100% airtight, those ingredients stay fresh.

Prada has formulated a range of products like no others. Prada skincare ingredients are 100% fresh, pure and active. And because every Prada pack is 100% airtight, those ingredients stay fresh, pure aand active with until the moment you apply.

PRADA
Beauty

TOP: **SEVENTY ONE GIN** ADVERTISING   BOTTOM: **PIRELLI** GRAPHIC DESIGN
OPPOSITE: **GOLD** MIXED COLLATERAL

71

WWW.CHLOE.COM/LOVE

self service

twenty five years reconsidered photography by craig mc dean

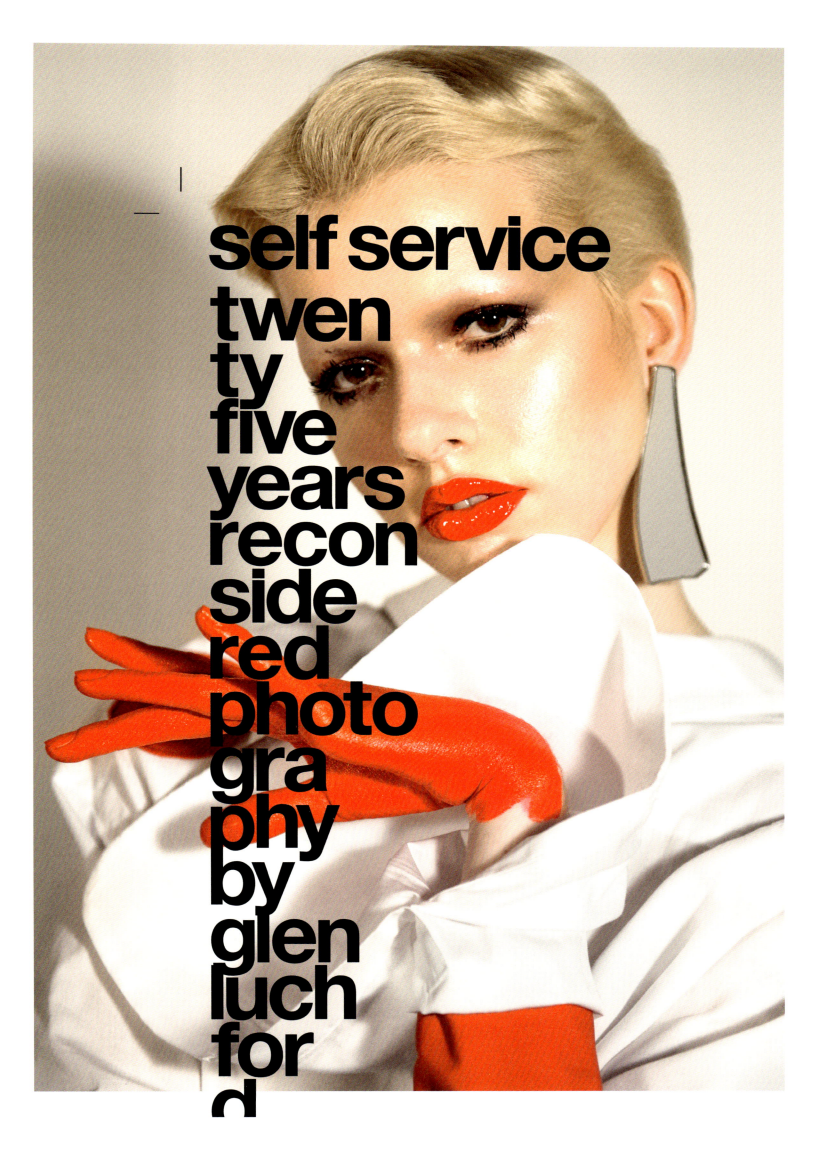

SEVENTY ONE GIN BRAND IDENTITY & PRODUCT DESIGN
OPPOSITE: PRADA PATTERN RESEARCH

SELF SERVICE POSTER

MANIFESTO:
A NEW
FASHION ORDER.
THE TRIUMPH OF SPIRIT.
THE RESOLUTE
ELEGANCE OF YSL.

YVES SAINT LAURENT SS10 MANIFESTO

MIU MIU GRAPHIC DESIGN

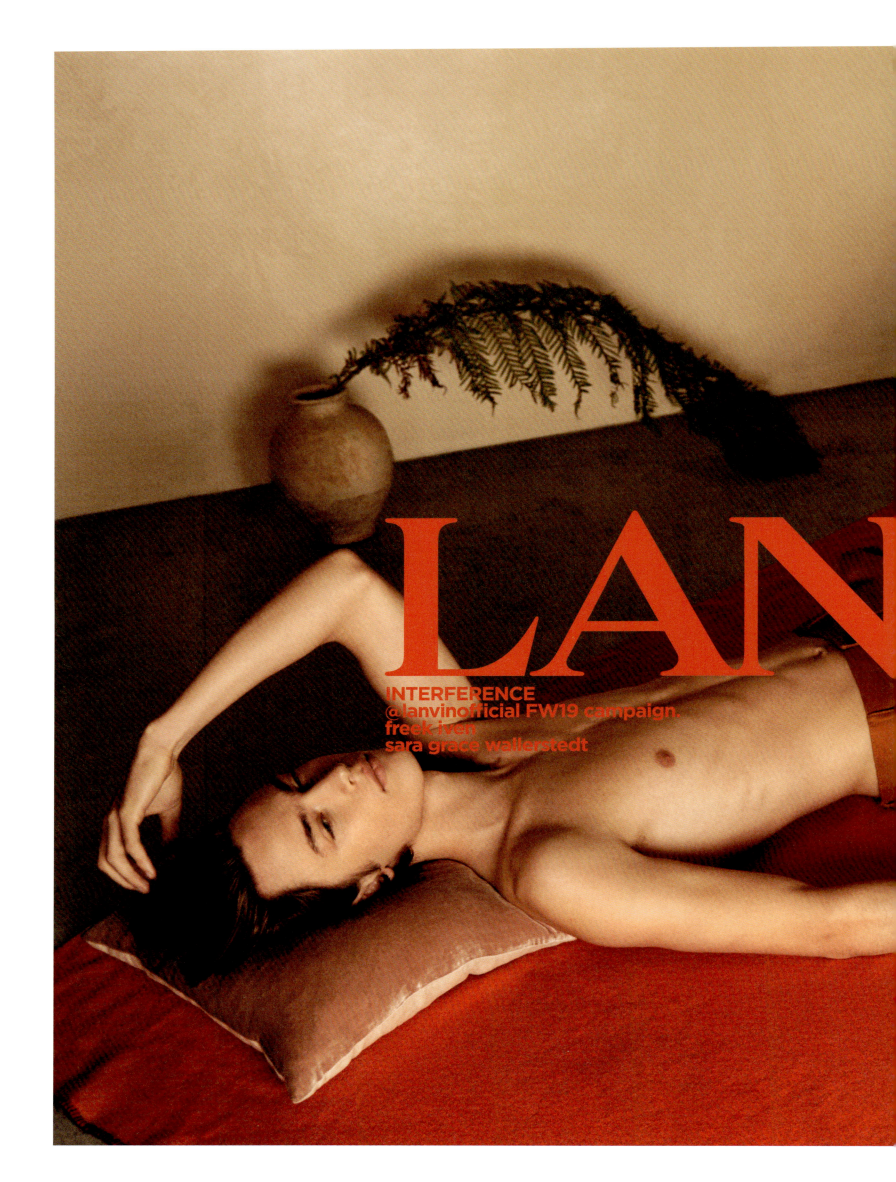

LAN

INTERFERENCE
@lanvinofficial FW19 campaign.
freek.iven
sara grace wallerstedt

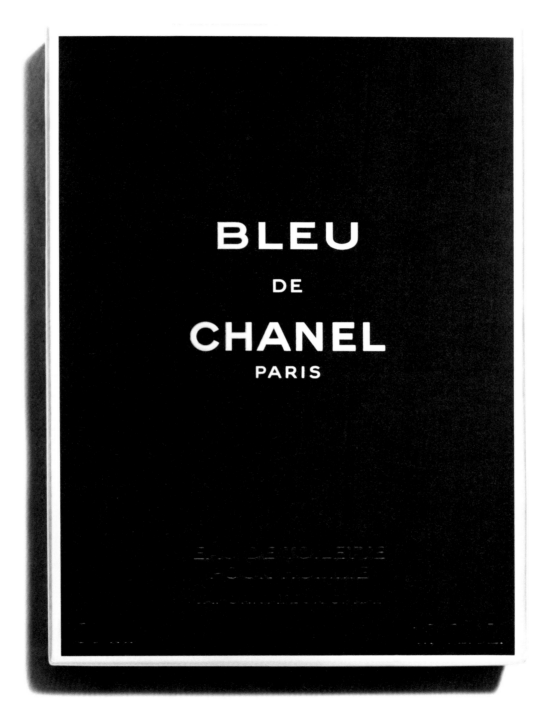

CHANEL PACKAGING
OPPOSITE: CHLOÉ PARFUMS ADVERTISING

UN PRINTEMPS
CHANEL

COLLECTION LES IMPRESSIONS

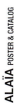

ALAÏA

PARIS

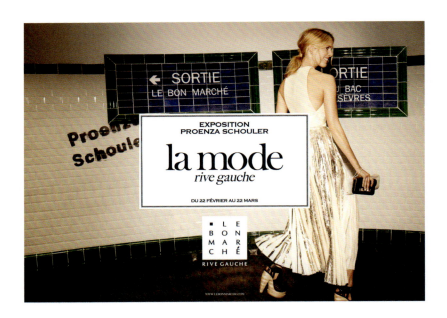

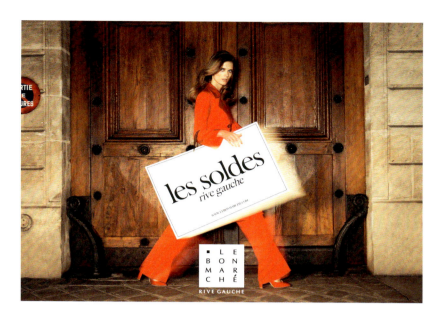

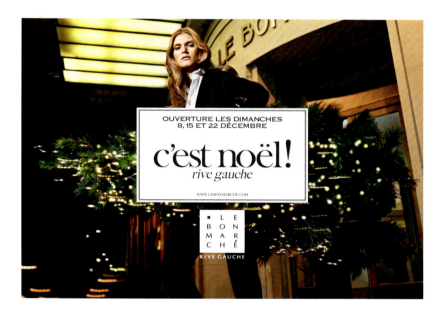
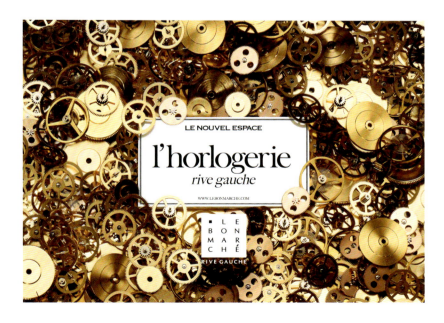

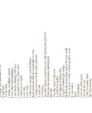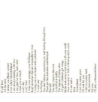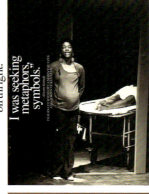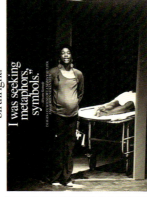

STUDY MAGAZINE ART DIRECTION & DESIGN
PREVIOUS SPREAD: **PRADA** GRAPHIC DESIGN

CHLOÉ BRAND IDENTITY
OPPOSITE: EMILIO PUCCI FW08 ADVERTISING

LANVIN BRAND IDENTITY
OPPOSITE: A.P.C. BRAND IDENTITY

A.P.C.
FALL/
WINTER
2013/14

ZARA PARFUMS PRODUCT DESIGN
OPPOSITE: PRADA PRODUCT DESIGN

JIL SANDER PARFUMS PACKAGING
OPPOSITE: LA BOUCHE ROUGE BRAND IDENTITY

la bouche rouge
MAISON DE MAQUILLAGE, PARIS

1. AFFIRM your revolutionary spirit 2. BE confident and determined 3. EMBRACE a certain parisian elegance 4. CELEBRATE your inner fashion spirit 5. ASPIRE to the artistic and intellect 6. LIVE color as an emotional state of mind 7. ENGAGE in a socially responsible act.

An infinite choice of colors to reflect a sense of true beauty and individuality.

#KISSFORLIFE

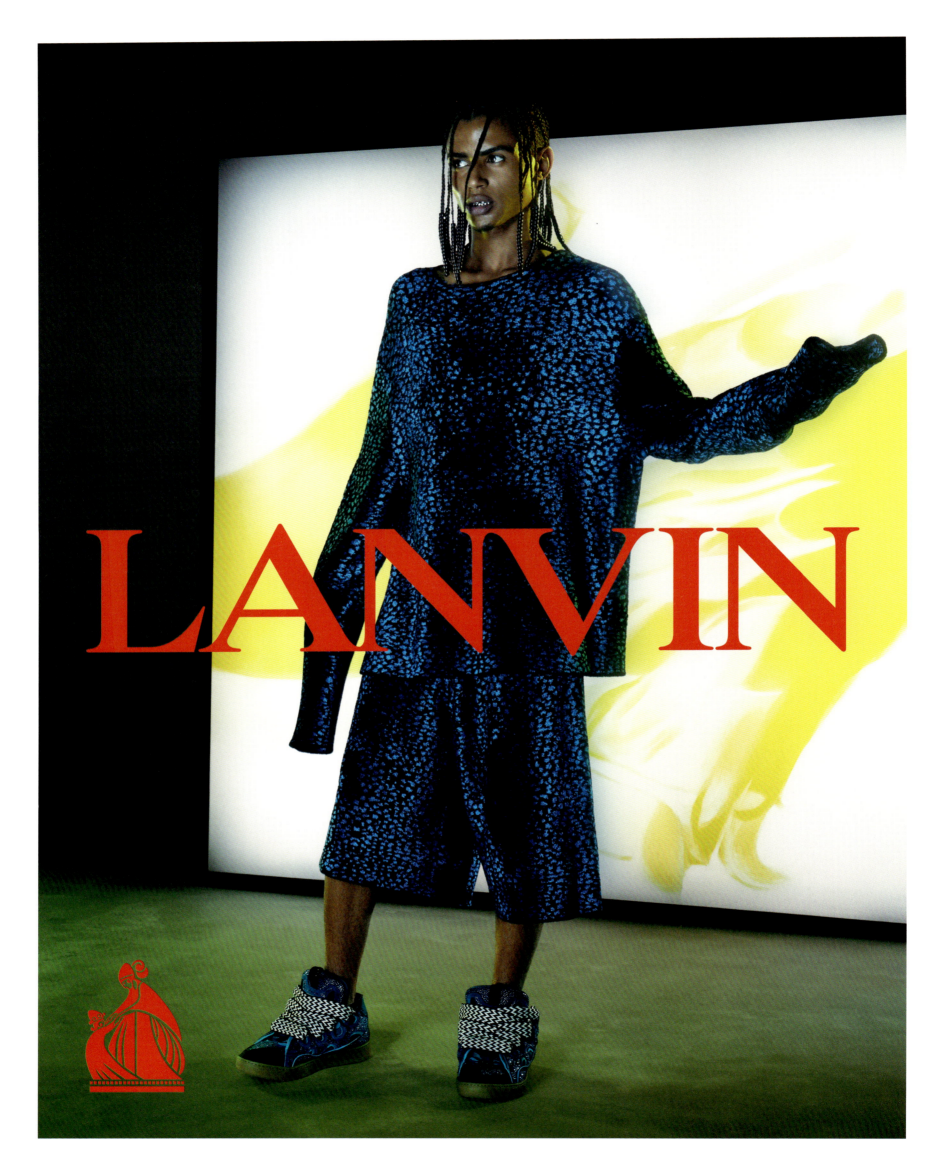

SAINT LAURENT RIVE DROITE DIGITAL CONTENT
OPPOSITE: LANVIN FW21 ADVERTISING

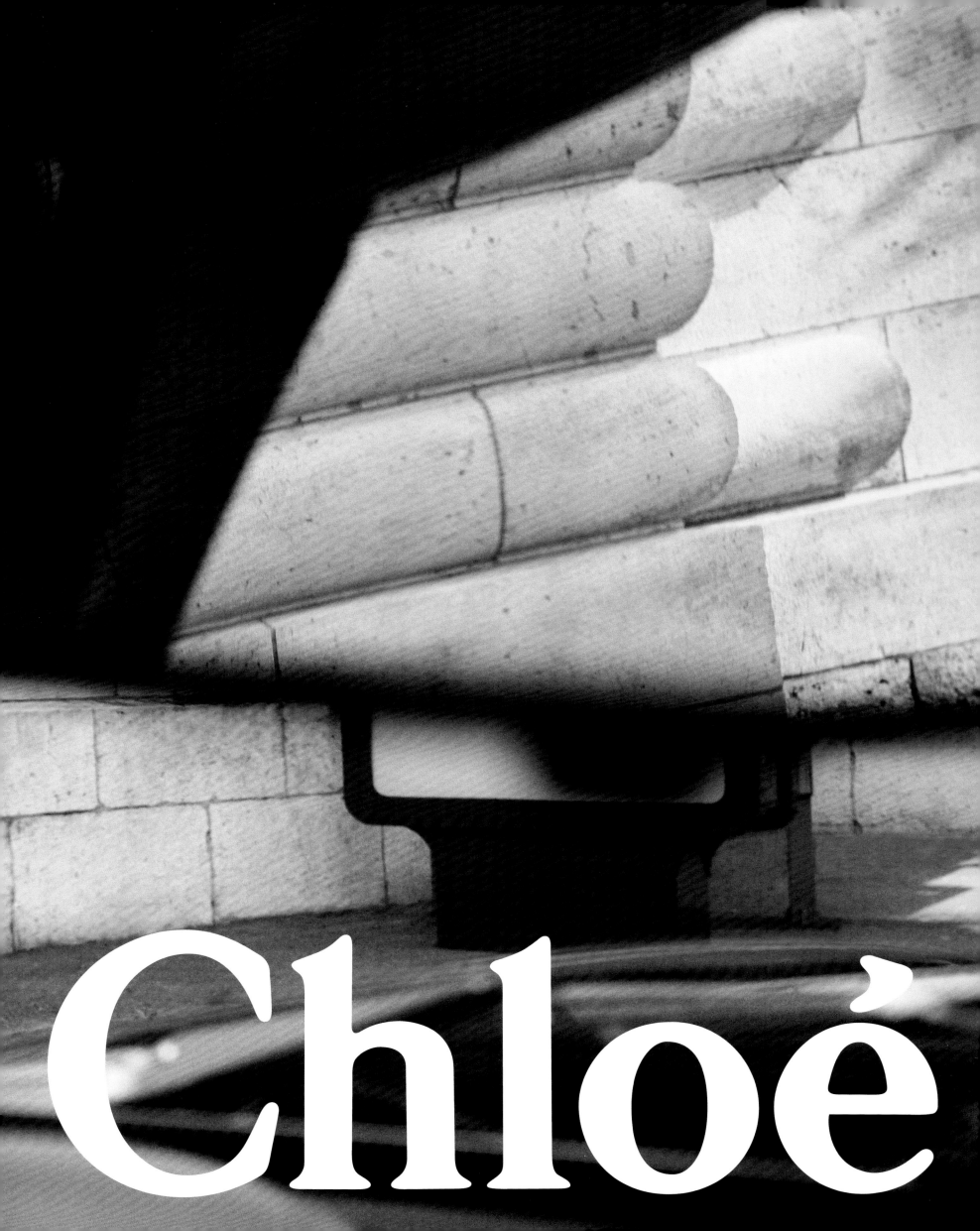

ON VISUAL THINKING
AN INTERVIEW BY CHARLOTTE COTTON

CHARLOTTE COTTON: Ezra, bravo to you and your collaborators for bringing this expansive book together. Tell me about the process of giving your multivalent practice a comprehensible form for the reader.

EZRA PETRONIO: It is difficult to define what would be the best representation of my body of work, drawn from multiple working groups and collaborations. I think what we have done is what I always tend to do, which is to portray the journey I am on. At the end of the day, the journey is way more important than the final destination.

CHARLOTTE: Tell me about the beginning of your journey.

EZRA: I am both French and American, born in New York in 1968. My grandfather emigrated with his family from Italy in 1900 at the age of one. He was a typesetter working for the newspapers and a senior trade unionist in New York. My father was born in Brooklyn. He studied at the School of Visual Arts, and his first job was as the art director of *New York Magazine*. He met my mother at the advertising agency Young & Rubicam. She was born in Bombay, India, of Jewish heritage, and her family immigrated to America when she was 19. My maternal great-grandfather was a famed astrologist and photographer who took large-format pictures of the British Raj.

CHARLOTTE: How old were you when your family moved to Europe?

EZRA: I was two years old. My father got a job in Geneva. Two years later, he was invited to participate in the creation of the advertising agency TBWA in Paris as its first art director. A few years later, my father started his own advertising and design agency in Paris. My mother became a renowned jazz tap dancer.

CHARLOTTE: That's extraordinary!

EZRA: They are extraordinary. It was a big risk at the time for a couple of young Americans to move to Paris to make their dreams come true. They were very involved in the jazz world and the American Center in Paris. My sister Leela and I would go to jazz festivals and clubs in Paris when we were children. We were raised in a very privileged creative environment. I followed in my father's footsteps as an art director, and my sister became a wonderful dancer like our mother.

CHARLOTTE: What was your mother's style of dance?

EZRA: My mother is a jazz tap dancer whose style is more like that of Gregory Hines than Fred Astaire. Every show is a unique performance. To accompany her dance, she performed in concerts with some of the finest American and French musicians in Europe and the U.S.A. She set up the leading tap dance school in France and was always doing shows, for which my father designed the posters. The energy and entrepreneurship they put into their projects had a great influence on my sister and me as young people.

CHARLOTTE: Were you able to observe your father's art direction and agency work at close hand?

EZRA: He would involve us as kids. I remember being on set with him and the film director Tony Scott in the Seychelles, and all my dad's work as an art director, such as creating the world of the fashion brand Kenzo in the 1980s. I remember being at shoots with photographers like Hans Feurer, Peter Lindbergh, and Oliviero Toscani. At my father's agency, I helped his staff on small projects and studied the typography books. He encouraged me to be very immersed in the processes and to intern at different design companies, to learn about everything from packaging design to typography. I saw my father, as an art director, entrusted with the aims and ambitions of clients and company C.E.O.s, being the holder of the overall creative vision, ensuring that your idea is executed beautifully and surprisingly by this great group of talent you've put together. As art director, you are there to protect the photographer and the talent, trust them to push the ideas and make magic happen, and make sure they have the space to creatively breathe.

CHARLOTTE: What did the young Ezra understand an art director to be?

EZRA: A job that required applying your creative thinking to an extremely wide and constantly evolving range of subjects, problematics, and mediums, while being solicited to exercise a wide range of artistic crafts such as graphic and type design, illustration, photography, film, editing, copywriting, and product design. The role also pertains to what you might think—it is directing artistic talent, and having the culture and vision to assemble the right group of talent required on a creative project.

CHARLOTTE: "Visual thinking" and "image-making" are the two constituent parts of the title of this book.

EZRA: Yes, and the idea of a creative journey that combines illustration, photography, fashion, graphic design, spatial design, architecture, shape, and volume. Creative strategies that can have forms and collaterals that range from logos to packaging to advertising billboards, with an increasing number of platforms that now include online and social media, and augmented reality. In my view, you have to know all these crafts to be able to apply your thinking. I dedicate this book to Henry Wolf, who was an Austrian-American art director, designer, and photographer who energized magazine design and advertising strategies in the 1960s. He was one of my teachers in my senior year at Parsons School of Design in New York and had published his seminal book, *Visual Thinking*, which I pay homage to in the title of this book.

CHARLOTTE: Did your journey as a photographer start at the same time, as a child?

EZRA: Yes. My father was a photographer, and he gave me an old Pentax camera when I was 15. I would take Kodachrome slides. I loved it. I had an internship that was very important to me in a lab in Paris called Picto, founded by Pierre Gassmann in the 1950s. He was a master printer for eminent photographers such as Man Ray and Henri Cartier-Bresson and created true excellence in the reprographic chain of photography. I spent the summer of my final year in high school in darkrooms learning how to print. He spent many hours explaining the magic of collaboration between a photographer and his printer: how one captures, and the other reveals.

CHARLOTTE: In hindsight, do you see your parents' drive to create situations and structures as their participation in the cultural shift that was happening in Paris at that time?

EZRA: Through them, I got to see firsthand the beauty of the trust and creativity between artists. Both my parents had creative ideas that brought people together to express and try new things. More than anything, I think that is a very great privilege that gave my sister and me high levels of self-confidence and belief in ourselves.

CHARLOTTE: I am listening to you and thinking about the journey you have been on, including the centrality of founding and editing *Self Service* magazine. I'm taken by the parallels between your parents being generous hosts, creating frames in which other creative people can participate, to be responsible peers with and for others, and what I see of your journey that is literally laid out in this book and on the pages of *Self Service* magazine since its beginnings. When did the young Ezra Petronio make his first magazine?

EZRA: It was during my senior year in high school at the Lycée Montaigne in Paris. I gathered my close friends and started it from scratch. We financed it through advertising sold to the local stores around the block! We addressed issues of art and culture, but also drugs, politics, and student-union activism.

CHARLOTTE: And did you take that burgeoning passion for creating editorial stories with you when you went back to New York in the late 1980s, for your undergraduate education at Parsons School of Design?

EZRA: I took with me the love that I already had for making editorial material and its political and social capacities. I immediately became the editor-in-chief of the student newspaper at Parsons. It was at the beginning of the first Gulf War in 1990-91, and we wanted the dean of the school to take a position on the potential drafting of students to fight in the war, and to take a position against silence and censorship. It was the moment when the impact of Senator Jesse Helms's vilification of the Robert Mapplethorpe posthumous retrospective exhibition in Washington, D.C. and the removal of federal funding were felt in every art school across America. We were hoping that the school would take a position on the culture wars as well. It was very important. Senator Jesse Helms was about to kill the National Endowment for the Arts. We supported the L.G.B.T. community in school as well. I realized the importance and influence a magazine can have in its capacity of voicing the needs and aspirations of the group and community it is representing.

CHARLOTTE: I'm really interested to know what your education was like at that juncture in design, reprographic, and digital history. I'm imagining that it was a very hybrid moment between the analog heritage of graphic design and art direction and the arrival of desktop computers.

EZRA: It was definitely the point on the verge of change. In class, graphic design was still done in the old-school ways, whether it be a magazine layout, an ad, or product packaging. The analog design mechanicals meant that you were sending very precisely stacked layers of design to the color separator to print. It was very slow. Let's say that you were designing a poster. You'd start by going to the typewriter, or you would hand-write the text. You'd have to write the specs of every block of text, the font, point size, kerning… It went off for rendering, and maybe two days later, you would receive a printout of that type rolled in a cardboard tube. You'd then cut out the lines of text, paste them into the design grid, mark in the crop marks with a blue pen, and position your type. Something that today takes 15 minutes took five days. All of this manual type of work on typography really taught you so much.

CHARLOTTE: When did desktop computers arrive?

EZRA: In my first year at Parsons, in 1987. It was an Apple Macintosh Mac Classic computer with the first desktop publishing program, PageMaker. I think it had three fonts: Times New Roman, Helvetica, and maybe Arial. We had a little printer so we could type something out, control and enlarge the point size, and print it out there and then. For us, that was a revolution, and it was the beginning of digitalization. In the ten years that followed, everything changed into desktop publishing. All the technologies got more compact and accessible, and you could edit and re-edit things. I'm part of the generation that has passed into the world of digital from the analog history of graphic design and art direction. I'm very grateful to have known the pre-digital, while being an early adopter who fully experimented with the digital creative workflow. I wouldn't have wanted to have started ten years earlier, nor five years later. I still received a rigorous training in the specificities of typography, which you just take for granted if you have only ever used InDesign software. The first two issues of *Self Service* in the early 1990s were done the old-school way of literally cutting and pasting, Xeroxing, and layering your layout designs.

CHARLOTTE: That's amazing context to think about.

EZRA: It was really beautiful to participate in digital tools coming into being and becoming the new creative processes. I feel lucky that my background was in the craft and analog techniques of design and art direction; I think that made the range of possibilities of digital processes even more amazing. What analog and digital design share is that in order to make anything of substance, you have to have rigor in your processes, and you still need to have a creative culture in the digital realm, despite it being a very different way of working. Because of the ways we were beginning to compact all the stages of typesetting and layout, it became undisputable that we had arrived at the new way of working.

CHARLOTTE: How do you ground yourself, within the potential for noisy distraction from new tools and technologies?

EZRA: I am grounded in the essentials of design. I understand the grid, and what balance and proportions are, how to size and space typography, how to be playful, how to create grids—all these rules and principles of visual display and graphic design. Mastering and owning these then give you so much freedom to decontextualize and restructure things, to play and experiment, create what can seem to be improbable layouts, break words, disrupt with your choice of proportions, overlay, mix, and shuffle. If I take type off the edge of the page, it works because somewhere else on the page something else will keep it balanced, with its own grounded style. I think there is always a sense of taste in what I design. Working typography requires precision, craft, culture, and the boldness to depart and explore. In our office, every single word is letter-spaced, for instance! It is dogmatic and obsessive.

CHARLOTTE: What is the greatest loss that you would lay at the feet of digital technology to the creative process of making an editorial story or ad campaign?

EZRA: Firstly, I would say the compression of creative time. Before computer screens were on set, the Polaroid was the image you would show to a client so that everyone knew and agreed what the intention was. Although it was not the final image, it was enough for everyone to be confident and happy that the image-making team were heading in the right direction. Then there was time to work with the photographer after the shoot to edit the contact sheets, try different layouts, and work progressively before presenting back to the client. It was three or four weeks of work after the shoot. That space and time no longer exist. The second major change is the exponential increase of deliverables we must produce on an advertising job. Today we tend to call these "content campaigns," in which we need to produce still images, films, and conceptualize social content. There are more deliverables, smaller budgets, shorter timeframes, and thus the unfortunate compressed creative journey.

The markets' increasing appetite for digital content was the reason Lana Petrusevych and I started our digital creative agency Content Matters, a sister to our main agency Petronio Associates, with a dedicated team that possess a digital and social mindset and culture. This is a way for us to ensure a total creative and strategic coherence in the work we produce for clients and ensure that all primary and secondary content created—whether it be the main film or a secondary Instagram "story," for instance—is creatively consistent and exciting.

The digital era and social media have obviously greatly impacted the fundamentals of our industry and its mechanics, including how we create and communicate. Channels have multiplied, and the need to create an increased flow of content is constant. As an art director, you need to work creatively on all these different aspects and layers. I have recently conceptualized a huge and expensive fragrance campaign that ended up only living on the company's website and Instagram for a week, rapidly disappearing in the abyss of its feed.

Simultaneously I have conceptualized an original Instagram filter for the same brand that could have even more impact and engagement with their customers. Sometimes, creating a simple Instagram filter has more impact than a multimillion-dollar campaign.

CHARLOTTE: How do you approach working on the overall image of a brand?

EZRA: I have always tried to first define and determine the fundamentals of how I see the brand I am working for, what I call my creative ideology and dogma—the basic principles that will guide and influence my creative executions, as well as those of the people working for the brand. When I started working with Miuccia Prada on different aspects of Prada, including the fragrances, I quickly came to realize that this creative dogma would reside in something essential and simple: classic with a twist. Prada was grounded in a love and respect for the traditional yet was also progressive and experimental. This is what led me to reintroduce their original Nodo logo and give it a contemporary, bold, and unusual twist by its off-register placement and overlays. We would use beautiful traditional papers and print-production techniques but disrupt this in the design and execution. Everything looked, at first, quite elegant and simple, but there was always something that would be "off" in an interesting way. Everything I would do for Mrs. Prada from then on would respect these fundamentals.

A few years later, I became art director for Miu Miu, and we also defined certain principles, especially for advertising. Whereas the Prada brand represented Miuccia's more formal personality, Miu Miu was the playground for her various current obsessions and vision of feminine incarnations. We decided that every Miu Miu campaign would be built upon her passions at that point in time. There were young cool girls, older empowered women, and Hollywood celebrity and cult figures over the seasons.

CHARLOTTE: One of the first case studies in this book's sequence is your long-term work with Chloé, and the selection takes us from the start of your art direction of the print advertising for Chloé through to the beginnings of creative experimentation with moving image and what is now the essential deliverable of any ad campaign.

EZRA: I wanted to highlight the Chloé campaigns as a case study in the book to show how it is possible to define certain constant creative guidelines and set principles for a brand's advertising and build a narrative over the course of many years. Chloé was never about a single incarnation of femininity but about a sisterhood of women. We decided that this would remain the case forever, and that each season's campaign would contextualize this grouping and capture the dynamics of their interactions, creating emotional pictures we knew the consumer would relate to—actually, that any woman would relate to, regardless of her interest in fashion or not. We started working on this with Inez Van Lamsweerde and Vinoodh Matadin, with whom we had developed a close and trustful working relationship. This complicity enabled us, on every shoot, to find that one magical "off moment" shot that most people would usually disregard, and we would run that as part of the campaign. Chloé has a special place in my heart as it is a great example of how we were able to completely revisit and create a renewed D.N.A. as well as a unique brand identity and experience that would exist and be recognized for decades. We started working there with Phoebe Philo, Ralph Toledano, and Hannah MacGibbon. Everything was reimagined. I found the logo to be a little clumsy, but decided to embrace it and enlarge it as a sign of renewed brand self-confidence. We built everything following the creative dogma we had defined: visual identity, packaging, digital and retail experience. I also had creative control over licenses such as eyewear, kids, etc., and also became art director in the fragrance and beauty joint venture with Coty.

CHARLOTTE: I'm fascinated by the precision and the rules of art-directing perfume and beauty brands.

EZRA: I launched the first four fragrances for Chloé x Coty, each one carefully crafted to represent one fundamental pillar of the brand. The first one featured three portraits of women, whose presence was intimate and soulful as a means to express the fact that the Chloé woman was truthful, real, and highly relatable. Chloé is about women plural, hence the three women portrayed as the brand's spirit, which will never be encapsulated in a single character. If the first signature fragrance explored the inner beauty and strength of the Chloé woman, the second launch—*Love*—was about her extraverted, fashionable personality that was a mixture of French nonchalance and British wit. The third launch explored the more youthfully romantic side of the Chloé woman. It centered on the very confident, free, and logical mindset that we were able to build for the brand, enabling both Chloé and Coty to fully benefit from each other and collectively grow and develop their businesses.

CHARLOTTE: I know it was a much shorter period of time, but I would love to know what your early experience of art-directing at Chanel was like.

EZRA: It was one of the most unique experiences I have ever had. I was hired in 2008 to take over the position, previously held for 40 years by Jacques Helleu, as Chanel's in-house art director for fragrances, beauty, skincare, watches, and jewelry. What made the job unique is that at Chanel, creative strategy and decisions always come first. I would get briefed on the season's objectives by each division's president. We would have simple conversations with no PowerPoints, and then I would go off and produce all the campaigns based only on my vision and with no approval whatsoever needed. Finalized campaigns would be presented to the C.E.O. and owner, and that was that! It was an incredible experience, exploring the splendor of their archives, rejuvenating the brand, and imagining what Gabrielle Chanel's voice would be today. I was able to bring into Chanel a whole new generation of photographers and stylists and talent. This was the ultimate freedom of creative expression.

CHARLOTTE: I want to ask you about this axis-shift moment in the story of the image industry, from your perspective as an art director. I am curious to know what you felt you were responding and answerable to, and where the challenges have been for you in a visual landscape that has changed perhaps beyond recognition during your creative practice.

EZRA: The digital world and social media are a totally new canvas with new materials—motion graphics, 3D, virtual and augmented reality, music—making it more extravagant with new, interactive behaviors. As a creative director, I find it is thrilling to have these new creative avenues to explore and play with.

CHARLOTTE: Looking at your work as it is collated here in this book, I see an equal balance of the traditional and new canvases of image-making and graphic design. There's a level of thoughtfulness and precision that cuts across these different platforms and types of engagement. And I wonder whether you actively pursue a set of common principles and methodologies across the board of your practice, from art and creative direction to publishing and photography, as well as across canvases.

EZRA: For me, it is also about engaging with the tools and the possibilities you have now and that are constantly evolving. You have to incorporate all evolutions from the technological to the societal into your work and what you do. As an art director, whether it is for your personal work in the context of a magazine or for the ad campaigns for clients, you need to have detailed knowledge of the visual landscape, including the digital landscape. I have had to step outside of fashion to see more broadly what is happening in our image environment. Fashion has been one of the last industries to see what was evolving in digital-image space and to make better creative decisions beyond digital banners and behind-the-scenes B-roll films. A lot of brands want to show that they are embracing the evolution of technology. In the working groups of our agencies, we try to help brands tackle this with ideas and designs that have commercial relevance and also animate user experiences in ways that are right for a specific brand. If you want to do good things in the digital space, you have to embrace it, however superficial it can seem. From a commercial point of view, it is still very expensive to produce interactive digital content, augmented reality, and motion graphic design because they take a lot of hours of labor to build. With my creative partner Lana Petrusevych, cofounder of our Content Matters agency, we constantly explore new technologies. For us, the creative journey is foremost about exploration, from which ideas will come. Economic relevance comes after. Even if one prefers a printed billboard on L.A.'s Sunset Strip because it appears to be timeless and appealing in comparison to an Instagram story, one cannot ignore what has become the default and most powerful platform for visual communication. Everything has to be done well and with precision. I am incredibly lucky to collaborate with Lana, who brings relevance and a point of view into the digital conversation and with whom I can shape expansive proposals for our visual futures.

I was very lucky early in my journey to have learned profound lessons from the best people about the lengths you can go to fully realize your vision. I was fortunate enough to have great mentors. In the 1990s, my first major client was Comme des Garçons, working with Adrian Joffe and Rei Kawakubo. I remember two things that Rei taught me. The first was when I came to them with some layouts, and Rei asked where the rest of the layouts were. I said, "Well, the rest are in my trashcan." She said to me, "Next time, bring your trashcan." She showed me that I was editing myself way too much and not bringing everything into the conversation, and that one has to trust and share with one's collaborators. The second lesson I remember was when Suzanne Koller and I were designing an invitation to the Comme des Garçons runway show. This was back in the day when urgent back-and-forth decisions across time zones were made via fax machines. A fax came in from Rei with the R.S.V.P. phone number at the bottom of the page in small type highlighted, and she had written, "Plus one point size increase." I thought then, "It is four in the morning in Tokyo, and Rei is actually looking at the point size of the R.S.V.P." I was blown away by her sense of attention to things. In a parallel way, my engagements with Karl Lagerfeld educated me in how precise you can be. It was a fascinating experience to even meet such an icon of fashion. He had the capacity to spontaneously embrace the potential in people. He did this all his life. Encouraging the talents of other people provided him with energy and stimulation.

CHARLOTTE: What was your first encounter with him?

EZRA: I met him when I went to see him with my Polaroid photographs. He published my first book, *Bold & Beautiful*, in 2005 as part of his 7L imprint with Steidl. Before I was employed at Chanel, I worked with Karl on a couple of projects, including a catalog. He had just shot a campaign, and he gave me the box of prints and said, "Do what you want." He had this capacity to follow his intuition and his instinct, not question himself, and trust those he invited into his universe. I returned a week later to present the design. Karl was always doing several things at the same time, every day of his life, and it was like waiting for a meeting with the ringmaster of a circus. After waiting for a few hours, it became my time to see him. I presented the layouts, which were essentially composed of black and white pictures yet with strong splashes of a pink color on certain pages. He liked it and said, "Wait a minute," and left the room. He disappeared for literally an hour, and I was getting worried. Then he came back holding this 1970s Shiseido lip-balm case that he had spent the hour searching for in his archive. Very gently and elegantly, he said, "I love everything, but do you mind if you could just change that pink in the layout to *this* pink, which is very close?" Once again, here is someone who teaches you about obsession, perfection, and precision.

CHARLOTTE: I think particularly in the fields of art and creative direction, there's such an overwhelming amount of responsibility and pressure to quantify and deliver end results and to stay on track rather than push beyond the safe or the already known.

EZRA: Responsibility is the right word. Responsibility and respect. You have to map out all the collateral, environments, and engagements through which your clients need their brand to be visible and intelligently present. The job of an art director starts when you're briefed by the designer in his atelier, when they are showing you their forthcoming collection and describing what their feelings and intentions are this season. You have to distill that into a creative interpretation and strategy, plan all the steps, and come back with the final concept for the campaign and all its ingredients. Our job, as art directors, is a very long process from conceptualization to the final sign-off from the client and their C.E.O. One of the challenges of making great imagery is not being able to have control over that whole process.

I also remember one of the first experiences I had of working with Mrs. Prada on the packaging and ad campaign for a new fragrance. We decided the ads would be quite classical still life images and that we would ask the legendary photographer Irving Penn to shoot the campaign. He was in his 80s at that point, and it was still everyone's dream to work with him. I was sent to New York to make the proposal to Mr. Penn. I arrived at his studio on Broadway, very nervous at the prospect of meeting him. I went inside and started pulling out all the Fondazione Prada books and the prototype perfume bottle, and Mr. Penn said: "Ah, put that away. Tell me about yourself." We started talking, and then he took a piece of paper and drew me this composition of the perfume bottles, all upside down so that I could see the image from across the table from him. He signed it. He said, "This is your campaign."

CHARLOTTE: What did you do?

EZRA: I folded the paper, went nervously back to The Mercer Hotel, and I faxed the drawing to the Prada offices in Milan. A driver took the fax to Mrs. Prada's house, and she called me up an hour later, saying, "I want something different, more modern and new." As I hung up the phone, I knew that it was going to be impossible to go back to Mr. Penn and ask him to give me something else.

CHARLOTTE: What do you think you took from this situation? What stood out to you?

EZRA: There was something to learn about the nature of my ego because I was very upset about having to let go of the chance to work with Irving Penn. But more than that, the thing that impacted me deeply was the strength of Mrs. Prada's convictions, ideology, and vision. She does not want to be a follower; she wants something truly original, whatever it takes. Working with her and observing how she worked with all the different people in her teams, you saw how there was always this quest to find the ultimate solution, and a willingness to throw an idea away and redo things. I think you see less and less people in fashion getting the chance or being allowed the luxury to surprise themselves—to look to either side or above or below what is accepted or has been done before.

CHARLOTTE: What do you think are the most significant factors that diminish the possibilities for such creative opportunities today?

EZRA: We have reached the point culturally where what matters for too many young people is succeeding. What matters is to accumulate. What matters is how fast you're able to rise. What example do we set if the industry celebrates these as the new role models young people should aspire to? We are allowing and tolerating too much mediocrity, rather than talent and expertise. A lot of people are getting work not primarily because of their original creative vision and craft expertise, but because of their following, community representation, and clout. In some ways, the mechanisms of social media do enable new talent to exist and be seen. I connect to that aspect and find it extremely healthy, but it has also created a lot of false illusions about what creative culture really is. I hope there will be a big cleansing of those misunderstandings about our creative industry at some point soon, where great new things will be forged, and we go deeply into the possibilities of the new canvases with which we now work. I think we're at a pivotal time, one that is the same in many ways as what felt possible for me back in the early 1990s—the same possibilities for young talent to create completely new and unexpected narratives.

CHARLOTTE: I think this brings us to the part in this conversation where you describe founding *Self Service* magazine in Paris in 1994 with your then creative partner, Suzanne Koller. What came together for you at that point in time that led to you creating your experimental proposal for independent magazine publishing? Looking back at those early issues of *Self Service* in the mid-1990s, I am reminded how new and established fashion and image-making talents have been interlaced in *Self Service* from the beginning. The graphic and formal qualities that you established for the magazine operate as the balance and the frame for a pretty diverse scope of creatives to sit alongside each other and to define culture.

EZRA: *Self Service* has always been about providing a creative place for emerging and established talent, and a context that supports strong fashion narratives. I think the reason that *Self Service* has survived this long is because we have stayed true to that objective. I never wanted it to be an ego-led publication—that wasn't our raison d'être. Since my first magazine experience in high school right through to today, I have constantly been trying to create editorial structures that unite different voices and creative fields. That gathering of perspectives is something that I have always done.

CHARLOTTE: What do you think that's about for you?

EZRA: I am sure it was because I was an American growing up in Paris, knowing I was different because of that, not liking dogmas or stereotypes, being politically engaged, having friends from lots of different countries.

CHARLOTTE: For me, one of the hallmarks of *Self Service* is its editorial quality of being incredibly open to the range of voices in cultural production well beyond its location in Paris, in ways that are very discerning without being exclusionary, cliquey, or superficial. *Self Service* is curious about creative practices and excited by who is genuinely animating cultural life at a point in time.

EZRA: When I go back through issues of *Self Service*, it's like entering these condensed and curated time capsules. I'll take Fall/Winter 2003 off the library shelf and have a vantage point onto what culture was back then—who were the people, what was the fashion, what was the art, what was the vibe that was defining that moment in time. Being in the *Self Service* library is like, "Let's see what happened in 2010." I'm sure you can say this for other magazines, but that's what I notice that we have.

CHARLOTTE: And it's not an incidental kind of time capsuling with *Self Service*—it feels intentional. I wonder if that is connected to it being a biannual form of publication.

EZRA: Yes, and that's not just about the timescale of publishing biannually versus monthly. A biannual is an editorial approach that navigates a very broad territory but does it in a highly curated and very concise style. It is structurally about creating a time capsule of creativity. When I look back at the early issues of the magazine, I also see how raw it all was. Or at least, it was very pure and spontaneous and directly mapping where we were exploring culture. I think it is also important to say that we weren't just looking to fashion for the frame of reference. Contemporary art movements like the Düsseldorf school of photography that were exploding in the 1990s galvanized us to take risks in how we approached editorial photography. We felt a real urgency in what we were doing, with an almost tangible innocence and a certain rawness. We would go in search of things that really touched us. Locally and regionally, there were creative people who were also trying to push ahead with new ideas. It was a very conservative time in Paris, so there was also a lot to push against. There was a real understanding and affinity that we felt toward Olivier Zahm, who had started *Purple Prose* magazine a couple of years ahead of us. Mathias Augustyniak & Michael Amzalag had established their art and design partnership M/M (Paris) in 1992. Suzanne and I started our own creative agency Work in Progress in the same year, in the basement of my parents' house. Jefferson Hack and Rankin started *Dazed & Confused* magazine in London in 1991. We all looked to the U.K. for inspiration and recognition. Daft Punk were selling their records out of Rough Trade in London, and you can't overestimate the importance that the British independent magazines *i-D* and *The Face* had for all of us emerging publishers and image-makers in holding our resolve to make our own cultural shifts because of their capacity to engage in the breadth of their contemporary culture. We saw the U.K. as having respect for its countercultures and a lot more intertwining of different forms of creativity than we had in France up until the 1990s. Cultural life in France was extremely segmented, and music, art, film, literature, and fashion did not mix with each other.

CHARLOTTE: You've reminded me of a great quote from Noël Coward about opera, which could possibly be applied to Paris in the early 1990s: "People are wrong when they say opera is not what it used to be. It is what it used to be. That is what's wrong with it." Tell me about the plan you made for *Self Service* and your proposal for some cultural change.

EZRA: We had a section at the back of the dummy issue of our magazine where we put images and texts about all kinds of different fun things, and it was called the "Self Service" section. A friend pointed out that this would be a great title for the magazine, so we went ahead and launched *Self Service*—a 64-page, stapled magazine. We had a Heineken beer ad and a photo lab that helped us, and Agnès B. kindly gave us 10,000 francs for our production costs. My sister and I drove around on a scooter to newsstands in Paris to drop off copies. A friend would follow behind us, wait 10 minutes, then buy up all the copies so that the newsagents would reorder *Self Service*. It was fun.

CHARLOTTE: That sounds fantastically resourceful of you. It also makes me pretty nostalgic for the 1990s as a pivotal moment when, if you could scrabble together enough resources, D.I.Y. skills, and materials, you could literally start a magazine or an art space. Did you have a long-term plan for *Self Service* when you started?

EZRA: I don't think we even had a business plan at the start. But we understood the values that *Self Service* would stand for and still does. We set out with the aim to attract and create a context for people who want to push themselves, who want to try to explore and do things they believe in, with high expectations and without filters or covert agendas.

CHARLOTTE: I understand what you are saying about how your creative journeys start with an intention and a concept and are materialized through your craft and trusted collaborations. I also appreciate that important, long-term projects like *Self Service* magazine can only be sustained by keeping true to your purpose. But I think I need to reframe my question to you about how you have sustained a living, breathing, relevant "canvas" for cultural ideas in the form of a magazine for close to 30 years. I would say magazines have increasingly prohibitive fixed costs—of paper, ink, distribution—that mean it is a Herculean venture to create a break-even publishing business plan. I also think that the shape and cultural value of independent magazine publishing have changed enormously during the lifetime of *Self Service*, and there have definitely been points where the relevance of a printed magazine has been questioned. How do you set the parameters that ensure that your magazine is sustainable and does not, despite all best intentions, become a vanity publication?

EZRA: At a certain point, we made an active choice to make *Self Service* a hardcover biannual magazine, which is obviously much less economical on a unit-cost basis. But you balance that with printing a fixed number of copies with no wastage, and you target and control your distribution to maintain the lowest percentage of unsold copies. We've stayed faithful to putting any money that is made back into the physical object and ensuring that people get paid for their work. We keep *Self Service* self-sufficient and take the pressure away from the magazine and its small team to economically perform brilliantly because I haven't made *Self Service* my prime source of income.

CHARLOTTE: I really appreciate you being so honest with me about this. Maybe it seems like the least interesting part of the story, but I think it's really important to know that true success and sustainability within creative industries can still be about a very pragmatic approach to what business actually means. Whether it be fashion, publishing, or image-making—or the combination of all these creative industries—there is no hiding that these are multibillion-dollar industries scaled on exploitation and a zero-sum game plan. It not only makes having a different business plan and demonstrating its sustainability worth acknowledging, but also incredibly important. We need inspiration and hope that there are going to be moments ahead of us that are parallel to the 1990s, when we are going to be able to start out on a journey, open to new ideas and manifestations of creative diversity.

EZRA: I think the biggest challenge for a young person wanting to establish themselves in the creative industries of fashion and image-making is knowing where to aim. We are disrupting journeys for new people by fast-tracking them or defining the goal as one of being in power, staying in power, and being as influential as possible. I think we provide poor role models, and that creates the challenges. I still believe that even today, if a creator can come up with a strong idea, be disciplined in honing the craft of their practice, focus on the best platform, take care of the community that constellates around them, and not get impatient for instant gratification, then they will find supporters and the sustainable scale for their ideas. Editorial projects like *Self Service* are still a healthy necessity in this business because we work with talent; we provide context, inspiration, experience, and visibility. I think you can argue that independent magazines have even more relevance and importance today because this is where the high benchmarks for creative excellence are still to be found.

CHARLOTTE: I really appreciate the way that you've structured this book as almost a "how to" of being creative, with the practices of graphic design, typography, creative direction, editorial language and design, photography, and art direction all present. You utilize these practices in the making of *Self Service*, and by separating out these layers of craft in this book's sequence, you clarify what a magazine is from the perspective of a maker. It's kind of overwhelming, but it's your journey, and it's also a route map for others.

EZRA: I hope it is. That is my intent both in this book and in every editor's letter that I have written for *Self Service*. I write to encapsulate the thought processes of that issue and that season of the magazine. I often use writing to send an open letter to the reader and call out what I feel we need to pay attention to, what is culturally at stake, what we are navigating, and the mindsets and motivations that our collaborators on that issue of the magazine are bringing into play.

CHARLOTTE: I enjoy your writing style, and I'm really glad that you have included a selection of your editor's letters from *Self Service*. They have an urgency and pace to them. I believe you. Do you enjoy writing?

EZRA: No! It's always hard to write. It has become a joke in the *Self Service* office because the printer is often waiting for my editor's note until the very last minute. I'm not a natural-born writer at all. I love language, but I have to work at it. First of all, you have to understand what you want to say. My writing style is never fluid or simple, and I wish I had more wit. I'm very wordy. I write my draft, then Lana reads it, then my father reads it. I value their help in putting words to what I am feeling in the moment. But ultimately, I think that part of visual thinking and your job as a magazine editor is to think and to have a point of view and to express these things in words. When you're lucky enough to have a magazine and the pretext of writing the editor's letter, then you do it. As I was reading them again, it became evident to me that I have an underlying need to restate the fundamental premise of *Self Service* and the intention of the magazine to support exploration, innovation, creativity, and new generations of thinkers and practitioners.

CHARLOTTE: The book section titled "The Juxtaposed" is about the relationship between image and text, and I read this section as not just a facet of how you are breaking down the practice of art direction and graphic design in order for us to see the elements of your practice. I also read it as the section of the book that openly analyzes the stylistic "signature" of your creative and art-directorial approaches and the tonal range and flexibility you have created within *Self Service*.

EZRA: I'm very, very sensitive to the way we structure the magazine, and sometimes intentionally *de*-structure to give the viewing experience its rhythm and flow, and that sequence of the book lays that out. So much of the work of crafting a magazine layout is making sure that everything—every story and every message—is distinct. From the start of the process to the end, we work in a traditional way where we look at everything together, make sure there is a coherent and wonderful journey through the front of the book, the ads, the editor's letter, conversations, essays, special portfolios, and through the editorial well of the magazine. I also have the luxury to play with print production for each issue of *Self Service*. We offset print the pages of the magazine to have better control of the ink and the quality and range of multiple paper stocks, helping to differentiate and amplify the various sections of the magazine. We have certain graphic grids that are recurrent and identify sections of the editorial pages. We play with type point size, line breaks, and changes in tone where we can. Story titles can be succinct or a quote, a whole page of text, and sometimes ironic or poetic or funny. As an art director and graphic designer, I am perhaps known for taking classic design elements and playing with them and shifting them up. My layouts are always underpinned by a grid system, even when I am pursuing the most experimental layouts. We might repeat an image or add further steps like reprinting or rephotographing pages that create layouts that are intentionally a little bit "off." Words are broken over multiple lines. I have always had a group of fonts like Caslon, Bodoni, Helvetica, Futura, and Avant Garde that I have learned how to flex and play with over the course of three decades. These are added layers of active choices that create the richness of *Self Service* as a physical experience. It's a combination of all these things that celebrates the congregation of talent in each issue of the magazine with bold intention.

CHARLOTTE: I think it's really interesting that on top of all these active choices and fine balances that you make as the creative director and editor of *Self Service*, you also manage to successfully bring your own photography, and principally your Polaroids, into the editorial conversation. We are so used to thinking of photography as one of the sacred grounds of authorship, and for your photographs to not destabilize the collaborative balance that you set up within *Self Service* is something that I note with all respect to you. Can you tell me more about how photography became such an important facet of your creative journey?

EZRA: I started to create a body of photographic work 20 years ago. *Self Service* was well established by that point and constantly provided me with such a privileged vantage point onto the broad terrain of creative cultures. In the context of *Self Service*—so, not independently—it felt urgent for me to work out how to document these incredible encounters with the creative communities who were participating in the cultural conversations that *Self Service* was tapping into. I first tried to document all the situations I was going into and the people I was meeting in the studio, at runway shows, at art fairs with a compact digital camera, but it really didn't work for me. I always admired Andy Warhol's Polaroids and saw how photography operated as the social documentation of who passed through the Factory. I felt there was a parallel potential for *Self Service*, and how in 20 or 30 years' time, a cache of Polaroids would be the visual record of all these energies and people of all kinds who came into the *Self Service* orbit. I tested a Polaroid setup and immediately fell in love with the results and the practicality of it. It just suited exactly what I wanted. It is a Land camera so you can shoot anywhere, but, ideally, it's meant for portraiture.

CHARLOTTE: What are the qualities of a Polaroid camera that mean it's a camera for portraiture?

EZRA: All you need is a subject and a tiny piece of a white or gray wall for them to stand against. You have these square flashcubes that fix on top of the camera; you can get a diffuser fitting that creates an absolutely beautiful glow of light that smooths out some of your facial lines and imperfections. I discovered that by placing my subject at a specific distance from the wall, a striking dark shadow can be created when the flash goes off that dramatizes and delineates around your subject against the pale background.

CHARLOTTE: The way you are describing the technical character of working with a Polaroid camera, it sounds like it is simultaneously very specific as well as flexible and mobile. It's like a photography equivalent to the layout grid of a graphic designer.

EZRA: In a way, yes. I have to create a very intimate space in which to work. If I'm on set in a big photo studio, I still have to create a little black box of a space to make portraits. I'm also very specific with the size of the table, a white tablecloth, a comfortable chair, a scented candle, music, my flashcubes lined up. You construct the moments of complicity between you and your photographic subject. I need to feel self-confident, and I need the person I am photographing to feel the same way. With Polaroid, it's a very participative process because you do not hide anything, you are not shooting on film, and you are sharing these unique images in real time.

CHARLOTTE: Do you choreograph your subjects?

EZRA: Yes, it's like a ballet where I move around them and ask the person to move into a position they want to hold as I search for the composition that will frame them.

CHARLOTTE: That's an intense bodily experience for both of you.

EZRA: It's exhausting! I thrive on those moments, but I also have to prepare and manage myself—get enough sleep, stay healthy, be in the right frame of mind for these photographic marathons. I would say that three-quarters of all the 3,000 or so portraits that made it to the final selection were either the first Polaroid or the final image, always at the point of the highest intensity of the shared moment between the subject and myself.

CHARLOTTE: I am struck by the way that your description of what frame of mind you have when photographing—the intensity of your being very present in the way that you engage with your subjects—mirrors a very present point of view and my experience as a reader/viewer of the two recent film issues of *Self Service* magazine that you created with Lana in 2021. At the height of the pandemic lockdowns, they are pretty remarkable digital translations of what you have established in print, with the same visual intensity, novelty, and overarching sense of order. I flag that because still—20 years down the line from Web 2.0—it is notable to experience highly finessed, truly creative visions of fashion culture using the "canvas" of digital media.

EZRA: Whether printed or digital, every issue of *Self Service* holds what we and our collaborators are feeling at the moment of putting a body of work together. The inception of every issue is a reflection on what we have just done, what we've gone through, and not just about the specifics of our creative silo but much more broadly than that. We stand for creative freedom, and I think you are responding to that being present in a film version of *Self Service* at the same level as in a printed version. I often say that we're like the postgraduate program for visual thinking because we feel the imperative to communicate directly and collaborate with creatives who want to do something incredible with us.

CHARLOTTE: If anything, the film issues of *Self Service* in 2021 were even more expansive than the printed versions that went before it.

EZRA: It had been a while since Lana and I were exploring the idea of launching a film issue as a complementary experience to its printed primary version. We were interested in providing the reader with a richer and unique sensory experience combining animated typography, advertising pages that came to life, still images, film, sound, the real voices of interviewees, a made-to-measure music score, and with pages flipping in a magazine-like manner and in a linear timeline mirroring the magazine page order. All of this was created in motion graphics and post-produced in studio as a film. It was the first time that something like this had ever been done. When we were hit with Covid, everything suddenly turned digital so it was the right moment to provide our industry with a new, innovative, creative experience.

This is also what the magazine and our agency are about—being the places and the vehicles to explore and create new digital experiences. We pioneered by creating the first bespoke digital fashion ads with Chloé, the first real relevant iPad application version of a magazine, one of the first to work with augmented reality in the industry. We are capable of creating an Instagram filter that is creative, interactive, and innovative all the way to a mass-market, worldwide augmented-reality retail experience for Zara.

CHARLOTTE: I really loved the editor's letter from issue 57 and that you were framing our coming back out of the various lockdowns. You describe this moment in a very hopeful way. You use the word "awakening" to describe what it feels like to emerge into a return to business and a hope that we will be "device-sober" and not rush to—or ever—return to normal and, instead, use this for a time to do things differently.

EZRA: I like the expression "device-sober." I don't want us to lose our ability to fully explore without restraint and in a place of unexpected excellence. We have been so formatted, and we naturalize conventions rather than rise above them—we are corrupted by them so easily. When I wrote this editor's letter, I was longing for a new age of innocence. I have hope that the new generations who are coming will navigate and communicate with new mindsets. I ended my editorial by saying, "To all you emerging talented people and new generations who decide to engage in the creative fields, be fierce, be disruptive. We do not want followers, but innovators, dreamers, pioneers. Take us out of our comfort zones and explore and define new forms of artistic expression. Live a new age of innocence in harmony with yourself, your past, where you want to go, and what you aspire to achieve." I think that's what I am hoping for. The only way to truly be creative or to do interesting work is to have the capacity to lose yourself in what you do. You have to be able to make mistakes without being afraid of making them, and to be intellectually and emotionally receptive to intuition. Our work is a way of engaging what is in front of and around us. Whether you're documenting it through a camera lens, or you're writing or putting it together in a magazine—these are just different ways that you engage, learn, and understand what is happening. Very early on in my journey, one of my taglines was, "Revisiting the past, engaging the present, to create the future." If you add in further ingredients of taking risks and being at play, then hopefully we move culture forward.

BE HIND THE LENS

Ezra Petronio's Polaroid portraits carry an elegant directness and still tangible sense of momentary, intimate, and revealing interactions between photographer and subject. Using a Big Shot Land camera, with its fixed focal length, integrated flashcubes, and the magic of the so-called "instant" image-making chemistry of Polaroid, Petronio finds and amplifies the gait and character of a constellation of cultural icons. They present an almost overwhelming sense of being in uniquely close proximity to this radical pantheon of thinkers and creators. We are also shown here a selection of Petronio's early fashion Polaroid grid and collage configurations as well as his experiments with the chemical properties of Polaroid. They represent the start of his authored fashion image-making practice and a key moment in the ongoing evolution of his photography.

Left to right, top to bottom: MICHAEL KORS, YOHJI YAMAMOTO, JUN TAKAHASHI, JIL SANDER, SONIA RYKIEL, JAY JOPLING, ANN DEMEULEMEESTER, JEAN PAUL GAULTIER, NICOLAS GHESQUIÈRE, GRAYDON CARTER, ALBER ELBAZ, HEDI SLIMANE, GIANFRANCO FERRÉ, PAUL SMITH, GIORGIO ARMANI, MARIO TESTINO.

Left to right, top to bottom: MARY-KATE OLSEN, PAQUITA PAQUIN, QUENTIN TARANTINO, GLENN O'BRIEN, FRANÇOIS NARS, JAN KAPLICKÝ, ASA MADER, CARINE ROITFELD, LOUISE WILSON, JOEL MADDEN, JEAN-BAPTISTE MONDINO, EMMANUEL PERROTIN, JEAN-PAUL GOUDE, TERRY JONES, NOOMI RAPACE, MARTINE SITBON.

Left to right, top to bottom: JEFF KOONS, KARL LAGERFELD, JUDY BLAME, JACQUES HERZOG, SYLVIE FLEURY, PHILIP-LORCA DICORCIA, GRACE CODDINGTON, HAMISH BOWLES, JONATHAN NEWHOUSE, VINCENT DARRÉ, MATTHEW MARKS, TIM NOBLE, ISABELLA BLOW, EDWARD ENNINFUL OBE, JOHN ARMLEDER, NICK KNIGHT.

Left to right, top to bottom: JEFFERSON HACK, JOANA PREISS, CHARLOTTE RAMPLING, PHILIPPE ZDAR, HORST DIEKGERDES, GIAMBATTISTA VALLI, CHRISTIAAN, JOE MCKENNA, KEHINDE WILEY, PIERGIORGIO DEL MORO, CLAUDIA SCHIFFER, KARL TEMPLER, KYLIE MINOGUE, AGNÈS B., BAMBOU, DICK PAGE.

Left to right, top to bottom: VANESSA BEECROFT, ARIELLE DOMBASLE, ALEXANDER WANG, ROLF SNOEREN, PEDRO WINTER, EMMANUELLE SEIGNER, ISAMAYA FFRENCH, PANOS YIAPANIS, MARIANNE FAITHFULL, STEPHEN GAN, CHRISTOPHER BAILEY, VIVIENNE WESTWOOD, MICHAEL CLARK, ALEXANDER MCQUEEN, DOMENICO DOLCE, STEFANO GABBANA.

KANYE WEST. 2013

LOUISE BOURGEOIS. 2004

Left to right, top to bottom: JENNY HOLZER, FRANCESCO CLEMENTE, CHARLOTTE GAINSBOURG, HUSSEIN CHALAYAN, RICK OWENS, ANDRÉE PUTMAN, MIUCCIA PRADA, RONNIE WOOD, LOULOU DE LA FALAISE, EILEEN FORD, FRÉDÉRIC BEIGBEDER, TRACEY EMIN, YANN BARTHÈS, CARLA BRUNI, RICHARD BUCKLEY, ALESSANDRO MICHELE.

Left to right, top to bottom: HENRY WOLF, VENETIA SCOTT, CAMILLA NICKERSON, MICHAEL STIPE, CHARLOTTE COTTON, MARY-KATE OLSEN, AZZEDINE ALAÏA, LÉA SEYDOUX, FRANCA SOZZANI, MIGUEL ADROVER, HAIDER ACKERMANN, CHRISTIAN LACROIX, TOMMIE SUNSHINE, TERRY RICHARDSON, VALERIA GOLINO, SARAH SOPHIE FLICKER.

Left to right, top to bottom: PETER LINDBERGH, MIKE MILLS, NATALIA VODIANOVA, LOU DOILLON, TRAVIS SCOTT, MARIO SORRENTI, STEFANO PILATI, HANNAH MACGIBBON, SPIKE JONZE, ADAM KIMMEL, BRYANBOY, JANET JACKSON, KIM JONES, MARY-KATE AND ASHLEY OLSEN, MARIA GRAZIA CHIURI.

Left to right, top to bottom: GAIA REPOSSI, PAUL SEVIGNY, POPPY DELEVINGNE, CHLOË SEVIGNY, JULIE GAYET, VANESSA PARADIS, XAVIER VEILHAN, HELMUT LANG, CLÉMENCE POÉSY, MICHÈLE LAMY, CHINA CHOW, NAOMI CAMPBELL, BRYAN ADAMS, JEAN-PAUL BELMONDO, JANE BIRKIN.

KYLIAN MBAPPÉ. 2021

VIRGIL ABLOH. 2016

TOM FORD. 2010

PHOEBE PHILO. 2010

Left: JUERGEN TELLER. 2011 *Right:* TILDA SWINTON. 2010

Left: PETER DUNDAS. 2011   *Right:* FRANCESCO VEZZOLI. 2010

Left to right, top to bottom: MALGOSIA BELA, MISSY RAYDER, LIZZY JAGGER, ANJA RUBIK, SASHA PIVOVAROVA, LEONOR SCHERRER, AMBER VALLETTA.

Left to right, top to bottom: ANNA SELEZNEVA AND MALGOSIA BELA, MARY-KATE OLSEN, CHANEL IMAN, ANJA RUBIK, DAPHNE GROENEVELD, RAQUEL ZIMMERMANN, STELLA MAXWELL.

Left to right, top to bottom: CARMEN KASS, KARLIE KLOSS, ANJA RUBIK, JERRY HALL.

Left to right, top to bottom: ANJA RUBIK, RAQUEL ZIMMERMANN, EDIE CAMPBELL, MALGOSIA BELA, DREE HEMINGWAY.

PAUL HAMELINE. 2016

Left: MAJA WEISS. 2016 *Right:* ELIZA DOUGLAS. 2016

KARLIE KLOSS. 2013

DAPHNE GROENEVELD. 2016

MALGOSIA BELA. 2010

LARA STONE. 2009

RAQUEL ZIMMERMANN. 2009

CARMEN KASS. 2010

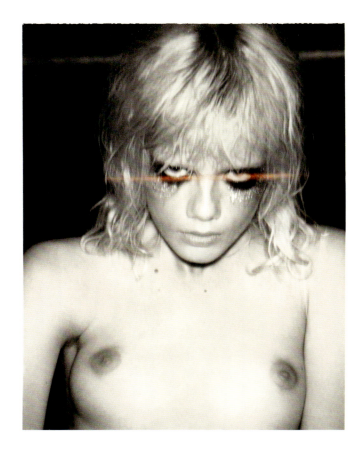

Top, left: ANJA RUBIK. 2016 *Top, right:* MARJAN JONKMAN. 2015 *Bottom:* ENIKO MIHALIK. 2009

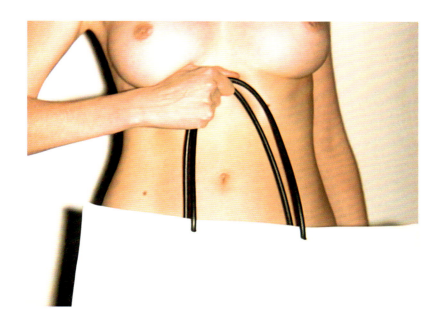

LARA STONE. 2009

MALGOSIA BELA. 2010

KARL LAGERFELD. 2003

LILY ALDRIDGE. 2016

KENDALL JENNER. 2016

If you were to ask fashion and magazine industry insiders how they see Ezra Petronio's graphic design style, they would most likely say that it is characterized as definite, instinctive, and bold, where combinations of images and language are abstracted, de-conventionalized, and taken to the very edge. Here is a compilation of the key graphic and typographic ideas that Petronio has developed since the founding of *Self Service* magazine. Always assured, never too precious, Petronio's exactitude with the classic fonts and grid layouts as well as the granular precision of his spacing of letters and control of language continually hold our attention.

IS THE ARTIST. HE'S FR
NCE HE PASSES THRO
F IT MAKES HIM UNH
Christophe Girard, 2

RCONS. UNL
OULD NOT TE
NER TO ADHE
ST. THEY WOU
O REMAIN FR
Rei Kawakubo, 20

TRY IS BEHIN
T PROMOTES
LLY FOR THE
CESSIBILITY
Betsy Pearce, 2003, n°18

ME INTERESTED IN
HATED – A COLOR
TO WORK WITH IT.
ST MY OWN TASTE
Miuccia Prada, 2003, n°18

STRONG CREATIVE
OMETHING GREAT
Rei Kawakubo, 2000, n°13

UP WITH
AT FEELS
ERE'S NO
NG POINT
Chris Cunningham, 2001, n°14

I THINK IF I
MAKEOVER
VER OF THE
ASON. THEN
TO SCREAM
Suzy Menkes, 2001, n°14

UT A LOT ON THE
REAL AUTHOR IS
EOPLE TRYING TO
E HUMAN THING

self service
embrace absurdity with bright clockwise

Photography by Nathaniel Goldberg.
Styling by Emmanuelle Alt.

9. 1998, N°9
THE BIGGEST NO-NO OF THE SEASON
IS HIGH HEELS WITH LONG SKIRTS
*Photography by David Sims.
Styling by Anna Cockburn.*

10. 2005, n°22
EXPLORE THE SUBTLETY OF CHANCE
*Photography by Suzanne Koller.
Styling by Camille Bidault-Waddington.*

COEXIST
HIGHER PU
Rosemarie Trockel, 2004, n°20

A GOOD PARTY IS A PARTY WHERE PEOP
Gaspard Noé, 2002, n°17

WHEN YOU'RE SEARCHING FOR SOMETHING AND YOU FIND
OF GREAT HAPPINESS. IT'S IN MY WORK THAT I'VE BEEN
Yves Saint Laurent, 2000, n°12

I SIMPLY GET TIRED OF
THE SAME CONCEPTS

IT'S NICE
WHERE P
THAN TO

SKY-HIGH'S THE LIMIT AS MINIS MADE A BOLD COMEBACK

PHOTOGRAPHY BY DIRK SEIDEN SCHWAN
STYLING BY ANDRE WALKER
HAIR BY SEB BASCLE@LIGHT HOUSE
MAKEUP BY MICHELLE RAINER@STREETERS
MODELS: KRISTINA S. AND MICHEL G.@NATHALIE, KIRSTY RICHARDS@MARYLIN
CECILIA ANDERSEN@KARIN, SOPHIE BADER@NEXT
STYLING ASSITANCE BY GUYA MARINI, HAIR ASSITANCE BY SEBASTIEN
OPPOSITE PAGE: PRINTED SILK BUSTIER DRESS WITH SEWN-ON SYNTHETIC HAIR BY JEAN-CHARLES DE CASTELBAJAC

THE OBJECT, THE SIGN, A STORY OF THE NINETIES

THE OBJECT, THE SIGN A STORY OF THE NINETIES. L'OBJET, LE SIGNE, UNE HISTOIRE DES ANNEES 90.
BY STEPHANIE MOISDON TREMBLEY   TRANSLATED BY BRIAN HOLMES

TEN YEARS RECONSIDERED

**10 YEARS. 23 ISSUES. 5145 PAGES. 11396 PHO[TOS]
1678 FEATURED PEOPLE. 221 INTERVIEWED [PEOPLE]
FASHION STORIES. 2961 FASHION PAGES. 14[__]
BRANDS. 102 CONTRIBUTORS. 73 PHOTOGR[APHERS]
21 STYLISTS. 3476 FASHION CREDITS.**

edited by Thomas Persson

100 THING

by Suzanne Koller, Carina Frey, Marie Chaix, Nicolas Trembley and Patrick Li.

1 **A small fortune.** "Mini" F…
2 **Intersection.** Installation …
www.lund.se/konsthallen/
3 **Emergency.** Pro Helvetia …
4 **The big apple.** Apple orch…
5 **Toppings.** Baseball caps, …
6 **Red light district.** Installat…

CONVERSATIONS WITH

NORMA KAMALI
WALTHER & KASPER KÖNIG
GERHARD SEIDL
LISA EISNER
ROMA VON ONO
CHRISTIAN LACROIX

TRANSCENDENTOBJECTIVITY

Photography by David Armstrong Styling by Panos Yiapanis

I'VE ALWAYS HATED OVERTLY POLITICAL MUSIC. I THINK THE THING WITH MUSIC IS THAT IT WORKS ON A KIND OF PURELY EMOTIONAL LEVEL

Jarvis Cocker, 2003, n°19

I'VE LIVED THROUGH HELL AND I'LL KEEP ON GOING

Jeremy Scott, 2000, n°13

A WORK OF ART THAT ISN'T SHOCKING IS NO GOOD, WHICH MAKES MAKING ART A COMPLETE WASTE OF TIME

Jake Chapman, 2004, n°20

TOP 10 TOPICS OF CONVERSATION

1. ON CHAOS IN WONDERLAND, 2003, n°18 2. ON ACCIDENTAL ART AND BRANDING A SOCIAL CAUSE, 2004, n°21 3. ON BEING AN OUTSIDER ON THE INSIDE, 2004, n°21 4. ON HIDDEN PLEASURE GONE UNDERGROUND, 2003, n°18 5. ON HYBRIDS IN HOLLYWOOD AND DRESSING A NARRATIVE, 2004, n°21 6. ON THE REFUSAL TO BE CATEGORIZED AND UNDERMINED, 2002, n°17 7. ON NEGOTIATING INTANGIBLES, 2003, n°18 8. ON THE SUPERFICIALITY OF AVANT-GARDISM, 2001, n°14 9. ON SEEKING PEACE FROM CONSUMERISM, 2003, n°18 10. ON DRESSING FOR THE REVOLUTION, 2002, n°17

WHEN I WORKED FOR FAIRCHILD, I WAS SEATED FIRST ROW AND EVERYBODY WAS KISSING MY ASS. WHEN I MOVED TO MIRABELLA, ALL OF SUDDEN I WAS SEATED BETWEEN THE 3RD AND 5TH ROWS, AND COULDN'T GET A PR PERSON ON THE PHONE. I KNOW HOW THE SYSTEM WORKS

Richard Buckley, 2000, n°12

I THINK IT'S DIFFICULT TO BE CREATIVE FOR A LONG TIME IF YOU DON'T HAVE ZILLIONS OF REFERENCES
Karl Lagerfeld, 1999, n°11

YOU CAN'T BREAK MY SPIRIT

Polly Mellen, 2002, n°17

OURTNEY LOVE
ROCK N'ROLL
On perpetually landing on one's feet
304

336

TOIRE DE TELLANE
HAUTE JOAILLERIE
On the thrilling appeal of the fake
316

340

CATHY HORYN
FASHION THINKING
gration of opinion in new journalism
322

346

JULIE & LUDIVINE
CINEMA TALK
On the inhabitation of a character
326

352

LUIGI MURENU
TRANSFORMATIVE BEAUTY
On the philosophy of the image
332

356

UNLEASHED JEANS GENIE

SEVEN IMPASSIONED DESIGNERS EXPLORE THEIR CREATIVE INSTINCTS BY RE-INTERPRETING AN ENDURING CLASSIC
PHOTOGRAPHY BY MAGNUS UNNAR STYLING BY MARIE CHAIX

OPPOSITE PAGE: CHARLES ANASTASE. AGE: 26. BRITISH. SECOND COLLECTION. ITEM GIVEN: ONE PAIR OF DIESEL JEANS. MADE AN OVERSIZED BERET. OVERSIZED JEAN BERET, CHARLES ANASTASE. WHITE COTTON OVERSIZED SHIRT, ALAN LE BLANC. GRAY SATIN OVERSIZED SHORTS, FADE. MAKEUP BY CHRISTINE CORBEL@JED ROOT. HAIR BY DAMIEN BOISSINOT@CALLISTE. MODEL: MICHAELA@ELITE. STYLING ASSISTANCE BY CAMILLE VINCENT.

SUBLIMINE THE PURPLE VARIATIONS

HELMUT LANG
EXCERPTS FROM THE LONG ISLAND DIARIES

To begin with, are these "Long Island Diaries" a work in progress? It is an excerpt of an ongoing work without title. I am working on some kind of a diary without the usual dynamics of diaries, because I am naturally unable to follow its conventional structure. I am planning to have parts of it indefinite and parts of it occasionally communicated. Some of the works are quite isolated and others are done in collaboration. *What inspired/inspires this project?* The idea of an indefinite structure. The idea of "self service" in the first place, to be shared with others later, and also the exploration of less urban contexts. *You have always had a very close and organic relationship with the art world. How do you see this relationship growing today and how important a place does it occupy?* My relationship with the art world has not changed. I think that it is an important relationship. *Have you found that art has progressively replaced designing as a vehicle for your creative expression?* It could be a possibility, but I am against putting myself in a situation of defining what I am doing right now because it would not allow an organic outcome. It is really more about formulating an alphabet for an unknown language. The content will vary on who will be exposed to it. I am less interested in the perfect communication right now. In this creative procedure it is not bad to not owe anything to anybody. *How difficult is it for you not to design collections?* Not at all. I wanted change in order to progress, wherever it will lead to. *Has the sudden change of pace affected you? Do you find that working within a stressful context or a more relaxed one changes the creative experience for you?* Being able to define one's own deadlines is rather priceless. I was always attracted by the idea that everything has its own time. Certain things are fast and certain things take longer. There is always a clear shot and then there is always the object, which you revisit as long as it seems right. It also promotes projects that do not need closure within a defined time, so the approach is immediately much more open and the outcome has a chance of being more unexpected. *Could you imagine redesigning a collection?* Only time will tell. *If so, would you come back with a radically different perspective on the business?* Radically different is always good.

MMER
APHY
S

OVERSI
CHNEI
GHER
LISTON
WKES

GOING FOR YOUR WOW EFFECT

The Cannes Film Festival is an endless nonstop ride of exhilaration and frenzy that threatens to consume you completely. The different levels of star wattage multiply year after year, from the genuine A-listers to the indie royalty to the porn stars to the Russian billionaires with their underage arm candy. Fashion has stepped up in an increasingly major way, with more and more brands installing fleeting showrooms in plush hotel suites. Although at times the Boulevard de la Croisette feels like nothing more than the ultimate jetsetter's spot to see and be seen, the festival is unparalleled as one of the world's foremost hubs of promotion and old-fashioned wheeling and dealing. The countless parties are not (merely) froth, but influential power-meetings cloaked in layers of glitter and lace. Glamour is as glamour does: French magazine *Madame Figaro* and the house of Chanel hosted a party for Karl Lagerfeld's photography exhibition at the Canal Plus studio, and the room swirled with actors, television journalists, fashion editors, designers, artists, semi-celebrities, and wannabes. There, amidst the crinkle of rustling silk and the glare of razor-sharp diamonds, we shone yet another blinding light in the eyes of the stunningly beautiful and influential. *Cannes, Canal Plus Studios, May 23rd 2007* **Photography by Ezra Petronio**

Claudia Schiffer, model.

Elodie Bouchez, actress.

STARS & STYLE
PORTRAITS LONDON

PHOTO BY EZRA PETRONIO

Our impulse for social documentation has again led us acro— intricate web of our "extended family tree." And what bega— and what make up our cultural and intellectual environme— fying experience. Traveling to a new city and meeting concentrated period of time, we perceived not only the si— and undeniable differences. While we

A unique collaboration with Supreme. Paris January 17th, 2016. Photography by Ezra Petronio. Styling by Alastair McKimm. Featuring the Supreme spring/summer 2016 collection.

RDASHIAN WEST, *media personality*
2012 (203 weeks), 3369 posts, 57.4 million followers
ER JACKET, GIVENCHY BY RICCARDO TISCI.

Me, Myself and I
Photographed by @ezrapetronio On documenting the digital influencers; a series of portraits of the Instagram players captured over a weekend during #pfw15

THE BIGGEST NO-NO OF THE SEASON IS HIGH HEELS WITH LONG SKIRTS.

WHAT MATTERS TO ME IS ALLURE, WHICH IS A LITTLE STRANGE BECAUSE IT'S NOT AN IDEA THAT IS OFTEN ASSOCIATED WITH GUYS

Hedi Slimane, 2000, n°12

RESISTANCE, WHEN PEOPLE SAY NO TO YOU, WHEN PEOPLE HATE YOU, IS VERY STIMULATING

Serge Lutens, 2003, n°18

I DON'T CONSIDER MYSELF AN ARTIST!

Rei Kawakubo, 2000, n°13

WHAT HELMUT (LANG) AND I FEEL IS, WHY DOES THERE ALWAYS HAVE TO BE A FORMULA? IN SUCH A CREATIVE INDUSTRY SHOULDN'T PEOPLE BE OPEN-MINDED, READY FOR CHANGE, ACCEPTING OF CHANGE? SHOULDN'T FASHION BE THIS JOURNEY THAT IS CONSTANTLY CHANGING AND KEEPING PEOPLE ON THEIR TOES? I JUST HATE ROUTINES AND CAN'T BEAR THIS ANTIQUATED SYSTEM

Melanie Ward, 1999, n°1

I WONDER WHY SELF SERVICE HAS NEVER DONE ANYTHING ON ME BEFORE?

Alexander McQueen, 2002, n°16

YOU COULD GIVE ME ANY COLOR, A COLOR PEOPLE THINK IS UGLY – BABY VOMIT, FOR INSTANCE – AND I COULD DESIGN A ROOM AROUND IT

Joseph Holtzman, 2000, n°13

A MAN WHO LOVES CULTURE IS SOMEONE WHO NOURISHES THE PRESENT WITH HIS KNOWLEDGE OF THE PAST

Jean-Jacques Picart, 2002, n°17

A BRAND LIKE DIESEL NEEDS TO BE GLOBAL BECAUSE, IF NOT, THE KIDS IN OTHER COUNTRIES WOULD FEEL POOR

Renzo Rosso, 2004, n°20

YOU HAVE TO EMPTY YOURSELF OUT, GET RID OF

INDULGE IN ESSENTIAL STYLE.

Photography by David Armstrong styling by Joe McKenna.

CEASE ESSLY NOND RING

...her Walter Pfeiffer is cult. Seen as the predecessor of artists such as Wolfgang ...an McGinley, the visual esthetic he has developed since the 70s is common fang-...temporary art world today. Working around the central themes of youth, sex, ...rs and still life, his studio was the Zurich equivalent of Warhol's Factory, where ...meet the art and fashion crowds as well as other "free-minded" individuals. A ...photography, Pfeiffer created elaborately colored sets in his apartment, placing his ..."kitsch" found objects. This series, The eyes, the thoughts, ceaselessly wondering, ...Service, was shot in the early 80s. Iconic portraits of anonymous boys, quickly ...ts of Paris, Milan, and Zurich, each image contains subtle references to the ener-...lture of the time.
—Nicolas Trembley

...Centre Culturel Suisse, April 30th – July 11th, 38 rue des Francs-Bourgeois, 75003 Paris. Phone 01 42 71 44 50. www.ccspa-
...a reprint of the book Walter Pfeiffer 1970-80 will be published by Editions JRP/RINGIER. info@jrp-editions.com

RETOURNEMENT DE LOOK

photography by Alasdair McLellan   styling by Olivier Rizzo

Photography by Mick Rock

KILLER
QUEEN
FREDDIE
MERCURY
MICK
ROCK

TRADITIONAL JESSICA
GDEN HEROES COLLECT
IVE IDEALS ANDRE WALK
ER ANTWERP BRANDING
SOCIAL LANDSCAPES EX
CESS MELANIE WARD HO
ME TERRITORY SUSAN CI
ANCIOLO FAMILIES NOKI
CUSTOM ECCENTRICITY
ANN DEMEULEMEESTER
NY JUERGEN TELLER EFF
ERVESCENCE CLANS AC
HIEVEMENTS FRONT 242

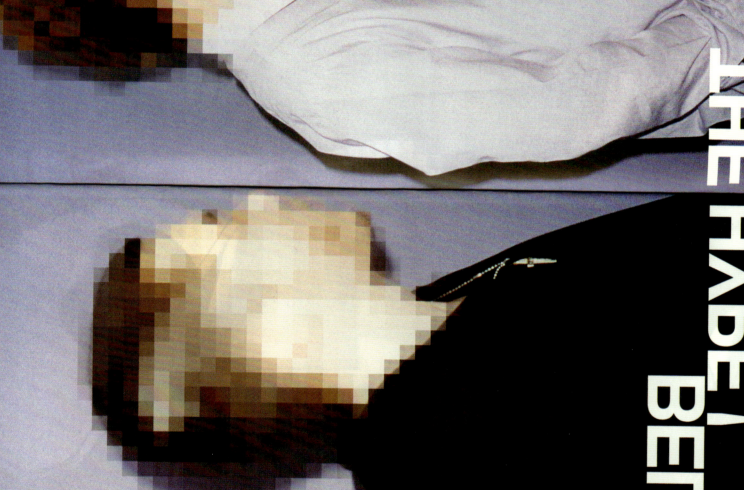

SELEC TED WORKS

PART II

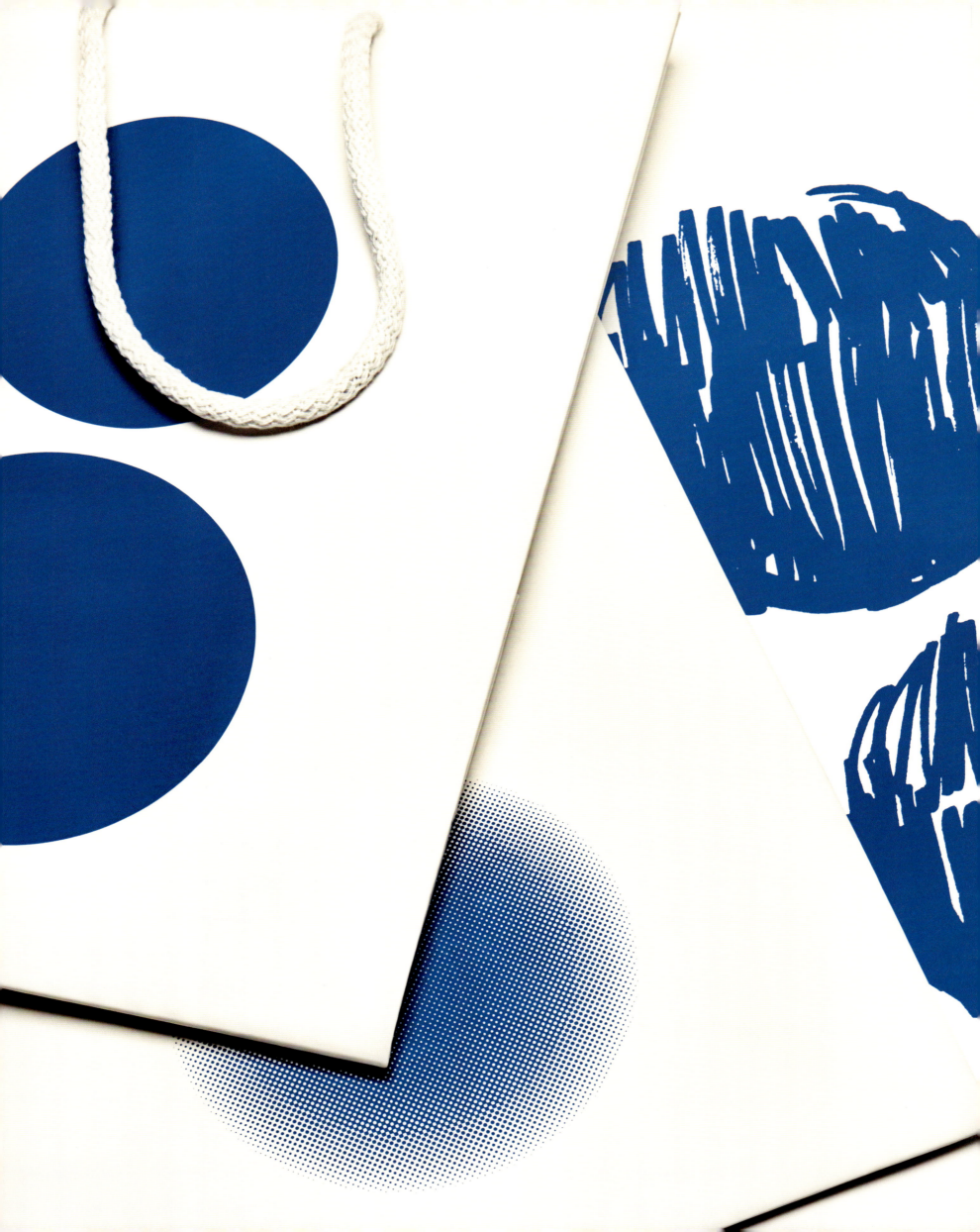

RESPECT IS BURNING

FEATURING DJ'S
DAFT PUNK
ROMANTHONY
CASSIUS
FRANÇOIS K

FRIDAY OCTOBER 16TH 1998
TWILO
530 WEST 27TH ST NYC INFO LINE: 212 462 9422
WWW.TWILOCLUB.COM

RESPECT POSTER
OPPOSITE: **COLETTE** PACKAGING

ODEUR 71
COMME des GARÇONS
*

EAU DE TOILETTE VAPORISATEUR / NATURAL SPRAY COMME DES GARÇONS PARFUM S.A. 16 PLACE VENDÔME 75001 PARIS. INGREDIENTS: ALCOHOL DENAT. 72% VOL., WATER (AQUA), FRAGRANCE (PARFUM), BENZYL SALICYLATE, BUTYL METHOXYDIBENZOYLMETHANE, HEXYL CINNAMAL, LINALOOL, BUTYLPHENYL METHYLPROPIONAL, EUGENOL, BENZYL BENZOATE, LIMONENE, ALPHA-ISOMETHYL IONONE, CITRONELLOL, BENZYL CINNAMATE, PROPYLENE GLYCOL, RED 33 (CI 17200). MADE IN FRANCE

℮ 200ML
6.8 FL.OZ.

3 488751 405317

71

COMME DES GARÇONS PARFUMS GRAPHIC DESIGN

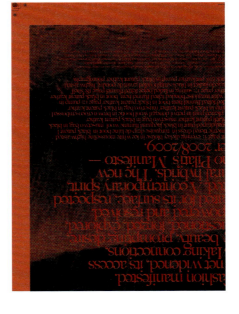

YVES SAINT LAURENT SS09 ADVERTISING & MANIFESTO

CHLOÉ PARFUMS ADVERTISING
OPPOSITE: SEVENTY ONE GIN BRAND IDENTITY & PACKAGING

EAU DE NUIT
SEVENTY ONE
GIN

GLOSSIER PLAY BRAND IDENTITY & PACKAGING
OPPOSITE: SAINT LAURENT RIVE DROITE BRAND IDENTITY & PRODUCT DESIGN

MIU MIU SEAT CARD
OPPOSITE: PRADA PACKAGING

TALK. TEXT. TIME. AN EXCEPTIONALLY SIMPLIFIED MOBILE EXPERIENCE
INTRODUCING THE PURENESS™ PHONE

TALK. TEXT. TIME. AN EXCEPTIONALLY SIMPLIFIED MOBILE EXPERIENCE
INTRODUCING THE PURENESS™ PHONE

TALK. TEXT. TIME. AN EXCEPTIONALLY SIMPLIFIED MOBILE EXPERIENCE
INTRODUCING THE PURENESS™ PHONE

Sony Ericsson
make.believe

TALK. TEXT. TIME. AN EXCEPTIONALLY SIMPLIFIED MOBILE EXPERIENCE
INTRODUCING THE PURENESS™ PHONE

Sony Ericsson
make.believe

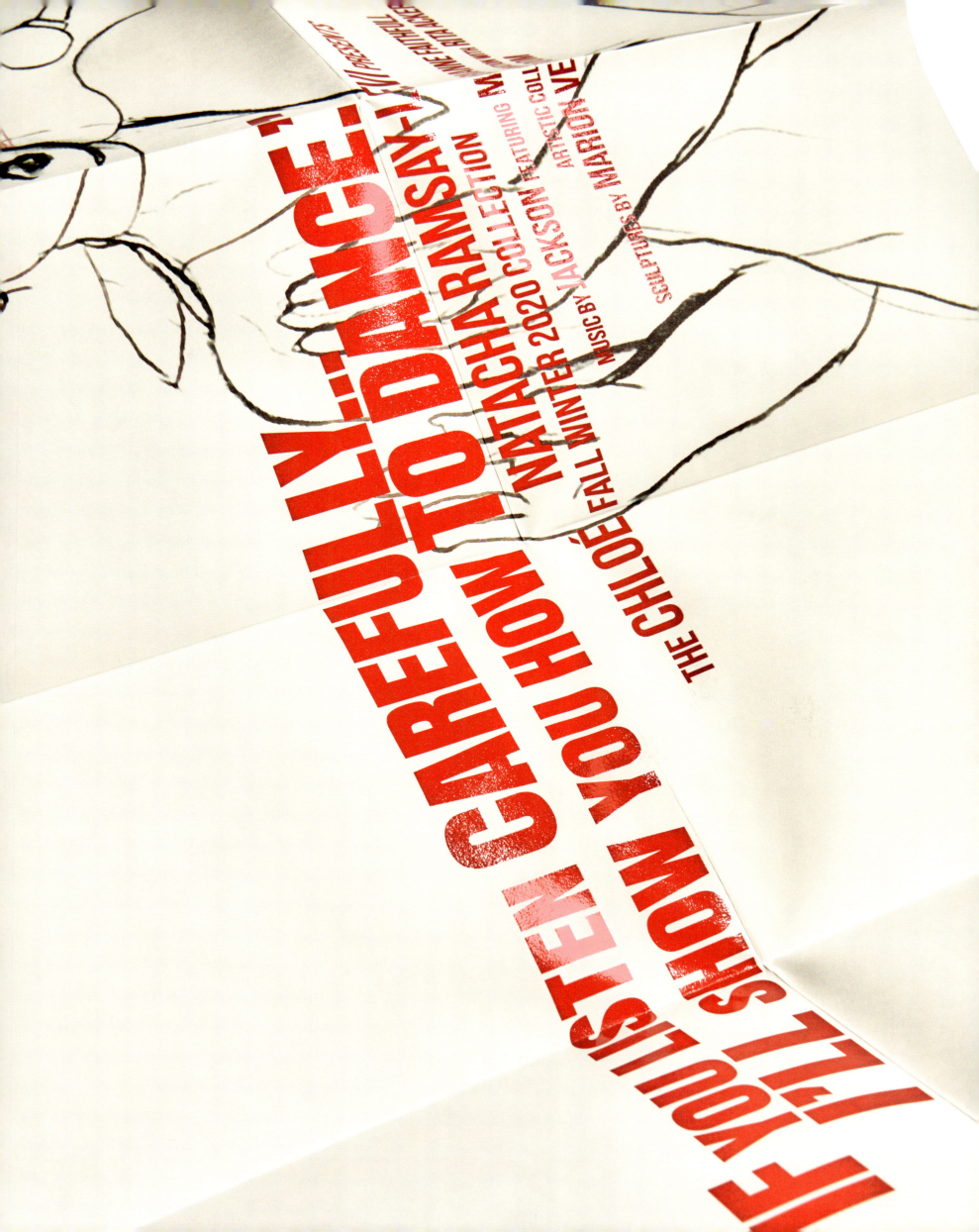

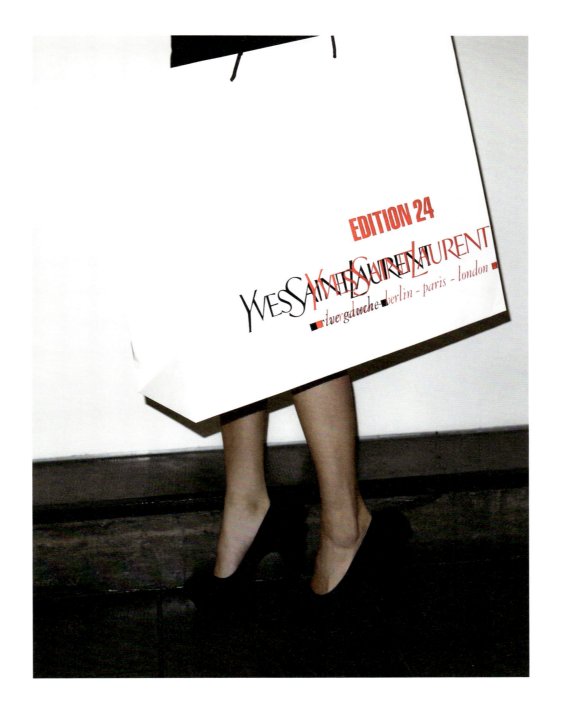

YVES SAINT LAURENT BRAND IDENTITY
OPPOSITE: **CHLOÉ** GRAPHIC DESIGN

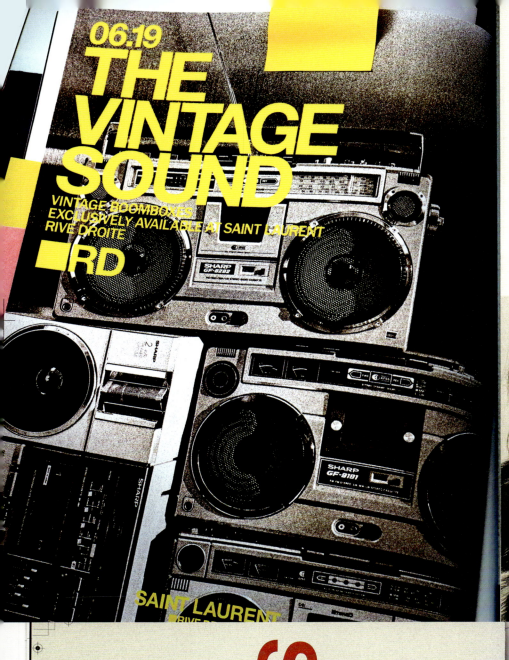

06.19
THE VINTAGE SOUND
VINTAGE BOOMBOXES
EXCLUSIVELY AVAILABLE AT SAINT LAURENT
RIVE DROITE
RD

06.19
THE LOUD MARBLE
MARBLE SPEAKER
EXCLUSIVELY AVAILABLE
AT SAINT LAURENT RIVE DROITE

SAINT LAURENT
RIVE DROITE

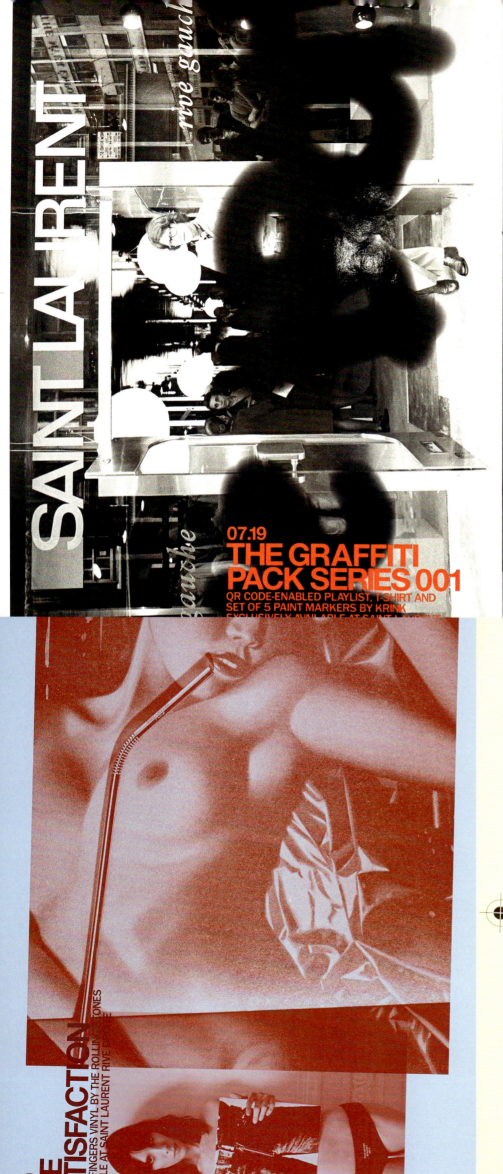

EMILIO PUCCI SS08 CATALOG
PREVIOUS SPREAD: SAINT LAURENT RIVE DROITE MANIFESTO

EMILIO PUCCI SS09 CATALOG

YVES SAINT LAURENT GRAPHIC DESIGN

EXCLUSIVE SCENTS
PRADA

N°1 IRIS, 2003
N°2 OEILLET, 2003
N°3 CUIR AMBRE, 2003
N°4 FLEUR D'ORANGER, 2003
N°5 NARCISO, 2006
N°6 TUBEREUSE, 2006
N°7 VIOLETTE, 2006
INTRODUCING:
N°8 OPOPONAX, 2007
N°9 BENJOIN, 2007
N°10 MYRRHE, 2007

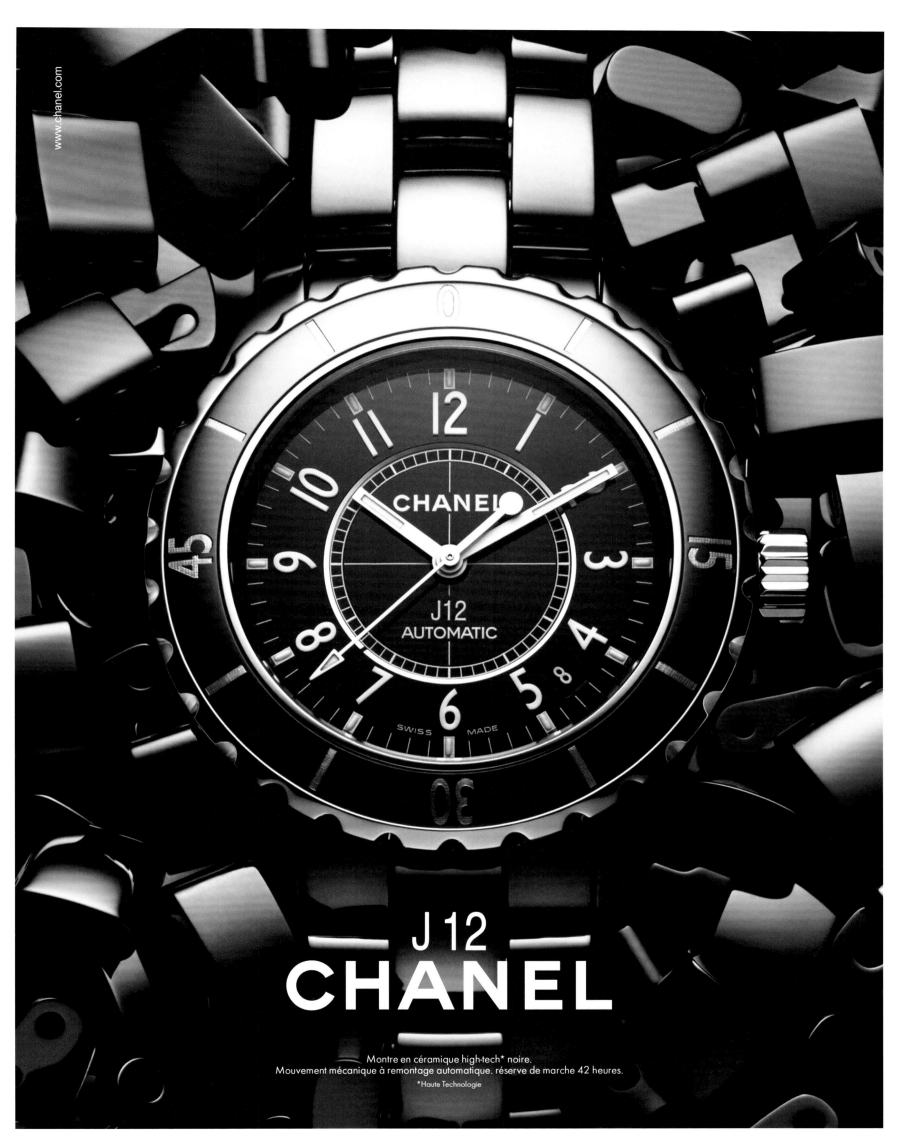

OPPOSITE: **COMME DES GARÇONS PARFUMS** GRAPHIC DESIGN
A.P.C. PACKAGING

CHLOÉ BOUTIQUE
152-153 SLOANE STREET
LONDON SW1
WWW.CHLOE.COM

CHLOÉ SS10 ADVERTISING

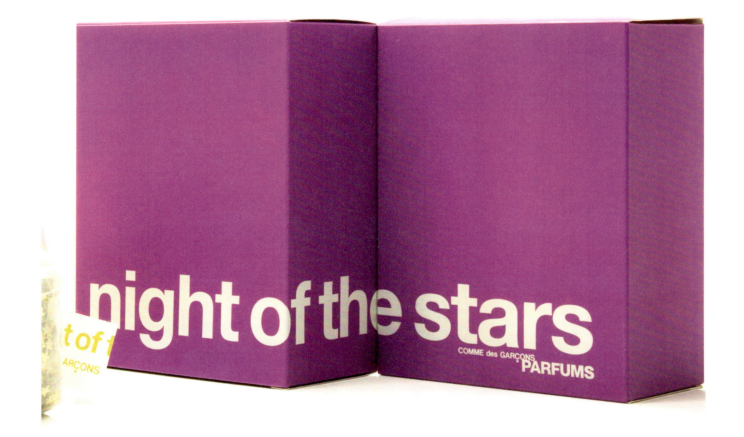

A.P.C. FW11 ADVERTISING
OPPOSITE: CONTENT MATTERS VARIOUS PROJECTS

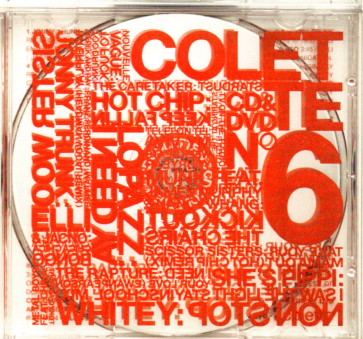

apc.fr

PRADA PARFUMS PRODUCT DESIGN
OPPOSITE: SAINT LAURENT RIVE DROITE X SELF SERVICE MATCHBOX SET

SAINT LAURENT PRODUCT DESIGN
OPPOSITE: PRADA PARFUMS PACKAGING

ysl.com

YVES SAINT LAURENT SS11 ADVERTISING

ALAÏA POSTER
OPPOSITE: COSTA BRAZIL ADVERTISING

ZARA AUGMENTED REALITY
OPPOSITE: **ZARA** BRAND COMMUNICATION

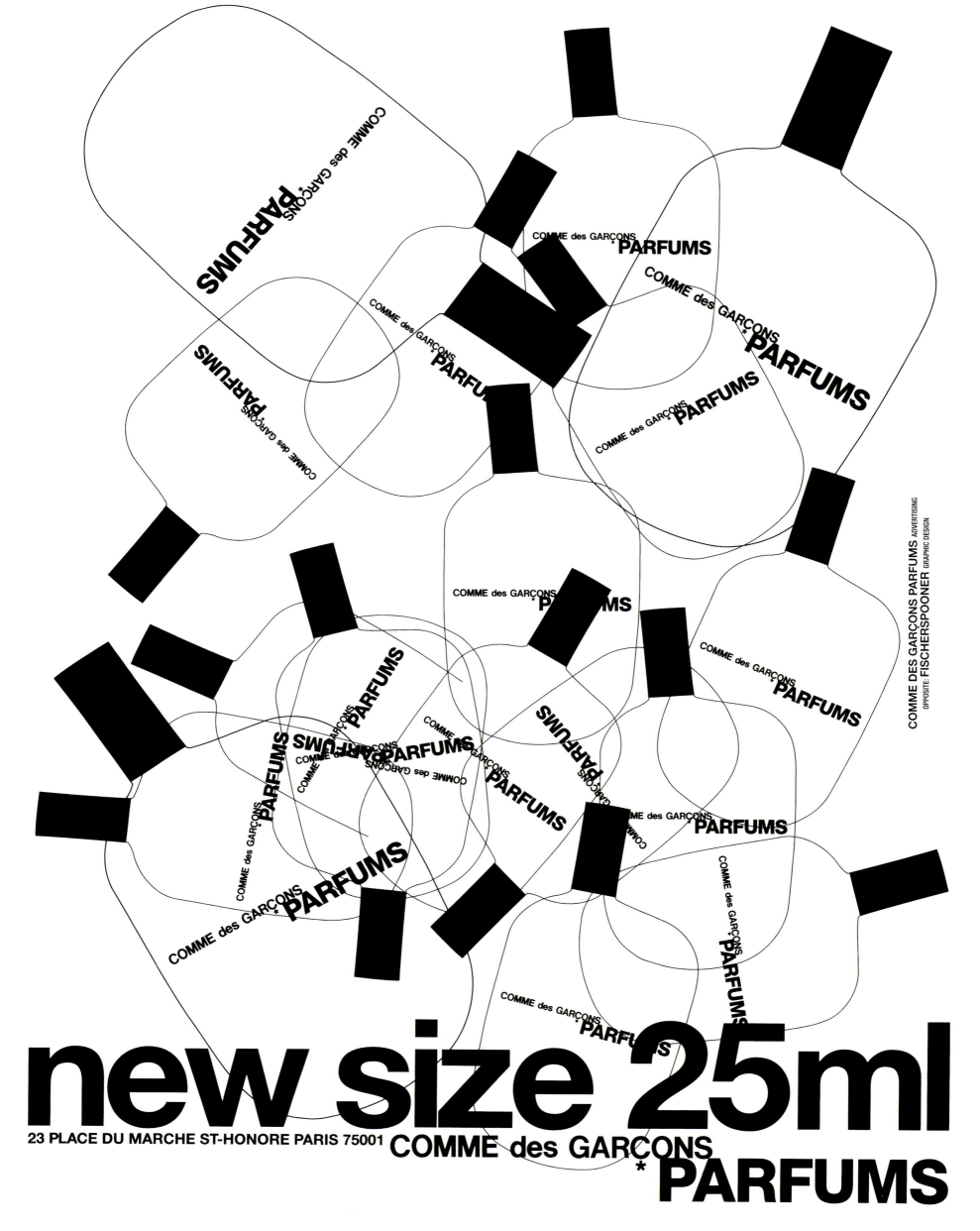

LOS-ANGELES, NOVEMBER 19-21 2007
Kirsten Dunst

LOS-ANGELES, NOVEMBER 19-21 2007
Kirsten Dunst

THE MISTINGUETT ROOM, PARIS, NOVEMBER 14–18 2005
Kim Basinger, Camilla Belle
CORSO VENEZIA 3, MILANO
VIA ROMA 8R, FIRENZE
TEL. 02 546701

miu miu

THE MISTINGUETT ROOM, PARIS, NOVEMBER 14–18 2005
Kim Basinger
CORSO VENEZIA 3, MILANO
VIA ROMA 8R, FIRENZE
TEL. 02 546701

miu miu

THE MISTINGUETT ROOM, PARIS, NOVEMBER 14–18 2005
Kim Basinger, Camilla Belle
CORSO VENEZIA 3, MILANO
VIA ROMA 8R, FIRENZE
TEL. 02 546701

THE MISTINGUETT ROOM, PARIS, NOVEMBER 14–18 2005
Kim Basinger
CORSO VENEZIA 3, MILANO
VIA ROMA 8R, FIRENZE
TEL. 02 546701

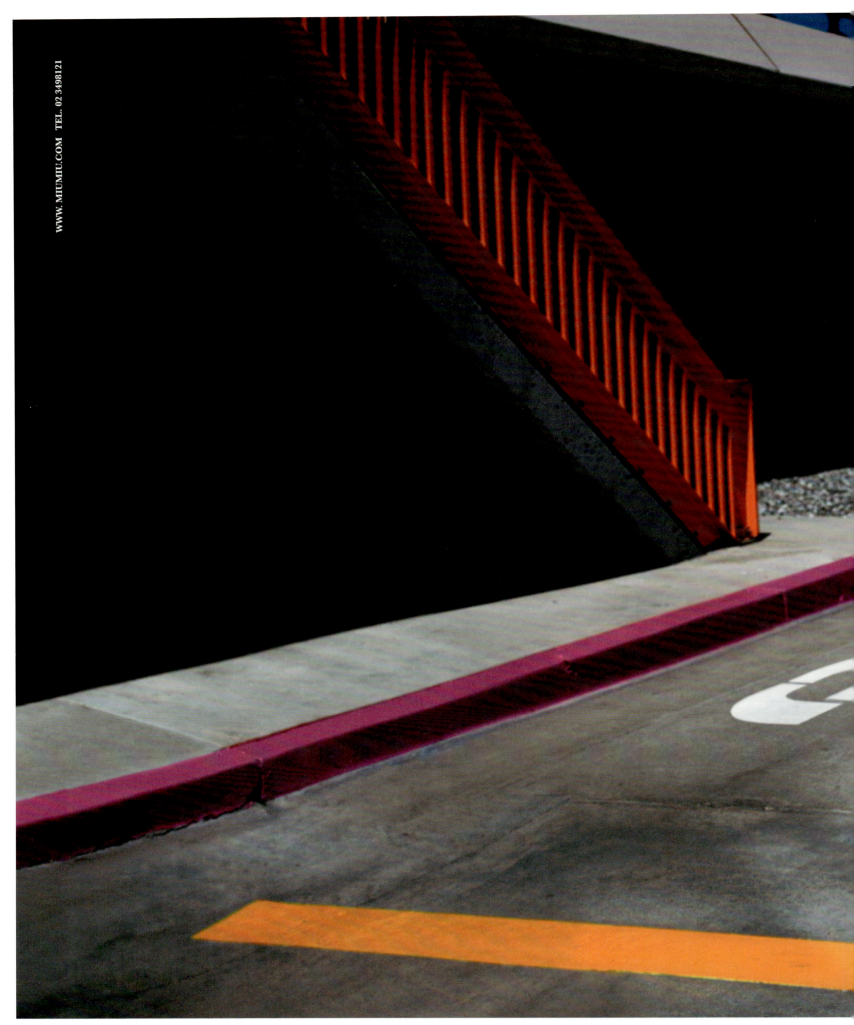

LOS-ANGELES, MAY 18–20 2008
Vanessa Paradis

LONDON, MAY 11–13 2007
Laetitia Casta

miu miu

LONDON, MAY 11–13 2007
Laetitia Casta

miu miu

LOS-ANGELES, MAY 18–20 2008
Vanessa Paradis

miu miu
eyewear

LOS-ANGELES, MAY 18–20 2008
Vanessa Paradis

miu miu

LONDON, NOVEMBER 18–21 2006
Lindsay Lohan
CORSO VENEZIA 3, MILANO
VIA ROMA 8R, FIRENZE
TEL. 02 546701

LONDON, NOVEMBER 18–21 2006
Lindsay Lohan
CORSO VENEZIA 3, MILANO
VIA ROMA 8R, FIRENZE
TEL. 02 546701

LAPEROUSE, PARIS, MAY 4–8 2006
Zhou Xun, Dong Jie & Rina Ohta
CORSO VENEZIA 3, MILANO
VIA ROMA 8R, FIRENZE
TEL. 02 546701

miu miu

LAPEROUSE, PARIS, MAY 4–8 2006
Zhou Xun & Rina Ohta
CORSO VENEZIA 3, MILANO
VIA ROMA 8R, FIRENZE
TEL. 02 546701

miu miu

SELEC TED WORDS

As editor-in-chief of *Self Service* magazine, Ezra Petronio has had the responsibility to write the "Letter from the Editor" for more than 25 years. Here is his curation of a collection of words that seems to have been summoned in anticipation of the current threats and hurdles many face in exploring without restraint. Petronio advocates for us to create the unexpected through excellence —to hold onto the capacity to lose ourselves in what we do, to make mistakes without being afraid of making them, and to be intellectually and emotionally receptive to intuition.

**editorial
can you
do less
and better
and do
so without
feeling
that you
will be out
of the
picture?**

THERE ARE THOSE WHO AIMLESSLY FOLLOW AND THOSE WHO EXPLORE. THOSE WHO REPRODUCE AND THOSE WHO DIVERT AND CREATE. THOSE WHO PLAY THE GAME AND THOSE WHO TRANSGRESS EXPECTATIONS. THOSE ON A STANDSTILL WHO ABIDE BY THE NORM AND THOSE WHO EMBRACE WHO THEY WANT TO BE.
IT IS THE SECOND KIND, THESE SELF-EMPOWERED INDIVIDUALS, WHO AREN'T SCARED TO EMBODY THEIR PERSONAL IDEOLOGY, WHO WILL MAKE A MARK AND FUEL INSPIRING AND QUALITATIVE CHANGE IN OUR CREATIVE ENVIRONMENT. BOLDLY RADICAL, EXCESSIVELY PERSONAL, EMOTIONAL AND CARING, UNAFRAID OF BEING WHO THEY TRULY WANT TO BE.

— *Ezra Petronio*

EDITORIAL_MOOD OF THE DAY

Now, Instant, Experience, Activations, Native branded content, Sentiment analysis, Power middle, Call to action, Millennials, Social media, Influencers, GenY, #instamood, Content, User-generated content, Content campaign, SEM, Daily feed, Following, Engagement, Endorsement, Storytelling, #fbf, Trending, Viral, Interactive, Digital experience, Live streaming, Sponsored, Dark posts, Impressions, Interactions, KPI, Comments, ROI, #igers, #tbt, Scale, Like, Influencer personas, Tag, Mention, Bots, Buzz marketing, eWOM, Mid-level influencers, PPC. —*Ezra Petronio*

EDITORIAL

The Quick Fix.
Let's hope our egotistical self-indulging fashion bubble explodes.
On a certain impoverishment of taste and design.
On influencers influencing no one.
On the obsession and oversaturation of millennial-targeted marketing.
On a growing fringe of the fashion industry's celebration of the tasteless.
On laziness and the acceptance of blatant copying and reappropriation of others' ideas, creativity and hard work.
On mediocrity too often becoming the "norm".
On lazy "yes-people".
On pretense.
On immediacy and the new new.
On being in a constant live-feed.
On fashion increasingly being devoid of elegance, femininity and imagination.
On the nonsensical meaning of novelty and inclusivity.
On greed.
On casting the spotlight on the wrong people.
On the ephemerality of a new establishment.
On the desecration of taste justified by a pretext of irony.
On the superficiality of the new "role models".
On an erroneous idea and meaning of professional success.
On speaking out on change and not really understanding what is going on.
On disruption for the marketing sake of disruption.
On the lack of ideology.
yet...
On the new luxury of time and living in the present.
On being unaffected by the pressures of social media.
On integrity and staying true to oneself.
On the return of a certain appreciation of quality and the meaningful.
On the return of self-made.
On sustainability and responsibility.
On adaptability, new networks and work patterns.
On the reinvention of business models.
On the emergence of individuality and doing things differently.
On humility, passion and standing the ground of one's personal ideology.
On the journey rather than the finality.
On making mistakes.
On looking the other way.
On keeping things simple.
On more emotionality.
On creative transgressions.
On sincerity and the authentic.
On our quest to find, support and embrace the future pioneers and creative revolutionaries who will forcefully engage our status quo. May the bubble burst!
– Ezra Petronio

The ability to nurture and maintain a creative flow in the face of the abounding environmental, societal, and economical disruptions has certainly proven to be a huge challenge to the new generations of creative and artistic minds. But this adversity has also proven to be a generative source and context toward progress and the exploring of novel ways of creative expression. Stepping back to reflect, redefining one's individual worth—this gained perspective has inspired a renewed radical honesty. When there is nothing to lose, there is often freedom and the ability to create and engage without compromising one's integrity or identity. With inspiring resilience, courage, and defiance, the young ignite disruption. The political becomes more relevant in the arts as they fight for a more inclusive, self-aware, and transformed future ahead.

—*Ezra Petronio*

RID YOURSELF OF COMFORT ZONES. FIND MEANING IN WHAT YOU DO. MAKE MISTAKES. REVISIT THE PAST, ENGAGE THE PRESENT TO CREATE THE FUTURE.

— *Ezra Petronio*

EDITORIAL

FEELING [one]: ON SEEKING APPROVAL – OR THE PREOCCUPATION WITH THE SUPERFICIALITY OF INSTANT GRATIFICATION
I need to be followed and crave to be liked. Am I a leader or am I a follower? Where does this urge for approval come from? As the popular definition states: when you have a need for approval, you value the beliefs, opinions and needs of others above your own. You sacrifice your own beliefs, opinions and values in order to have their approval. Then don't you risk losing your ability to be true to who you are?
> *"We should extricate ourselves from the seductive clutches of the instant image."* [SELF SERVICE N°18/SS 2003]
> *"Our era is one of instant sensation and immediate effect, where the all-important thing is image. Personal style is orchestrated whereas true authenticity has become a rarity."* [SELF SERVICE N°26/SS 2007]

NOTE: FOR ADDITIONAL INSIGHT, REFER TO THE STORY ON PAGE 204 OF THIS ISSUE, "ME, MYSELF & I".

FEELING [two]: ON FASHION'S STATE OF CULTURAL AMNESIA OR A PENCHANT FOR A SORT OF STALINIST WHITE-WASHING OF THE HISTORY OF FASHION, PHOTOGRAPHY AND AUTHORSHIP
If one can and should celebrate the fact that a tremendous amount of visual information is available today on the Internet, one must remind oneself that a lot of this information has been filtered—an involuntary kind of rewriting of the history of fashion and visual culture in the making. Some of it on purpose and some of it by chance. A lot of the things that existed in print and analog form have been scanned by someone, and that's how they exist online. Nothing is properly catalogued or properly documented and, most sadly, a lot of it isn't justly credited. And in the words of Jo-Ann Furniss (see p392), "There's a randomness mixed with weird Chinese whispers and there's a sort of Stalinist white-washing of history."

FEELING [three]: ON ADDRESSING THE ISSUE OF THE TRANSMISSION OF THE KNOWLEDGE, CULTURE AND VISUAL LEGACY OF FASHION
"The access to a creative online life means that everybody grows up in public, and that the apprenticeship period is not filtered with the help of an editor or with the help of somebody else's eye—it's just all 'there', just hanging around. And so there's never the time for people to fully form themselves. With Instagram or other online sources as our sole cultural 'reference', it's like getting a DVD and watching all the extras first and not the feature film— like watching all this nonsense. You aren't getting the time to develop yourself and your talent, you are simply perpetuating other people's taste." – *Jo-Ann Furniss* (see p392)

NOTE: FOR ADDITIONAL INSIGHT, REFER TO THE CONVERSATION WITH CHARLOTTE COTTON & JO-ANN FURNISS ON PAGE 390 OF THIS ISSUE.

FEELING [four]: NEW PATTERNS AND LOOSE NETWORKS OF CULTURAL RADICALS
Seeds continue to be planted and the first flowers of change are blossoming in our fashion industry. I feel there are signs that many are rising up to the challenge of provoking change. Fuelled by artistic intention and unpredictability, suddenly a loose network is emerging with greater confidence.
> *"They will increasingly start challenging all conventions and depart from what has become the norm, creating new networks, innovative forms of presentation, representation and communication, exploring and developing new forms of production and distribution…"* [SELF SERVICE N°23/FW 2005]
> *"These new cultural radicals embody some of the ideals that drive us forward. They don't merely reflect, they react. With grace and ease, their actions, while thought-out, are not over-thought."* [SELF SERVICE N°21/SS 2004]

FEELING [five]: ON INTUITION, INSTINCTS AND PERSONAL DOGMA
Daily mental exercise: why do I do what I do and how should I be doing it? Why is what I do worth doing?
> *"True creativity, true progressive and critical thought is something personal; it is an attitude, an ambition, an intrinsic desire for freedom."* [SELF SERVICE N°24/SS 2006]

FEELING [six]: STRIPPING BACK THE UNNECESSARY SO THAT THE ESSENTIAL CAN SPEAK
> *"As an independent publication, we want to explore the importance and the social responsibility of fashion in pushing ahead new ideas, to ask our readers to question what is presented to them."* [SELF SERVICE N°19/FW 2003]

What should fashion design and fashion photography be if not the questioning, the creating and the suggestion of a certain lightness of human emancipation through the embracing of individual elegance and personal style, a personal vision of the beauty and strength of men and women...?
> *"When will fashion be fashion again: that is, a means to challenge the boundaries of convention, a spirit that does not run away from risk, a driving force that redefines, enlightens, and provides a stylistic and visionary glimpse of the future?"* [SELF SERVICE N°14/SS 2001]

I think that the contributors in this issue reflect this feeling; that is, the mixing of tradition and technology, emotion and memory in order to create a relevant and personal photographic language and an intelligent and insightful method of dressing, as they cross boundaries from photographic documentary to social iconography and reflect our cultural background with an eye on the future.
> *"…and finally, and most significantly, a rediscovered pleasure and joy of experimenting in creating fashion images. Something more emotional and personal."* [SELF SERVICE N°25/FW 2006]

– *Ezra Petronio*

SELF SERVICE #6   FASHION ORIENTED
OBSERVING, LEARNING, FEELING, REDEFINING LINKS AND INTERACTIONS   BETWEEN VISUAL FIELDS EXPERIMENTING, SUGGESTING, TESTING   NOURISHING CURIOSITY,   CREATING NEW PERSPECTIVES NETWORKING, CYCLING, RECYCLING. PERIPHERY, CENTER CITIES, CITY CENTERS, NEW TERRITORIES, FUTURE, HOPE, TOMORROW, FREEDOM OF EXPRESSION, RESISTANCE, CHOICE, GENERATIONS, SUBJECTIVITY, WILL, DESIRE, GENEROSITY PLATFORM DISPLAY, GLOBAL ART, FASHION, REFLECTION IN PROGRESS,   IMAGE, TEXT, BEAUTY, TRENDS, PROJECTS CONTEMPORARY CONTEXT,   EVOLUTION, SHAPES PROCESS, FOOD FOR THOUGHT...

EZRA PETRONIO

COVER PHOTO BY INEZ VAN LAMSWEERDE AND VINOODH MATADIN
STYLING BY NANCY ROHDE   ASSISTED BY SARAH ELLIS
HAIR BY EUGENE SOULIEMAN @ STREETERS FOR AVEDA
MAKE-UP BY LISA BUTLER @ STREETERS   MODEL DEVON@STORM
SELF SERVICE 3

editorial

reach carefree abandon. immerse yourself in stimulating futility. deviate from the obvious path, explore the oblique. decontextualize your creative process, make unrestrained mistakes. document the insignificant, collect spontaneously. transcend existing patterns, explore random networks. cultivate singularities, multiply anticipations. forget today's fundamental shifts. obsess, confront, produce provocative thought. celebrate the opposite, be wrong. stretch your sensibility, urge for limitless boundaries. overthink, overreact, wander aimlessly. think absurd, proceed with lightness. research constructive contradictions. forget stylistic presumptions, arrive at uncertainties. stretch possibilities, stimulate frivolity. go deep, go deeper, work your inner metaphor. adorn excessively, decorate accordingly. embrace the idyllic lightness of fashion. indulge in a little *je ne sais quoi*. Ezra Petronio

To the memory of Henry Wolf, a great mentor who inspired and taught me to seek out and explore the unexpected. Thank you.

EDITORIAL

What is the essence of creativity? Is creativity part of human nature or is it something that must be learned and nurtured? Is not being afraid to fail an essential aspect of creativity? How does creativity differ from inspiration? How much is intuition part of how you work? Do you resist following your instincts? Is inspiration irrational? If so, how can you be more irrational? How can we free our minds so that inspiration can happen? Can inspiration be found in obsession? What is your obsession? Does inspiration come to you without questioning it? Is inspiration an ongoing process? Is imagination more important than knowledge? Is imagination the beginning of creation? Why do you do what you do? Why is what you do worth doing? Do you ask enough questions, or do you settle for what you know? Which is worse: failing or never trying? If we learn from our mistakes, why are we always so afraid to make them? If life is so short, why do we do so many things we don't like and like so many things we don't do? Does the 'new norm' of constant change require that we master 'perpetual transformation'? If you could do it all over again, would you change anything? When it's all said and done, will you have said more than you have done? — *Ezra Petronio*

EDITORIAL

Longing for an age of innocence.

Ever since its inception in the mid-1990s, the fundamental mission of *Self Service* has been to encourage and celebrate artistic creative freedom within the industries in which we navigate. Today's climate proves how essential and relevant this remains today.

Self Service's quest is to ensure an undiluted and creative space continues to prevail. This undeterred mindset perpetuates this creative dogma by continuously engaging and creating with its community of people and creative minds who believe in the power and relevance of a certain vision of fashion, image-making, and ideas.

The purpose and philosophy of our magazine were born in the pre-Web 1.0 era and desktop publishing, and it will survive the influencers, metaverses, "financial market pressures," or other challenges that it may encounter because of a commitment and state of mind to maintain its essence and purpose, which is simply about preserving freedom. *Self Service*'s resolve and determination are set in stone—fueled by our creative principles and those of all our contributors—the real tastemakers.

This stringent ideology defines who we are, what our values are, and that we will never compromise, however difficult a fight it may be. How else would our craft, artistry, and purpose make any sense? Why would we do what we do half-way?

The world we live in is fast-paced, volatile, and insatiable for novelty and ephemera. In an era when a college degree is no guarantee of work yet social media's abhorrent stupidity can provide more financial wealth and superficial recognition, where and who are the true role models for the next generations? This perverted circus of hype, nothingness, and extreme pressure to be who you are not, to look like who you are not, to possess what you do not have, is daunting and extremely intimidating.

These times should shake us out of our lethargy; be a form of renaissance, of rediscovery —an emotional and creative awakening. We should take the time to look within, ask ourselves the right questions, find deep inside of us what has true meaning, what we truly desire, what makes us happy.

To all you emerging talented people and new generations who decide to engage in the creative fields: be fierce, be disruptive. We do not want followers but innovators, dreamers, pioneers. Take us out of our comfort zones and explore and define new forms of artistic expressions.

Live a new age of innocence, in harmony with yourself, your past, where you want to go, and what you aspire to achieve.

Device-sober and noise-free, exempt from nostalgia but with the baggage of culture and awareness, be true to who you want to be. —*Ezra Petronio*

SELF SERVICE MAGAZINE

Since its inception in 1994, each biannual issue of *Self Service* magazine has been structured as a sensitive and acute journey through creative and fashion culture. Like a Tetris puzzle of unique stories and experiments, images and texts, design and sequence, and paper and ink, each issue's flow, rhythm, and tenor have been intentionally, meticulously structured to shine full light onto the message and meaning of its contributors. The selection of covers and spreads shown here creates a catalog of overwhelming evidence of the constantly energetic and sensitive ways in which Ezra Petronio and the *Self Service* team celebrate creative expression as well as cultural movements and presences. The many facets of editing and design and the collaborative work that result in the final form of a seminal magazine underpin the longevity and relevance of *Self Service*'s ongoing journey of experimentation and renewal in the fashion industry.

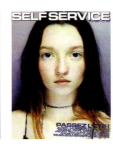
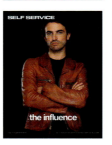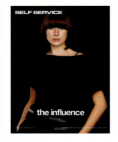
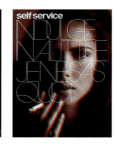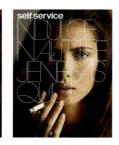

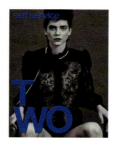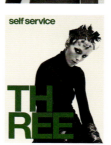
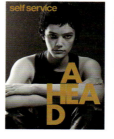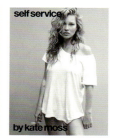

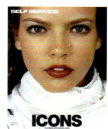
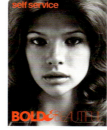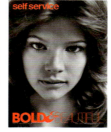
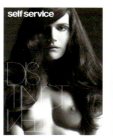
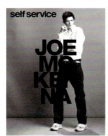
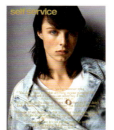
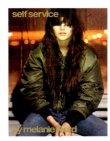
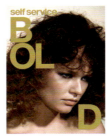

self service embrace absurdity with a bright clockwise motion to escape the ever present possibility of imminent change

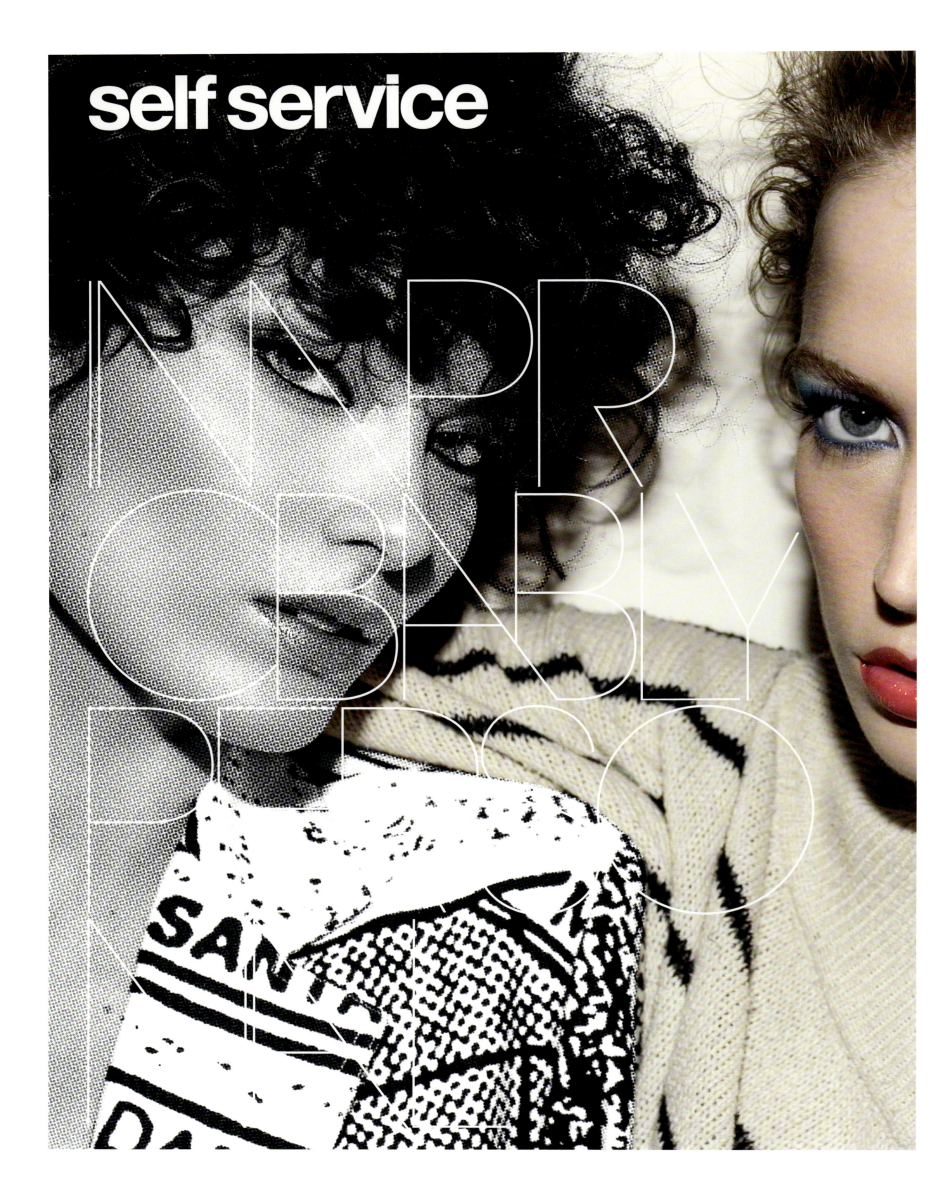

SELF SERVICE

the influence

ISSUE N°13 AUTUMN WINTER 2000 90F

NICOLAS GHESQUIERE PHOTOGRAPHED BY ANUSCHKA BLOMMERS AND NIELS SCHUMM

Then&Now: Nicolas Ghesquière for Louis Vuitton, S/S 2019.

Then&Now: Nicolas Ghesquière for Balenciaga, S/S 2001 & S/S 2003.

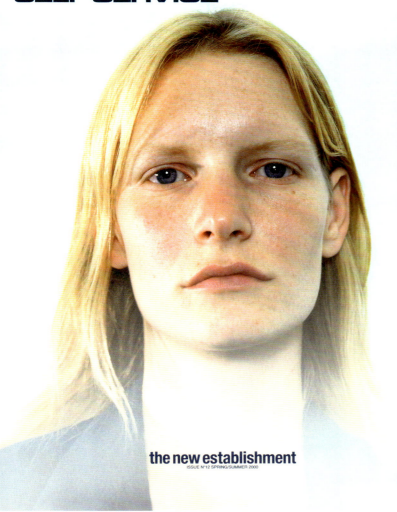
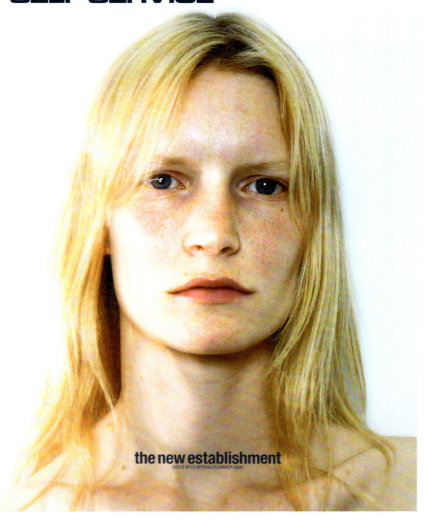

self service

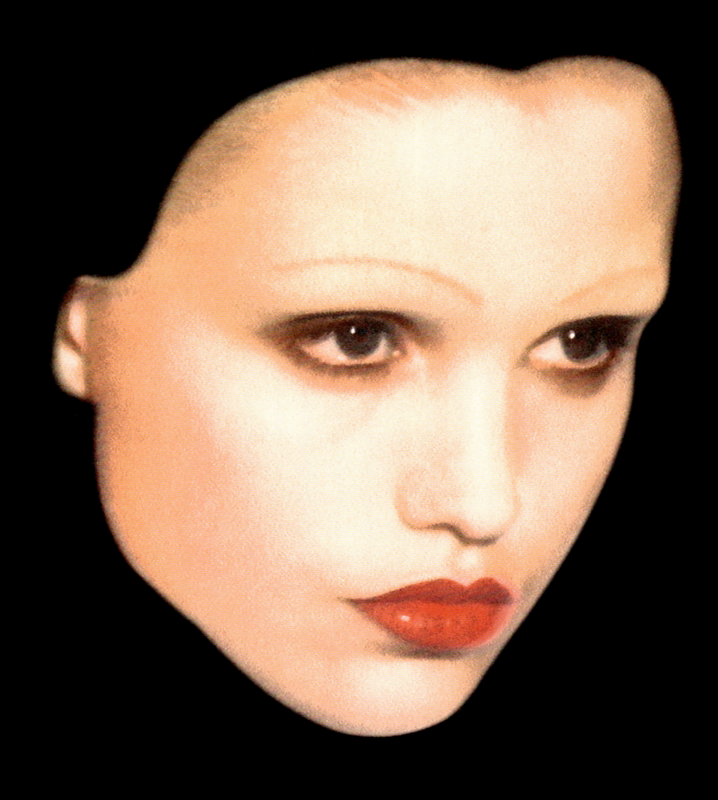

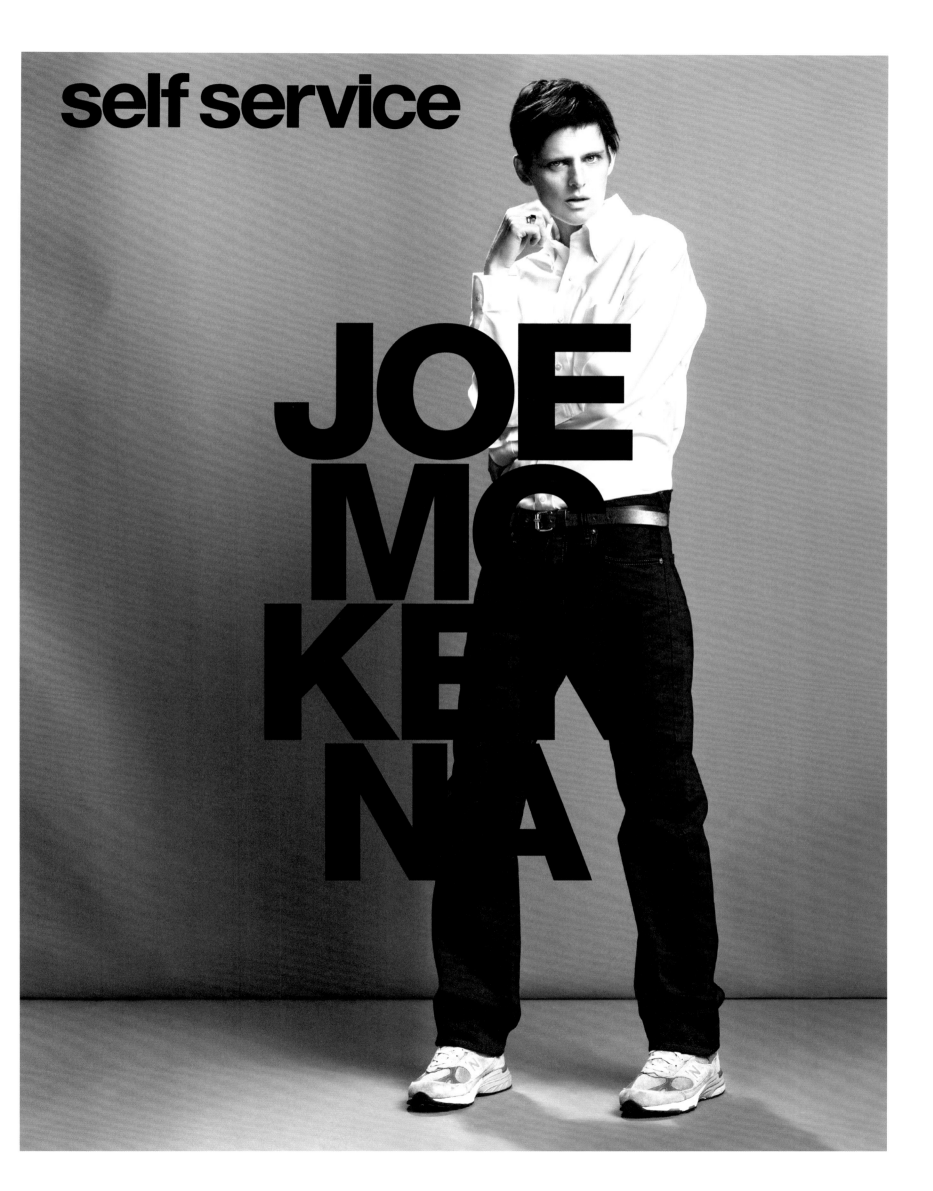

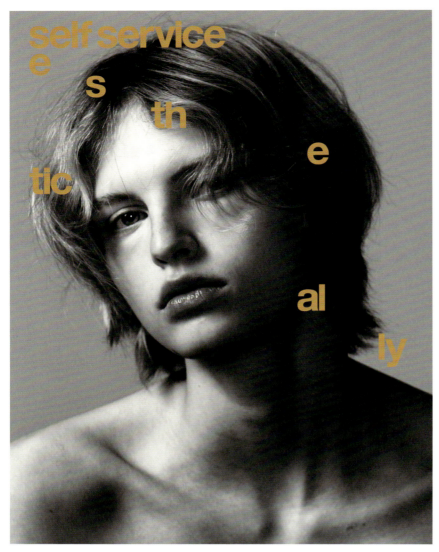
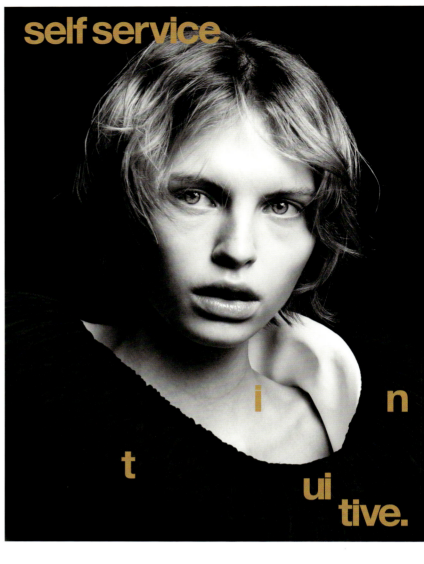
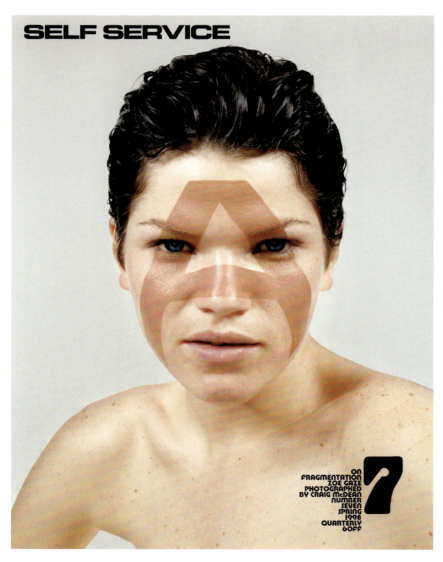
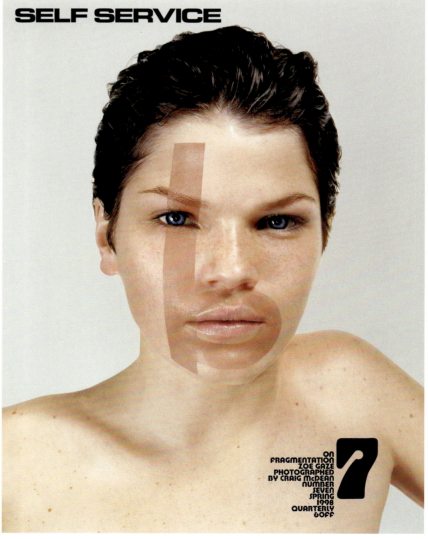

GLOW

Photography by Harley Weir. Beauty by Thomas de Kluyver.

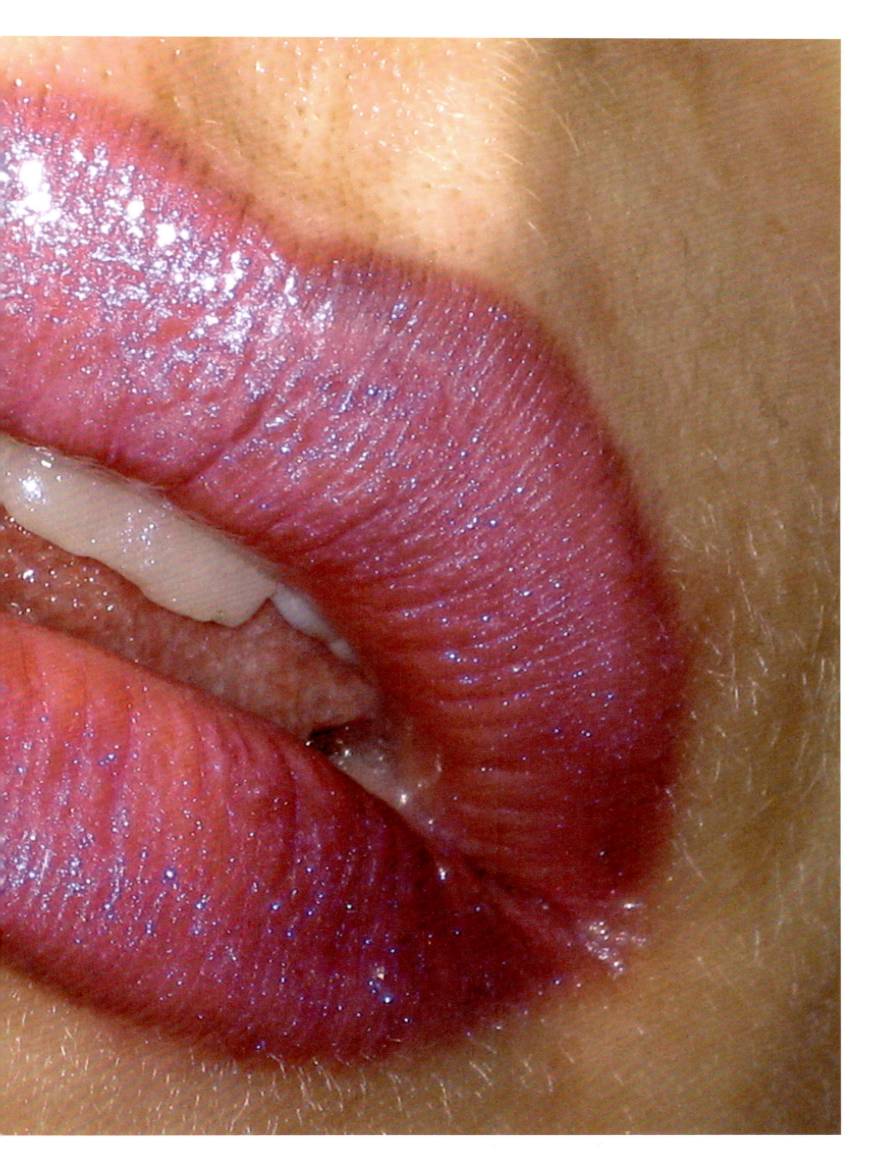

DUALISTIC

Photography by Inez & Vinoodh. Styling by Emmanuelle Alt.

I THINK

Photography by Inez & Vinoodh. Styling by Alastair McKimm.

CANDID

Photography by Alasdair McLellan. Styling by Benjamin Bruno.

YES I DO

Photography by Glen Luchford. Styling by Jane How.

INTO THE

Photography by Cara Bird. Styling by Chioma Azunday.

POP

Photography by Alasdair McLellan. Styling by Benjamin Bruno.

THEM

Photography by Alasdair McLellan. Styling by Marie Chaix.

I AM

HAT

SHE IS

Photography by David Sims. Styling by Alice Goddard.

JE M'ATTACHE AU ROUGE

photography by Paolo Roversi styling by Jane How

L'ARTIFICE DES LIGNES DROITES

photography by Magnus Unnar styling by Bay Garnett

What was the first song you snogged to? —JEFFERSON HACK

"Careless Whisper, at a friend's school disco. I never saw him again." —KATE MOSS

Photography by Johnny Dufort. Styling by Jane How.

Kate, if you could swap wardrobes with anyone in history, who would it be? —ANNA WINTOUR

"THE MARCHESA CASATI" —KATE MOSS

Photography by Alasdair McLellan. Styling by Elodie David Touboul.

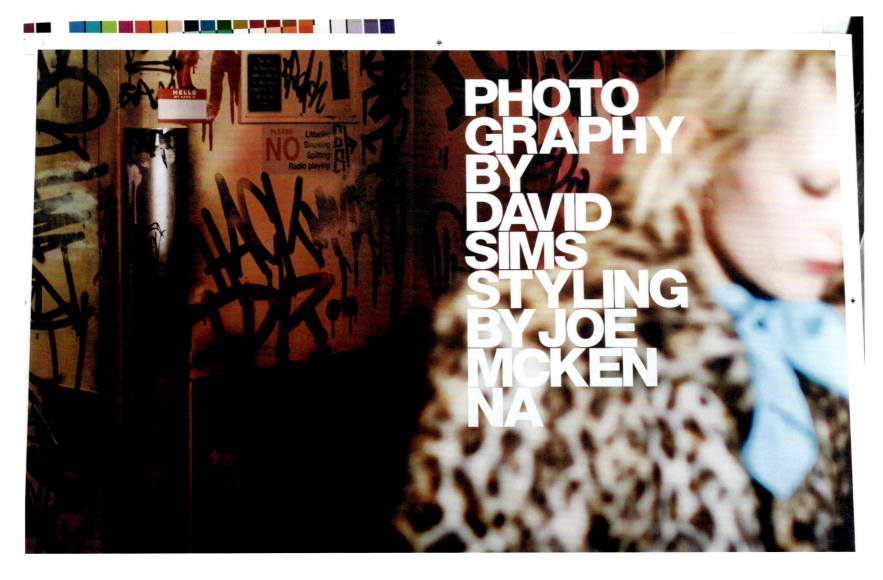

PHOTOGRAPHY BY DAVID SIMS STYLING BY JOE MCKENNA

PHOTOGRAPHY BY BRYAN LIST ON STYLING BY MELANIE WARD

PHOTO GRA PHY BY WILLY VAND ERPER RE ST YLING BY JANE HOW

PHOTO GRAPHY BY ALA SDAIR MC LELLAN STYLING BY JA NE HOW

I'VE BEE
DDICTE
GRAY C
ANS SIN
IGH SC

PHOTOGRAPHY BY TERRY RICHARDSON STYLING BY CAMILLE BIDAULT WADDINGTON
* QUOTE FROM HOUSE & GARDEN, JANUARY 2007

NADIA TO HARDCORE DIG TO ICE HIGH SCHOOL

100 Things

by Suzanne Koller, Carina Frey, Marie Chaix, Nicolas Trembley and Patrick Li.

1 **New neighbour.** APC shop, opening March 2004. 112 Rue Vielle du Temple. www.apc.fr.
2 **Vertigo.** Apartment building, Munich.
3 **Risingstar.** "Amanda Lear, Colville Terrace", 1973, by Peter Schlesinger GBE (Modern) 212 827 5258.
4 **About a boy.** Larry Clark videostill, Biennale de Lyon 2003. www.biennale-de-lyon.com
5 **Bootycall.** Colored satin cowboy boots, Undercover.

100 Things

by Suzanne Koller, Carina Frey, Marie Chaix, Nicolas Trembley and Patrick Li.

1 **A small fortune.** «Mini» Ferrari, Harrod's, London. www.harrods.com
2 **Intersection.** Installation by Dolores Zinney and Juan Maidagan, Lunds Konsthall, Lund. www.lund.se/konsthallen/
3 **Emergency.** Pro Helvetia for Switzerland Bag, Zen & Speed exhibition, Dortmund.
4 **The big apple.** Apple orchard, Constance lake.
5 **Toppings.** Baseball caps, Nike. www.nike.com.
6 **Red light district.** Installation by Olivier Blankhart, Marco, Geneva, www.mamco.ch.

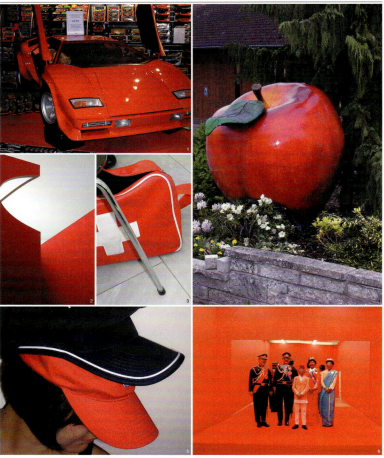

1 At Work. Book by Lee Friedlander, published by Steidl. www.steidl.de.
2 Step by Step. Window installation, by Emmanuelle Mafille, MK2 bibliothèque, www.mk2.com.
3 Straight edge. House wall. Paris.
4 Have some balls. Limited edition game by David Artaud and Xavier Veilhan, Xn editions, 01 43 43 12 01.
5 Take away. Travelling office project by Roman Coppola for APC. www.apc.fr.
6 On air. The history of Air France, Union Centrale des Arts Décoratifs. Starting October 2003. www.ucad.fr

100 THINGS

by Suzanne Koller, Carina Frey, Marie Chaix and Patrick Li.

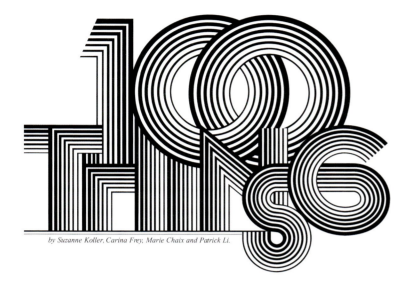

100 THINGS

by Suzanne Koller, Carina Frey, Nicolas Trembley, Patrick Li and Leela Petronio.

1 Greenpiece. Panda painting by Rob Pruitt. www.airdeparis.com. Photo by Nicolas Trembley.
2 All that Do'. Adidas sneakers by Jeremy Scott.
3 Liz. Versace exhibition at the Victoria and Albert Museum, London. www.vam.ac.uk.
4 Pink Rocks. Necklace. Prada, Spring/Summer 2003.
5 Good Stuffing. Doggies at FAO Schwarz, New York. www.fao.com.

Photography by Alasdair McLellan. Styling by Max Pearmain.

curate your dress essential sins ilk

Photography by David Sims. Styling by Emmanuelle Alt.

I WANT IT CURLY BUT I WANT IT STRAIGHT

Photography by Craig McDean. Hair by Duffy.

MY BOYFRIEND STILL THINKS MY EYELASHES ARE REAL

Photography by Zoë Ghertner. Styling by Carlos Nazario.

THE OBJECT THE SIGN A STORY OF THE NINETIES

UNIFORMISATION KNICK KNACK TRANSGRESSIONS GLITTERIA CAT POWER ANNA PIAGGI BERLIN DISNEYLAND STEREOTYPES KARL LAGERFELD ICONS TRADITIONAL JESSICA OGDEN HEROES COLLECTIVE IDEALS ANDRE WALKER ANTWERP BRANDING SOCIAL LANDSCAPES EXCESS MELANIE WARD HOME TERRITORY SUSAN CIANCIOLO FAMILIES NOKI CUSTOM ECCENTRICITY ANN DEMEULEMEESTER NY JUERGEN TELLER EFFERVESCENCE CLANS ACHIEVEMENTS FRONT 242 INDEX ERWIN WURM MEDIA FANTASIES •••

THE OBJECT, THE SIGN A STORY OF THE NINETIES. L'OBJET, LE SIGNE, UNE HISTOIRE DES ANNÉES 90. BY STEPHANIE MOISDON TREMBLEY TRANSLATED BY BRIAN HOLMES

CONVERSATIONS WITH POLLY MELLEN GASPAR NOE ANDREAS GURSKY DJ HELL VANESSA BEECROFT CHICKS ON SPEED JEAN-JACQUES PICART MAJED AL-SABAH

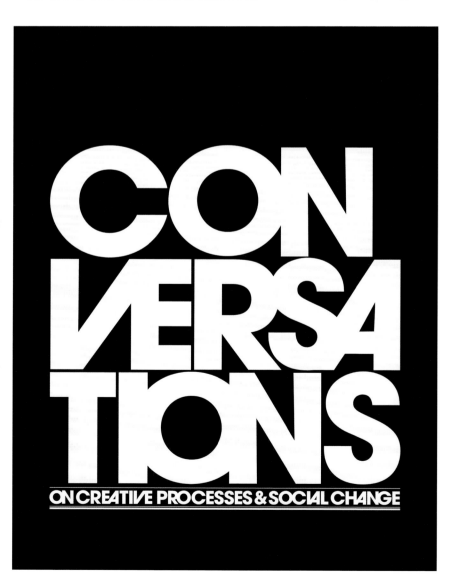

CONVERSATIONS ON CREATIVE PROCESSES & SOCIAL CHANGE

OBVIOUSLY&SIMPLY CHLOË

A BAD ECONOMY IS A BIG CHANCE FOR CREATIVITY
Helmut Lang, 2003, n°19

TOP 10 MOST CREDITS FOR A SINGLE DESIGNER IN ONE ISSUE
1. RAF SIMONS, 32 credits, n°8
2. YVES SAINT LAURENT, 32 credits, n°2
3. BALENCIAGA, 25 credits, n°15
4. CHANEL, 23 credits, n°20
5. HERMES, 22 credits, n°15
6. CHANEL, 21 credits, n°15
7. BALENCIAGA, 21 credits, n°19
8. BALENCIAGA, 19 credits, n°21
9. GUCCI, 18 credits, n°15
10. DIOR HOMME, 18 credits, n°17

I USED TO CARE WHEN THEY SAID I WAS A MISOGYNIST, BUT THE MORE YOU MEET THESE PEOPLE, THE MORE YOU DON'T GIVE A SHIT. THEY DON'T KNOW FUCK ALL!
Alexander McQueen, 2002, n°16

WHY DO THINGS ONE WAY WHEN YOU CAN DO THEM DIFFERENTLY?
Desirée Heiss, 1999, n°10

I THINK A CAREER IN FASHION, OR IN MY CASE OBSERVING FASHION IS ONE NEAR PURE SELF-INDULGENCE
Ginia Bellafante, 2000, n°13

THE IDEA THAT CELINE DION CAN BE SIMULTANEOUSLY NUMBER ONE IN 46 COUNTRIES IS SURELY ENOUGH TO MAKE ANYONE WITH ANY INTELLIGENCE CONSIDER MURDER OR SUICIDE
Paul Davis, 1998, n°9

YOU ALWAYS HAVE TO LOOK IN THE MIRROR AND TRY TO RATIONALIZE YOUR STANDARD OF TASTE. TASTE IS REALLY THE FILTER THAT EVERY DECISION IS SEEN THROUGH.
Brian Grazer, 2004, n°20

TOP 10 FAVORITE VERBS
1. CELEBRATE 2. CHALLENGE 3. DEFINE 4. EMBRACE 5. EXPLORE 6. EVOLVE 7. INDULGE 8. INFLUENCE 9. PERSONALIZE 10. TRANSCEND

TOP 10 MOST USED WORDS
1. ESTABLISHMENT
2. INTEGRITY
3. INFLUENCE
4. PERCEPTION
5. GENERATION
6. INDIVIDUAL
7. INFILTRATING
8. POWERFUL
9. PERSPECTIVE
10. STYLE

ABOUT COINCIDENCES AND 20-YEAR-OLD BOYS. DO YOU KNOW THAT IN THE FIRST BEAUTY PICTURE EVER SHOT THE FACE OF THIS BEAUTIFUL WOMAN WAS NOT THAT OF A WOMAN BUT OF A YOUNG BOY CHOSEN FOR THE EXTREME PERFECTION OF HIS/HER FEATURES. THE PHOTOGRAPHER WAS BARON ADOLPHE DE MEYER AND THE PHOTOGRAPH WAS FOR ELIZABETH ARDEN.
Anna Piaggi, 1997, n°6

I MISS LOOKING OUT THE WINDOW AND SEEING A GRAY DAY.
Chris Cunningham, 2001, n°14

I GUESS I MUST HAVE 30 BLACK TURTLENECKS
Polly Mellen, 2002, n°17

I'VE ALWAYS HATED OVERTLY POLITICAL MUSIC. I THINK THE THING WITH MUSIC IS THAT IT WORKS ON A KIND OF PURELY EMOTIONAL LEVEL
Jarvis Cocker, 2003, n°19

I'VE LIVED THROUGH HELL AND I'LL KEEP ON GOING
Jeremy Scott, 2000, n°13

A WORK OF ART THAT ISN'T SHOCKING IS NO GOOD, WHICH MAKES MAKING ART A COMPLETE WASTE OF TIME
Jake Chapman, 2004, n°20

WHEN I WORKED FOR FAIRCHILD, I WAS SEATED FIRST ROW AND EVERYBODY WAS KISSING MY ASS. WHEN I MOVED TO MIRABELLA, ALL OF SUDDEN I WAS SEATED BETWEEN THE 3RD AND 5TH ROWS AND COULDN'T GET A PR PERSON ON THE PHONE. I KNOW HOW THE SYSTEM WORKS
Richard Buckley, 2000, n°12

TOP 10 TOPICS OF CONVERSATION
1. ON CHAOS IN WONDERLAND, 2003, n°18 2. ON ACCIDENTAL ART AND BRANDING A SOCIAL CAUSE, 2004, n°21 3. ON BEING AN OUTSIDER ON THE INSIDE, 2004, n°21 4. ON HIDDEN PLEASURE GONE UNDERGROUND, 2003, n°18 5. ON HYBRIDS IN HOLLYWOOD AND DRESSING A NARRATIVE, 2004, n°21 6. ON THE REFUSAL TO BE CATEGORIZED AND UNDERMINED, 2002, n°17 7. ON NEGOTIATING ENTANGIBLES, 2003, n°18 8. ON THE SUPERFICIALITY OF AVANT-GARDISM, 2001, n°14 9. ON SEEKING PEACE FROM CONSUMERISM, 2003, n°18 10. ON DRESSING FOR THE REVOLUTION, 2002, n°17

I THINK IT'S DIFFICULT TO BE CREATIVE FOR A LONG TIME IF YOU DON'T HAVE ZILLIONS OF REFERENCES
Karl Lagerfeld, 1999, n°11

YOU CAN'T BREAK MY SPIRIT
Polly Mellen, 2002, n°17

GOING FOR YOUR WOW EFFECT

The Cannes Film Festival is an endless nonstop ride of exhilaration and frenzy that threatens to consume you completely. The different levels of star wattage multiply year after year, from the genuine A-listers to the indie royalty to the porn stars to the Russian billionaires with their underage arm candy. Fashion has stepped up in an increasingly major way, with more and more brands installing fleeting showrooms in plush hotel suites. Although at times the Boulevard de la Croisette feels like nothing more than the ultimate jetsetter's spot to see and be seen, the festival is unparalleled as one of the world's foremost hubs of promotion and old-fashioned wheeling and dealing. The countless parties are not (merely) froth, but influential power-meetings cloaked in layers of glitter and lace. Glamour is as glamour does: French magazine *Madame Figaro* and the house of Chanel hosted a party for Karl Lagerfeld's photography exhibition at the Canal Plus studio, and the room swirled with actors, television journalists, fashion editors, designers, artists, semi-celebrities, and wannabes. There, amidst the crinkle of rustling silk and the glare of razor-sharp diamonds, we shone yet another blinding light in the eyes of the stunningly beautiful and influential. *Cannes, Canal Plus Studios, May 23rd 2007* **Photography by Ezra Petronio**

Claudia Schiffer, model.

Karl Lagerfeld, couturier.

Elodie Bouchez, actress.

Kylie Minogue, singer.

ORCHESTRATE IMPROBABILITY

Elaborating on reality is the force that propels the Art Basel Fair. So it is apt that for his last year as director of the world's most influential art fair, Samuel Keller commissioned noted curator Stéphanie Moisdon to transform the Art Lobby from its previous incarnation as a lackluster passageway into a lively space of intellectual exchange, rife with confusion and performance. The Art Lobby thus became an engineered space of unexpected freedom within the confines of a highly regimented institution. Moisdon orchestrated a series of unrestrained talks over five days, involving fifty participants who had carte blanche over their subject matter, media, and collaborators. This project resulted in iconic pairings such as artist Elaine Sturtevant and curator Beatrix Ruf, and artist Jim Shaw with curator Fabrice Stroun. Their aim: "Secret Conversations" that encourage intense intimacy despite the hype of the fair (two hundred private planes, sixty thousand collectors). Moisdon approached the project in a definitively curatorial manner, using the transient space to exhibit ideas and discourse. Ezra Petronio was invited to take part in this exceptional installation to record its fleeting passage. From his strategically placed booth at the nexus of this encounter, Petronio chronicled the parade of personalities that make up the international cosmos of the art world. *Basel, Messeplatz, June 11th to 15th 2007* **Photography by Ezra Petronio**

HEAD HUNTING
TALENT & TALENT BEHIND TALENT
Photography by Ezra Petronio

Matthew Williamson, designer.

Hurley Hughes, menswear designer.

Peter Dundas, designer, Ungaro Paris.

STARS & STYLES PORTRAITS OF PARIS

There are certain times in certain places when particular faces come to the fore. Those times and those faces demand to be documented. Over the period of one month more than 100 people stepped through our doors to pose in front of the flash of our original 70s Polaroid camera: intimate moments, one-on-one conversations, the camera revealing the amazing strength that each individual projects. Designers, musicians, artists, photographers, writers, thinkers, people who make up our world - establishment and avant-garde, artistic, creativity and fashionable society, old friends, new friends and friends of friends. The upshot is a very special document, a social commentary of the beautiful minds and faces that make up our "scene" - a loose network of personalities immersed in their own worlds, centralized yet fragmented by their work, satellites circling each other, the occasional correlation occurring, people who love-in, live in and create one of the world's most inspiring cities. **Photography by Ezra Petronio**

Anna Mouglalis, actress.

Paquita Paquin, journalist, Libération.

STARS & STYLES PORTRAITS OF LONDON

PHOTOGRAPHY BY EZRA PETRONIO

Our impulse for social documentation has again led us across borders, organically following the intricate web of our "extended family tree." And what began as a desire to be in touch with who and what make up our cultural and intellectual environment has led to a fascinating and glorifying experience. Traveling to a new city and meeting so many cultural players in such a condensed period of time, we perceived not only the similarities we expected, but also some very remarkable and undeniable differences. While we may share interests and professional goals, each city's artistic community has a genuine and remarkable distinct flavor all its own, differing from each other in general atmosphere, relation and approach to work. Under the auspices of our London host Nick Knight's SHOWstudio, fashionable society, artistic community, establishment and avant-garde thinkers, photographers, writers and designers, all sat for our original circa-1970s Polaroid camera. A series of spontaneous meetings, one-on-one conversations and separate entities interconnected. The whole as the sum of its parts, a random cross-section representative of a precise time and place. An instant image of the soul of a great city.

STARS & STYLES PORTRAITS OF NEW YORK

PHOTOGRAPHY BY EZRA PETRONIO

The process of social documentation can be addictive, especially when it involves investigating our own environment. This time our curiosity took us and our circa 1970s Polaroid camera to New York City. In an attempt to document the creative forces who share and shape our cultural landscape, we shot 150 New Yorkers in a little under six days. Not a pre-mediated grouping, but rather an organically unravelled network of people, acquaintances, friends, and friends of friends, 15 minute, one-on-one encounters, intimate and personal moments resulting in the revelation of each subject's inner beauty and stature, a subtle combination of genuine sincerity, truth, and an inevitable touch of glamour. A portfolio symbolic of the innumerable possible combinations that can occur at any given time, on any given day, random and yet revealing of the personalities and most certainly the spirit of New York. From varied social circles, communities, and backgrounds, many of these people have come together for the first time on these pages. Unsuspecting members of the cultural community to which they all belong, they reflect individually and collectively the very essence of the city's creative soul.

UN LEASH SELF STYLED TH EA TRICS

James Main, bon vivant.

Millie Brown, performance artist.

The following portraits epitomize a wide-ranging cross-section of our creative landscape. Although culled from radically different milieus and contexts, the photographs taken as a whole could not be more representative of our magazine's commitment to the documentation of our world at this moment in time. As part of our quest to document the fascinating faces that make up the texture of today, we have entered three disparate microcosms, poles of contemporary creativity and influence: the BoomBox party, the Basel art fair, and Cannes Film Festival. The first, a voyage into London's Shoreditch, the Hoxton Square Bar and Kitchen. There we find the now-notorious BoomBox soirée, a hotbed of raw original energy and home to a thoroughly radical genre of face-painting and sparkle-donning. Gareth Pugh cast an overdressed crowd of fashion students, drag queens, starstruck squatters, and artists, all augmented by a myriad of curious freaks and fashion types from previous generations. Although the over-mediatized party is definitely reminiscent of London 80s parties and clubs such as The Blitz, the authentic lack of inhibition, passion for style, and inspiring music, is a mix all its own in our time.
Boombox London, Hoxton Square Bar, May 13th 2007
Photography by Ezra Petronio

Lucas Leclère, fashion student.

Kiki Lotta, student.

The new issue celebrates femininity and female empowerment because we love women

PHOTOGRAPHY BY
London, June
Styling by

STELLA TENNANT PHOTOGRAPHED BY INEZ VAN LAMSWEERDE AND VINOODH MATADIN
New York, July 12–15th, 2010
Fashion editor: Joe McKenna. Hair by Christiaan. Makeup by Lisa Butler.

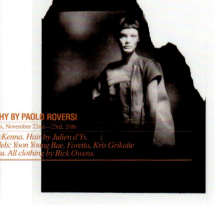

PHOTOGRAPHY BY PAOLO ROVERSI
Studio Luce, Paris, November 22nd–23rd, 2016
Styling by Joe McKenna. Hair by Julien d'Ys. Makeup by Linda Cantello. Models: Yoon Young Bae, Faretta, Kris Grikaite and Alexandra Micu. All clothing by Rick Owens.

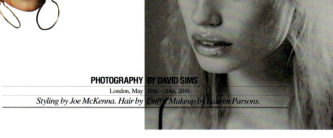

PHOTOGRAPHY BY DAVID SIMS
London, May 29th–30th, 2016
Styling by Joe McKenna. Hair by Duffy. Makeup by Lauren Parsons.

PHOTOGRAPHY BY GLEN LUCHFORD
Bray, County Wicklow, December 17th–18th, 2015
Styling by Jane How. Hair by Anthony Turner. Makeup by Yadim.
Models: Lina Hoss, Suzi Leenaars and Maggie Maurer.

PHOTOGRAPHY BY CRAIG MCDEAN
Ole Studios, New York, December 8th, 2016
Styling by Alastair McKimm. Hair by Shay Ashual.
Makeup by Francelle.

ARIZONA MUSE AND DAPHNE GROENEVELD PHOTOGRAPHED BY ALASDAIR MCLELLAN
Hampstead Heath, London, June 17th–19th, 2011
Styling by Suzanne Koller. Hair by Anthony Turner. Makeup by Lucia Pica.

KATE AND IRIS

"Inspiring, beautiful, funny, tasteful, kind. Kate Moss. A true friend."
— MARIO TESTINO

Photography by Robin Galiegue. Styling by Elodie David Touboul.
All clothing, Saint Laurent by Anthony Vaccarello.

What incredible fashion piece do you regret losing the most and still kick yourself about?
— JAMES BROWN

"I LOST A JOHN GALLIANO DRESS THAT HE GAVE ME FOR MY 21ST BIRTHDAY, AND I STILL THINK OF THAT DRESS. I'VE NO IDEA WHERE IT WENT."
— kate moss

Photography by Nikolai von Bismarck. Styling by Alister Mackie.

If you had to describe yourself by choosing only three objects, what would they be?
— VAL GARLAND

"A DUNHILL LIGHTER, ONE OF CHARLOTTE TILBURY'S LIPSTICKS, AND A CHAMPAGNE GLASS, LIKE THE OLD ROUND ONES THAT I MODELED MY TIT ON ONCE. THEY TOOK MY TIT AND CAST IT AS A CHAMPAGNE GLASS FOR 34 MAYFAIR. THEY TURNED OUT TO BE GOOD PRESENTS TO GIVE TO PEOPLE."
— kate moss

Photography by Mert Alas and Marcus Piggott.
Styling by Emmanuelle Alt.

Let's

Directed by Call This Number (Steve Mackey & Douglas Hart) with Katie Grand. Styling by Jeanie Annan-Lewin.

Pin Up

Photography by Ezra Petronio. Styling by Marie Chaix.

once

Photography by David Sims. Styling by Joe McKenna.

Photography by David Sims. Styling by Max Pearmain.

Me

Photography by Senta Simond. Styling by Marie Chaix.
All clothing, Bottega Veneta.

I want it

Glossy

Photography by Mert Alas and Marcus Piggott. Styling by Jane How.

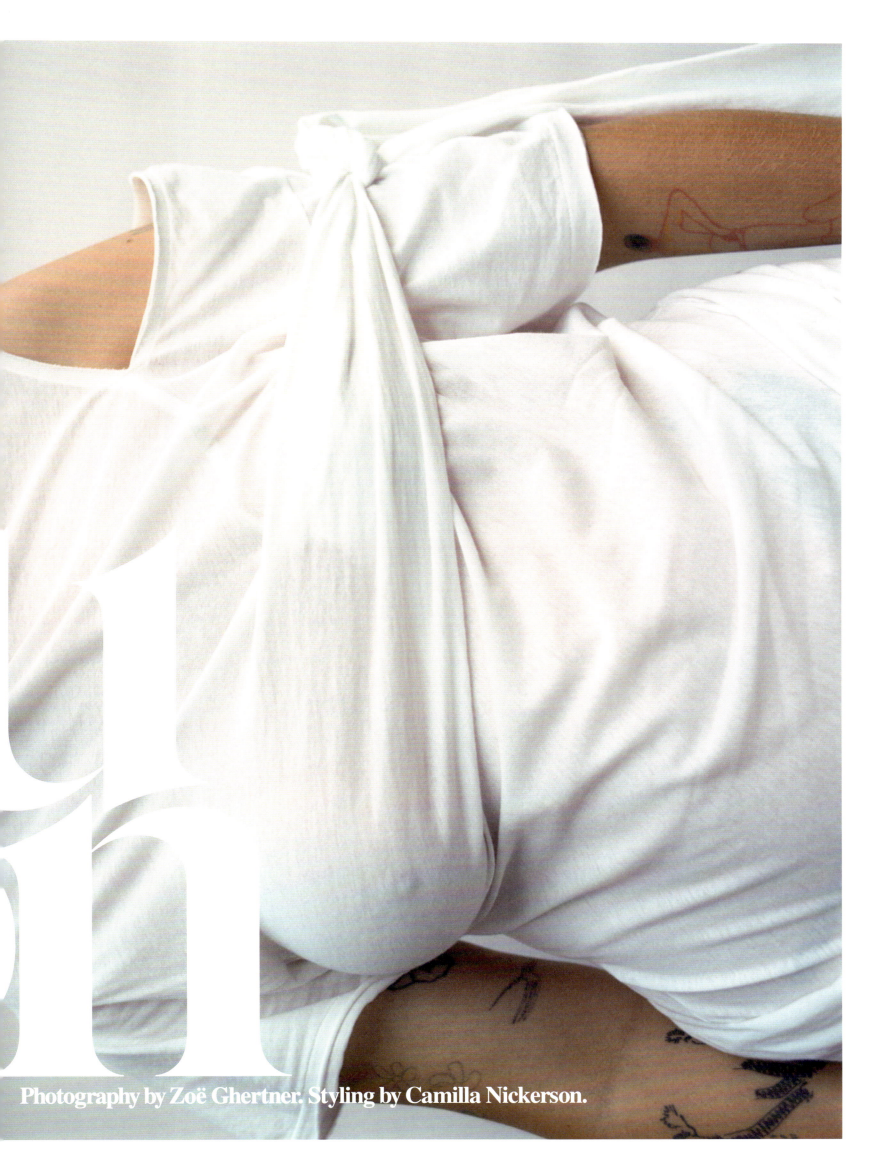

Photography by Zoë Ghertner. Styling by Camilla Nickerson.

SKY-HIGH'S THE LIMIT AS MINIS MADE A BOLD COMEBACK

PHOTOGRAPHY BY DIRK SEIDEN SCHWAN
STYLING BY ANDRE WALKER
HAIR BY SEB BASCLE @ LIGHT HOUSE
MAKEUP BY MICHELLE RAINER @ STREETERS
MODELS: KRISTINA S. AND MICHEL G. @ NATHALIE, KIRSTY RICHARDS @ MARYLIN
CECILIA ANDERSEN @ KARIN, SOPHIE BADER @ NEXT
STYLING ASSISTANCE BY GUYA MARINI, HAIR ASSISTANCE BY SEBASTIEN
OPPOSITE PAGE: PRINTED SILK BUSTIER DRESS WITH SEWN-ON SYNTHETIC HAIR BY JEAN-CHARLES DE CASTELBAJAC

DRESSING DOWN NEVER HURTS.
PHOTOGRAPHY BY KAREN COLLINS
STYLING BY CAMILLE BIDAULT WADDINGTON

BJÖRK
PHOTOGRAPHED BY
JUERGEN TELLER

STYLING BY VENETIA SCOTT
MAKEUP BY DICK PAGE @ JED ROOT
HAIR BY EUGENE SOULEIMAN FOR VS SASSOON
PHOTOGRAPHIC ASSISTANCE BY JON BAKER
STYLING ASSISTANCE BY FENTON AND ZELDA SELLERS

JARVIS COCKER
DARREN SPOONER

Photography by David Sims. Interview by Ezra Petronio.

TOSS ON A SKIMPY CITRUS SWIMSUIT ADD WATER CREATE STIR
PHOTOGRAPHY BY CORINNE DAY
STYLING BY JANE HOW

HAIR BY NEIL MOODIE @ PREMIER USING AVEDA
MAKEUP BY INGE GROGNARD @ AUSTIN
PHOTOGRAPHIC ASSISTANCE BY DANNY GLASSER AND MARC
STYLING ASSISTANCE BY ANNA FOSTER AND EMILY JERMAN
MODELS: ROSEMARY FERGUSON @ SELECT AND DELPHINE @ FORD SHOT AT STUDIO P1, LONDON

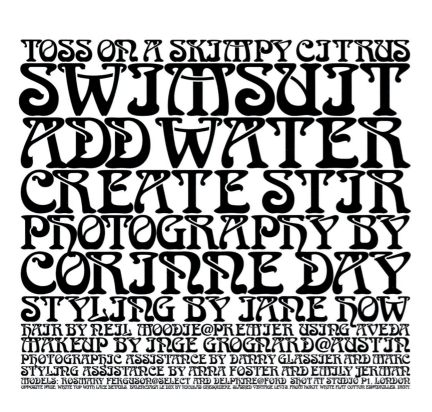

DRESSING RIGHT IS DE RIGEUR

PHOTOGRAPHY BY DAVID ARMSTRONG
STYLING BY PANOS YIAPANIS

WHITE IS THE NEW BLACK

PHOTOGRAPHY BY ALASDAIR McLELLAN
STYLING BY SUZANNE KOLLER

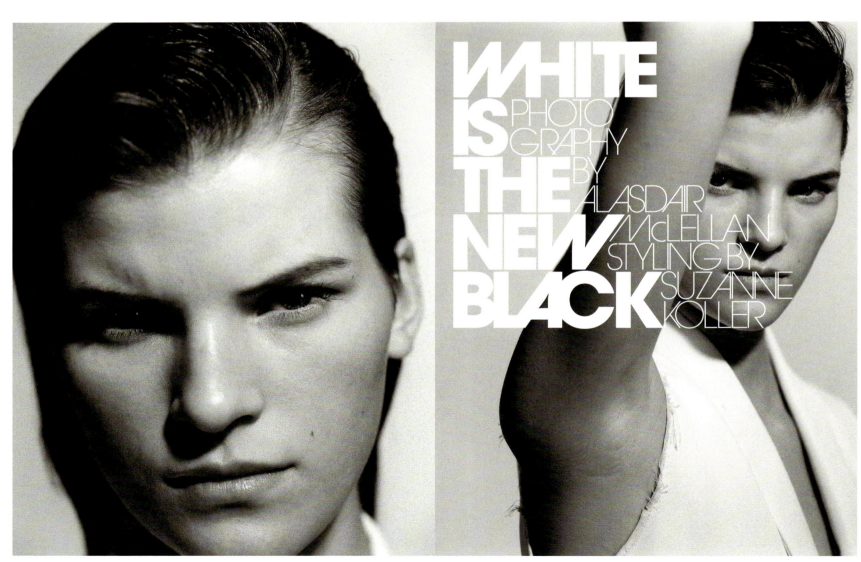

INDULGE IN ESSENTIAL STYLE

photography and styling by Suzanne Koller

ACHIEVING INSTANT ELEGANCE

photography by David Sims   styling by Anna Cockburn

ILLUSIONARY FRONTIERS
DAVID BLAINE
PERFORMER
ON THE POTENTIAL FOR MAGIC TO INFLUENCE MEDICINE AND BITING A QUARTER FOR HARMONY KORINE. ON THE DEFINITION OF DANGER AND ACCELERATING HEARTBEATS.

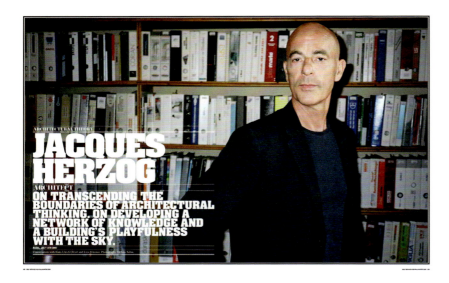

ARCHITECTURAL THEORY
JACQUES HERZOG
ARCHITECT
ON TRANSCENDING THE BOUNDARIES OF ARCHITECTURAL THINKING. ON DEVELOPING A NETWORK OF KNOWLEDGE AND A BUILDING'S PLAYFULNESS WITH THE SKY.

PERSONAL STYLE
ANDRE LEON TALLEY
EDITOR AT LARGE, VOGUE
ON THE IMPORTANCE OF MENTORS AND LIBERATION FROM THE SHACKLES OF AMERICAN PURITANISM. ON THE VISUAL INTERPRETATION OF FASHION NARRATIVE AND READING TO DIANA VREELAND AFTER DINNER.

In an industry often critiqued for its trend-driven conventionality, Andre Leon Talley stands out as a beacon of idiosyncratic personal style as well as a torch-bearer from the glittering epoch of Diana Vreeland and Andy Warhol. Despite fashion's commitment to invention, there are few characters that incarnate true personal style, audacity, and exuberance on par with Talley. His individuality and freedom escape categorization. Born in Durham, North Carolina, Andre Leon Talley was raised by his fastidious, church-going grandmother, whose sense of propriety and elegance would be a lasting influence on his life and career. After attending North Carolina Central University, Talley continued his studies in French at Brown University, making frequent trips to New York City. In 1974, André met one of his most inspirational mentors, Diana Vreeland, while interning at the Metropolitan Museum of Art. Ms. Vreeland would prove to be an important force in the young man's life, both personally and professionally. The following year, at her suggestion, André began working at Andy Warhol's Factory, answering phones and sweeping the floors in knee socks and boater hats given to him by Karl Lagerfeld. In the late '70s André joined the Women's Wear Daily team, ultimately shipping off to Paris to run its Paris bureau. He has been an integral part of Vogue since 1983, serving as both its Creative Director and Editor at Large, while style.com invites V and style.com correspondent Derek Blasberg to Michael's to chat about buying the best you can afford, the rareness of Manolo Blahnik furniture, fortuitous encounters that change a young man's life, knowing everything about someone before you meet them, Oprah as an entity unto herself, the instinctual editing style of Anna Wintour, the Obama family's realization of the American dream, and the representational power of classic white gloves.

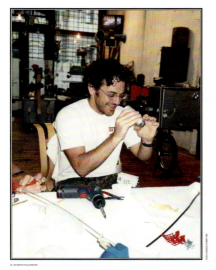

ARTISTIC FRONTIERS
TOM SACHS
CONCEPTUAL ARTIST
ON MILITARY POWER AND THE PSYCHIC AND PHYSICAL DANGERS OF CONTEMPORARY LIFE. ON A PERSONALIZED USE OF MATERIAL AND THE PROCESS OF MAKING CONCEPTUAL ART.

Tom Sachs is one of the most important conceptual artists working today and at the same time a true art-world outsider. His process-oriented, sculptural installations and movies, such as Nutsy's, "McDonald's Teaser", "Prada Death Camp", and "Chanel Guillotine/Breakfast Nook", and his weaponry made from urban debris, are physical representations of his humanistic and sociological reactions to everything from physicality, functionality, branding, globalization, and consumerism, to attempts to control the "uncontrollable." His work has been shown and collected by the Prada Foundation, the Metropolitan Museum of Art, The Costume Institute, the Solomon R. Guggenheim Museum, and the Whitney Museum of American Art. Author, journalist, director, and all-round pop guru, Glenn O'Brien, has been an arbiter of style and a creatively present critic on cultural matters and movements for the last 30 years. His mix of genres, ranging from former editor of Interview and creative director of Barneys New York and Calvin Klein, to the directorial success of Downtown 81, and novels and poetry and contributions to Vogue Italia and Artforum, illustrate his genuinely unique mastery of not only the intricacies of the modern consumerist world but also the depth and intellectualization of art. The two friends sit down together to discuss sympathetic magic, war as a metaphor for life, the distraction of the market when making work, anti-elitism, asserting power, artistic conscience and getting away from the lowest common denominator.

PERSONAL STYLE
STEFANO PILATI
CREATIVE DIRECTOR OF YVES SAINT LAURENT
ON ELEGANCE AND SOPHISTICATION. ON UNDERSTANDING THE HISTORY OF A BRAND WHILE BRINGING IT INTO NEW TERRITORY.

INFLUENTIAL MEDIA

JONATHAN NEWHOUSE

CHAIRMAN OF CONDE NAST INTERNATIONAL LTD.

ON THE ROLE OF INSTINCT AND INTUITION IN SUCCESSFUL PUBLISHING, ON CORPORATE VISION, MANAGEMENT STYLE, AND LUXURY AS HUMAN NATURE.

At the helm of the second largest publishing group in the world, Jonathan Newhouse has successfully developed Condé Nast International Ltd. to include over 100 magazines in 15 countries around the globe, as well as 22 daily newspapers and 37 business journals throughout the United States. Under his leadership the company has also expanded its magazine influence into new markets such as China, Japan, Korea, Taiwan, Russia, South Africa, and Portugal, as well as various important and complementary sites on the World Wide Web. An independent thinker from an historical newspaper-publishing family, Jonathan is easily one of the great managers of our times. He is equally inspiring for his gracious yet hands-on management style, a capacity for detail as well as overview, and his marriage of high moral standards with market realities. Jonathan meets Ezra Petronio at Vogue House for a rare interview about the human necessity of luxury, long-term expectations, cultural dialogue, anticipating the desires of the readership, celebrity culture, finding talent and expression in unexpected places, the avant-garde versus the establishment, the self-indulgence of nostalgia, and most importantly, the eight golden rules to successful magazine management.

LONDON, JULY 28TH 2005

Conversation by Ezra Petronio. Photography by Juergen Teller

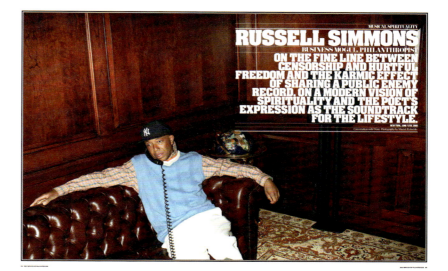

MUSICAL SPIRITUALITY

RUSSELL SIMMONS

BUSINESS MOGUL, PHILANTHROPIST

ON THE FINE LINE BETWEEN CENSORSHIP AND HURTFUL FREEDOM AND THE KARMIC EFFECT OF SHARING A PUBLIC ENEMY RECORD, ON A MODERN VISION OF SPIRITUALITY AND THE POET'S EXPRESSION AS THE SOUNDTRACK FOR THE LIFESTYLE.

NEW YORK, JUNE 13TH, 2005

Conversation with Diane. Photography by Marcelo Krasilcic

SOCIETY CHRONICLES

BOB COLACELLO

JOURNALIST, AUTHOR

ON BEING SO IN YOU'RE OUT AND SO OUT YOU'RE IN, ON EDITING OUT THE BALCONY OF STUDIO 54, THE PROFUSION OF HYPE BUBBLES, THE IDEA OF PARIS HILTON ON ANDY WARHOL'S ARM.

Although Bob Colacello came of age as the editor of Interview and the close confidante of Andy Warhol, he has managed to avoid the inevitable nostalgia of his past to become a true anachronism and individual: a staunch Republican with a debauched, artistic past, a devotee of the typewriter, and above all an old-school journalist with a commitment to indefatigable research (laced with a 70s-style taste for dishy gossip). Within six months of meeting Andy Warhol as a Columbia grad student, Colacello became editor of the fledgling magazine Interview, where he began writing and taking pictures for the nightlife column 'Out.' After leaving the editing of the magazine to Glenn O'Brien, Colacello toured the world with Andy as his biographer and sold portrait commissions. He left the Factory in a huff in 1983 and published the acclaimed Warhol memoir Holy Terror: Andy Warhol Close Up seven years later. Since 1984 Bob has been a Vanity Fair special correspondent, and spent many years researching his 2004 Reagan opus, Ronnie and Nancy: Their Path to the White House 1911-1980. The photos from 'Out' have recently been compiled into a book called Bob Colacello's Out. Bob talks to fellow Georgetown, Columbia, and Interview alum Glenn O'Brien about the contrary nature of a Republican at the Factory, the tragedy of text messaging, the invasive tendency of the past, radical chic, and niche scenes.

NEW YORK, JANUARY 21ST, 2006

Conversation with Glenn O'Brien. Photography by Jonathan Becker

PERSONAL STYLE

DIANE VON FURSTENBERG

FASHION DESIGNER

ON ETERNAL TRANSFORMATIONS AND NEW INCARNATIONS AND ANDY WARHOL'S BEAUTIES, ON THE MASCULINE/FEMININE DICHOTOMY OF DESIGN AND FOUR MILLION DOLLAR A MINUTE OBSTACLES.

NEW YORK, JANUARY 10TH, 2006

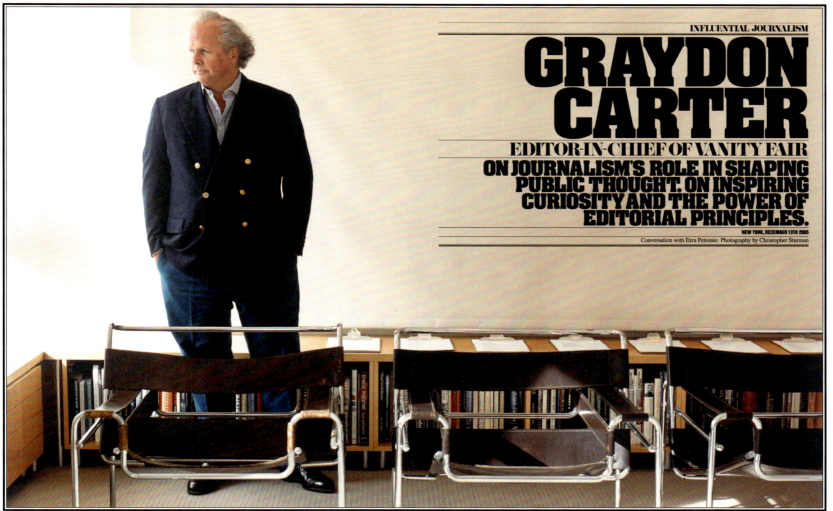

INFLUENTIAL JOURNALISM

GRAYDON CARTER

EDITOR-IN-CHIEF OF VANITY FAIR

ON JOURNALISM'S ROLE IN SHAPING PUBLIC THOUGHT, ON INSPIRING CURIOSITY AND THE POWER OF EDITORIAL PRINCIPLES.

NEW YORK, DECEMBER 13TH 2005

Conversation with Ezra Petronio Photography by Christopher Sturman

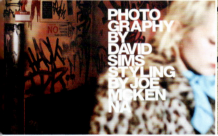

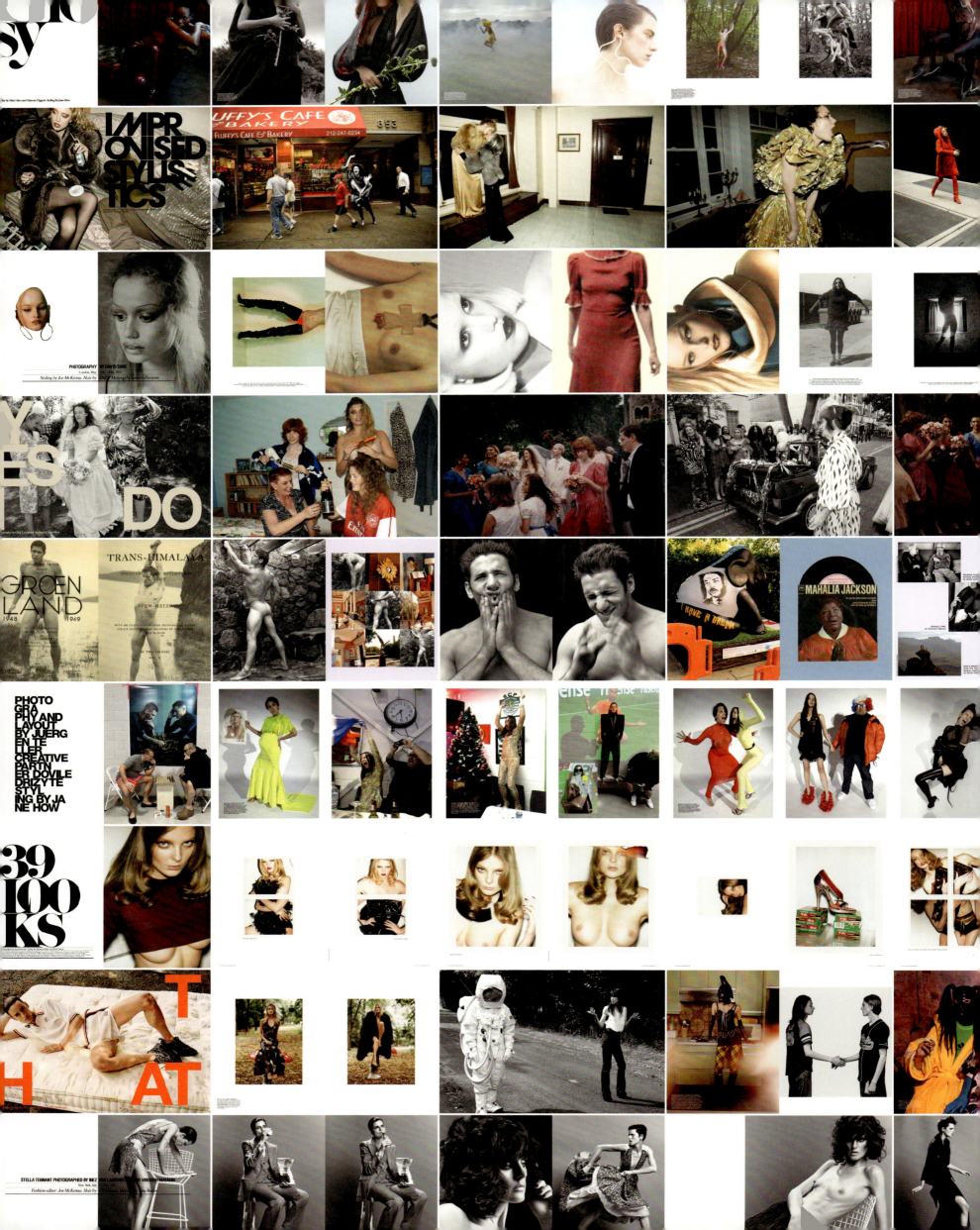

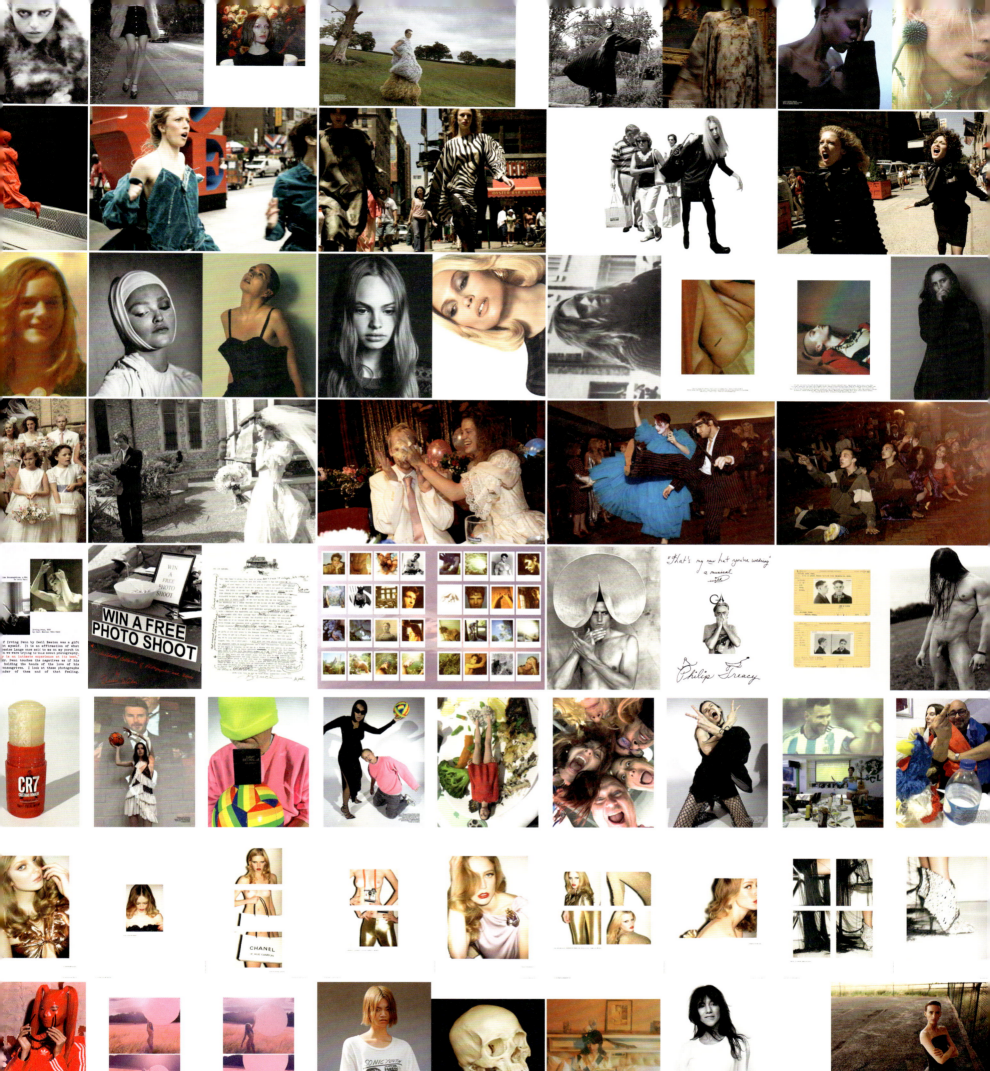

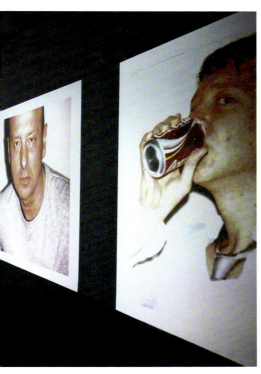

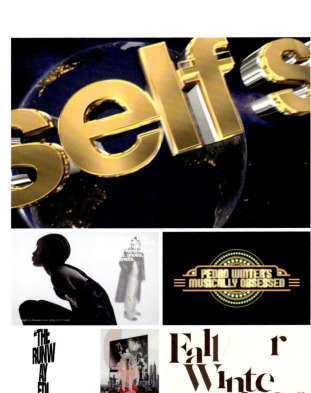

SELF SERVICE ISSUE N°53 — THE FILM

SELF SERVICE ISSUE N°54 — THE FILM

SELF SERVICE EXHIBITION: 25 YEARS OF FASHION, PEOPLE AND IDEAS RECONSIDERED — TEASER

SELF SERVICE 1994-2022, THE ADS — BOOK

THE VINTAGE YOU — BOOK

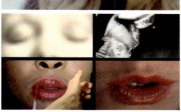

SELF SERVICE — VARIOUS FILMS

SELF SERVICE — IPAD APP

SELF SERVICE — DIGITAL CONTENT

ON INDEPENDENT PUBLISHING
A CONVERSATION WITH JEFFERSON HACK

JEFFERSON HACK: *Visual Thinking*: it's such a great title for a book.

EZRA PETRONIO: It was the title of my teacher Henry Wolf's book and the subject of the senior-year class he taught at Parsons School of Design in New York. Henry was a groundbreaking art director who worked with Alexey Brodovitch and did amazing covers for *Harper's Bazaar*. He was part of a generation of art directors who could do anything from designing magazines, advertising campaigns, and film titles to picking up a camera and taking memorable photographs.

JEFFERSON: You were fortunate to have him as a teacher and mentor.

EZRA: Do you have fond memories of your early days, when you look back at your journey?

JEFFERSON: Of course, it's always a bit rose-tinted because you look back at the past, and you kind of edit out the bad bits. I think we all have the capacity to do that. There were no boundaries between work and play. It was all a lot of fun. We were just very driven to create the next issue and to go through whatever the process was that needed to happen. In the analog days, even though we were the first generation to inherit desktop publishing, it was still pre-Internet, pre-email. It was the era of the fax machine. You were calling a lot of people and trying to get them to answer their phones, which were landlines. The production process was time-consuming.
We were busy trying to make things happen, but it was a lot of fun. We had three telephones, magazines as furniture instead of real furniture—you're sitting on magazines, it's funny. And that was the vibe. It was always a bit like a club. It was like, "When does the party start and the work begin?" I never really understood when to switch one off and switch the other one on—they both merged into each other. For the first 10 years, I met every person I hired for *Dazed & Confused* in nightclubs. They were the petri dishes of culture at the time.

EZRA: I have very fond memories of the way we were all very competitive but, in a very joyous way, stimulating each other. I have fond memories of going to the Milan shows. We were young and all staying at the Diana Hotel. I remember you were there, Katie Grand, Olivier Zahm from *Purple*. We would all go from room to room to share the minibars. There was this sense of wanting to enter the establishment. There was something quite lovely about the idea that we were very driven to succeed, but we understood that there was a certain time that was required to get there.

JEFFERSON: I still get the same buzz today when I meet independent publishers. I'm like, "Oh, you understand me." It is such a peculiar thing that we do, to make magazines, to make printed media. When I meet people who are making magazines that I really like, who know the craft, who know real graphic design, real photo editing, good commissioning, really good text—these are the people who are doing something that is progressing the media. They are doing something that is traditional but also new. It is coming from a place of intellectual curiosity, and that excites me. I loved meeting you because it was very rare. There were not a lot of us, and we needed each other to prove that the alternative press, the independent scene, was relevant. We could not prove that it was relevant to the industry, to the advertising industry, or to the fashion industry. We needed to get clothes, we needed to shoot, we needed access, we needed to get the advertising support. We couldn't prove that if there was just one of us.
A lot of the avant-garde magazines that had exploded in the 60s and 70s had closed, stuttered, or were being bought, or had become commercial. It was the rise of these big, commercial magazines. I remember the biggest magazine in the U.K. when we started was something like *Loaded*, *Maxim*, or *FHM*, and Time Inc. was launching *InStyle*. This was what people were talking about. I was looking at magazines like *Avant Garde*, or the early issues of *Interview*, or *Égoïste*. And I knew that you were looking at those things, too. That was our bond. When we met, that was what we talked about, like guys in bands get together and meet and talk about the avant-garde, the 60s, garage rock…

EZRA: To fast-track to today, both of us have always been quite fascinated with digital. You have clearly been able to bring classic print to a new level with your video channel, *Nowness*. You were one of the first pioneers in evolving your platforms. And you keep on doing that. How do you embrace the change? How do you see all of this playing out?

JEFFERSON: For me, it goes back to the same core principle, no matter the medium: curation and quality storytelling are what matter. So, whether that is visual journalism, like short-form documentary or short-form video, or a fashion film, or straightforward Web journalism, the core is that it has to be original, or made by you, meaning you're the first to premiere it. It is not a copy—you're not just republishing something. And it has to be a curation: you have to publish from a point of view, not just include anything and everything.

EZRA: It definitely has to be extremely original and with a unique personal point of view.

JEFFERSON: That kind of went against the grain of what we were sold by Silicon Valley, which was really about clickbait and numbers, these weird kinds of memes and fun stuff. I am not saying that everything we do is overly serious, but I just think that the quality and the curation come first, over and above the junk-food mentality that Silicon Valley is pushing. They don't care about quality, they don't care about people, they don't care about the consumer.
All of these tech platforms that have launched, every single one of them is really about owning your attention and turning you into the product. The product is you, and that goes against quality. It's always about reducing to something quick, disposable, tabloid-like. Very much like what tabloid journalism is.

EZRA: What made you decide to launch your own digital platform?

JEFFERSON: When we first started developing *Nowness*, it was very simple. It was like, "Okay, there is a generation of young people with cameras who are doing moving image and who are hungry in the same way that the photographers whom we were publishing in *Dazed & Confused* were hungry to express themselves through photography." And these were people coming out of college, university, or graduating from high school, and they were shooting and filming everything. But they were filming everything in a moving-image way, in the same way that photographers in the past were shooting everything with cameras. Where *Dazed* was a platform for photography through print, *Nowness* was going to be a platform for moving images using the same principles of curation.

EZRA: And you found the time and means to develop it, while maintaining complete creative control?

JEFFERSON: We were very lucky when we got backing from LVMH. And that they helped support it, because it took quite a lot of time to define itself, and it took quite a lot of money to invest in commissioning and curating that content. It would have been impossible to do it as a completely independent platform. But where they were fantastic was that they gave me complete control: they let me curate it like we curate our other publications.

The problem with digital is that the numbers always get so high, so quickly. It's like a casino. And everyone gets so excited about numbers that they want to push everything to get bigger numbers. It is ego-fulfilling. People think, "I'm better if I have a bigger number." And I think what we now know about the numbers, or the way the metrics work, is that the bigger number is not always the better result for the brand, for the photographer, for the artist. If you're interested in the avant-garde, if you're interested in culture, it is never about being the biggest — it is always about being the most influential. Sometimes influence is about scale, but sometimes it's not about the scale. Sometimes it has absolutely nothing to do with scale — it could actually have to do with the opposite, which has to do with authenticity, and then people find you, and they talk about you, and they amplify you, and they copy you, and then you have a huge influence from not having to be the biggest.

EZRA: So, in terms of your audience, you're interested in quality and influence, not quantity.

JEFFERSON: With digital, I think the mistake a lot of people made was chasing numbers. And we just always felt that we would grow like an onion: we would grow very slowly but keep to our principles, and over time, we would build a very true and honest audience who cared about what we cared about. We did that with *Dazed & Confused*, and we did it with *anothermag.com*, which I'm very proud of. Having more than one platform has helped because we could share the knowledge between them all. I would be totally bored if I was digital only. The beautiful thing about what now exists is that we have always done a lot of real-world events, as well as the physical publications, as well as the digital. So, it's a 360° approach.

I think that it is great that a lot of young publishers can use digital to express themselves and have an Instagram account as a magazine, have a TikTok as a magazine, have their own media, their own magazine now. I love that everyone is their own media. I am very excited about that idea. But for me, as more of a traditional magazine-maker who's also a futurist — I like to have all the 360°.

EZRA: During confinement, we decided to introduce two simultaneous experiences of *Self Service* — our usual print version as well as a film version following the same narration. We wished to creatively embrace the digital age, recontextualizing the narrative of our printed magazine in a multilayered film experience, expanding our reach and vision beyond boundaries. We want to engage our readers with two ways to experience a magazine — this juxtaposition being our vision for a possible future of magazine publishing. It was very experimental. When we entered the full-on lockdown, there was that big moment of panic when we were all wondering if we're going to get advertising, if campaigns were going to be shot, and what was going to be the revenue flow for the coming year. Funnily I realize that it is always in very unstable times that I take the most risks to explore. Our film issue was an interesting alternative media experience.

JEFFERSON: I saw it and thought it was so innovative. I think that you're a real master of motion graphics, which is not easy to do, but it's an art form in its own right. When we get pushed into a corner, we find ways to still be creative. I think that's so important.

EZRA: Even if it is not economically viable, it is still our role to explore and to create benchmarks.

JEFFERSON: What did your first issue look like?

EZRA: The first issue was 64 pages, in black and white, with 16 colored pages, stapled together. It was a Mark Borthwick and Jane How cover. My editorial was a quote by John Cassavetes, talking about the collaborative aspects of things. Our advertisers were Kodak, our photo lab Picto, Heineken, and Agnès B.

JEFFERSON: Agnès B. is such an important supporter of the arts. She is not recognized enough for her contribution to the avant-garde and alternative arts. Where did the name *Self Service* come from?

EZRA: It had a very boring name at first, like very nerdy — I think it was *Alternative* or something literal. And we had a section called "Self Service" at the end that had a lot of little visuals and lots of blurbs on different topics, that you could pick and choose from. A friend of mine said that's what the magazine should be called because basically it was about Paris at that moment, gathering all of our friends' points of view and contemporary art. Fashion was not the priority — it was the music scene, contemporary art, and cinema.

JEFFERSON: It's interesting because you say that it's the industry that supported you the most, but I also feel that you make a magazine that supports the industry so much. It's circular, but your magazine is like the reference point for so many designers. It's also the reference point for so many creatives to get hired from, and so many ideas go on to influence campaigns. It's an amazing insider toolkit for the season.

EZRA: The same goes for you. We are these time capsules of a condensed version of what we each curated in our own way. If you pull out a Fall/Winter issue of 1998, your magazine or mine, you'll see the most relevant advertising, who are the people photographing the clothes, the mood of the moment — so you're right to say that we are fundamental in enabling this industry to stay healthy because without our magazines, talents would not get the support to emerge. We are like postgraduate college programs for the new generation to come and learn. Ultimately, the industry, by supporting us all these years, has justified the relevance of our type of magazines in the market. I think we've succeeded.

JEFFERSON: This creative expression can happen anywhere. It can happen in any medium, in any way. But somehow, the format of a magazine is still a beautiful framing and, like you say, a time-capsule-type framing that maintains its value. What I mean is that you can publish fashion stories straight on the Web, you can publish them straight onto Instagram, you can publish them straight into many different formats, you can make fly posters of them and put them on the wall, you can stick them on billboards. You can do what you want with fashion pictures: you can make an exhibition, you can do a pop-up, you can paste wallpaper of your shoe all around a gallery and invite your friends and the industry to come and see it. But somehow, the format of the fashion story, laid out in a magazine, over pages, still has a thrill when it is viewed, when it is experienced, when it is selected, when it is put on a coffee table. That magic in paper, in that format, is not replaceable. You must feel that, too?

EZRA: For sure. And you experience that every time you put it together. The way everything's assembled, until the last minute... It's like cooking: each story is laid out in a way that every picture does not overkill the other, that every story follows a rhythm and a flow that celebrate each story, that your type design is there to enhance this narrative. That is our art as publishers: to have that capacity of words, images, and all these layers and juxtapositions to tell and to express people's visions. I'm sure you feel the same way, too — every time I get a new issue that comes in on my desk, and I look at it, I still get goose pimples because there are so many shoots, and you know that everyone has put so much energy and love and care into every story. The younger photographers, the older photographers... You feel that everyone — the styling, the hair, the makeup, the producers, the writers—has contributed so much love, and that is beautiful. And that is what keeps me going because I know that it resonates and that people care. They work for you, they work for me, they work for these different publications because we love them, and there is a sense of care, of support, and on top of that, it has a purpose. So, yes, we have, as we say, a lot of gratitude and pride.

JEFFERSON: It's good to hear what gets you going with what you do. And that is important: the psychology or, let's say, the reality of what gives you the buzz for what you do. People are a big part of it, obviously. I feel like I am less in the weeds these days than I used to be, and my role now is definitely much more about creating the conditions for my teams to be able to do their best work, and I work hard to create an environment where they have as much freedom and support to create *AnOther* magazine or *Dazed* in print and digital in the way that is most pure to their vision. And now I am taking more of a managerial role.

EZRA: Go on, you're the leader. I've always wondered: how did you come up with *Dazed & Confused* as a title?

JEFFERSON: We were listening to Led Zeppelin, and it is a track on a Led Zeppelin album. It was playing a lot in the background, and it was how we felt. We discussed it, and we felt excited by having a brief as a name, not just a name.

EZRA: There is a very cute story because my daughter is about the same age as yours. She is a young, aspiring photographer, and she was asked to go to New York to shoot your daughter.

JEFFERSON: The kids are taking over. I feel like we are fashion insiders now, and so are our children, even though I came into this industry as an outsider. I think that there is an incredible value in the young people who are exposed to culture and creativity at a young age—that's a wonderful thing because they are full of ideas and inspirations that are important. But I think our role at *Dazed* is also to bring people into this industry who are not from the fashion families or the elite schools, who are not the sons and daughters of the cool musicians and artists. We work really hard at creating outreach programs, and we do a lot of work in our community to make diversity and inclusion a very real thing, both in our own staffing and hiring, but also in the contributor set. We have to not just reflect those politics through image or text—we also have to live them in the behavior that we apply to the way we run our businesses. And that is what this new era in publishing really represents to me. What I hope is that *Dazed* continues long after I'm gone.

EZRA: One vital part of our job is transmission...

JEFFERSON: Absolutely! Because it's not about me. It's about them. We now work very hard to create a system where it's self-sustaining, where it sustains itself independently of just any individual. I love new magazines. I just helped to establish a bookshop and library at our offices called Reference Point. It is independently curated by two friends of mine. I helped birth it and make it happen. And we have a lot of young publishers coming there and making their first magazines there, doing their launch parties. And there are a couple that I am really proud of: one is called *New Currency*, a fantastic magazine. And the other one that just launched recently is called *Twist*. I am a real fan of a new one called *Boy.Brother. Friend* from London. Very, very cool fashion magazine.

EZRA: I think the U.K. is unique in its capacity to create new magazines, in terms of volume and consistency. There is a deep culture of the independent press in the U.K.

JEFFERSON: I am always very encouraging to new publishers, and I, like you, would love to meet them and give them some advice or support, help them with an ad. *Dazed* is only relevant if it connects to the culture, if it's truly connected to the culture. As an institution, we have a responsibility to break down the barrier between the street and the institution. The whole idea of Reference Point and what I'm doing now is that any kid can come in off the street and walk straight into the magazine. And it's a coffee shop, it's a hang, it's like a coworking, it's a little library space, it's free. You can come in, you can work there, you can make it happen. The older the magazine, the longer the magazine has been around, the more it becomes the establishment. For me, it is important because with *Dazed*, the ethos was always to be anti-establishment. So, how do you deterritorialize your position? How do you subvert your own success? How do you stay true, without becoming a victim of that success? And this is something that really bothers me about the fine art of staying true.

EZRA: You answered it: it's by transmission, it's by helping, it's by giving back, it's by supporting, it's by using the position you're in to help support change.

JEFFERSON: Because otherwise, what the fuck is it for? I always believed that you, Olivier Zahm, I, and several other publishers—whom we identify as part of the independent press—have always been part of a cultural resistance movement. Fighting for change, having to change, like guerrilla warfare.

We have to support each other against this kind of military-industrial complex of corporations that want to own and take over the world, that do not value people. The same players are behind the big Silicon Valley platforms. It is corporate mentality—they don't give a shit about people. They give a shit about the shareholder and corporate value, and they suck the life out of culture. Everything is disposable. We're disposable. But what the cultural resistance movement says is: "No, people are not disposable. Ideas are not disposable. We are going to resist the tide of your intervention into our lives and create space that we can hold as sacred for what we believe in."

EZRA: I love our little Marxist conversation.

JEFFERSON: We've got to be more than magazines—we are more than magazines. I believe that we are part of something bigger than just being publishers. On the cover of the first issue of *Dazed*, I wrote, "This is not a magazine." There was a bit more explanation after that, but I think this spirit of walking the walk, talking the talk, is important for those who want to outlast the moment. If you want to be around for a while, you are going to get found out if you are faking it. This is what I say to young talent.

EZRA: "Don't schmooze, you lose": that was a quote that you gave to us a long time ago. It was so good.

JEFFERSON: Don't schmooze, you lose.

ON IMAGE MAKING
A CONVERSATION WITH DAVID SIMS, JANE HOW, AND LANA PETRUSEVYCH

EZRA PETRONIO: I would like this conversation to be an inspiration to younger creative people—a discussion of the evolution and the process of image-making over the past 30 years, and how we have adapted. Both of you are part of a generation who were my heroes and inspiration when I started, and you were very instrumental in defining what fashion photography and styling were to become decades later. What would you say to a young person with sparkles in their eyes who came to you today for advice? What would be the mindset you'd tell them they should have?

JANE HOW: Work really hard because success doesn't come without hard work. It is important to have a really open mind, to be flexible, to keep on being inspired. Research a lot, go out, search for stuff because it is not going to just land on your lap.

DAVID SIMS: Hard work always leads to good things. Trust your instincts. If you're going into an assisting role, make yourself as indispensable as possible. I always say to young photo assistants: "If you hear somebody complain, fix that thing first, and then don't try and take credit for it because they will just love you, and then it puts you in a place where you can start to develop your involvement in a picture. It is the worst thing to be an assistant on the margins, where you are not part of the energy. You want to be a part of whatever energy is being created. Do not stand away from it."

LANA PETRUSEVYCH: What do you remember about being an assistant, when you were starting out?

JANE: Before I became a stylist, I was a hairdresser, and I remember assisting Ray Allington on early John Galliano shows. I was a baby, but I remember just being amazed. And I think that's what made me want to be a stylist. It was wonderful. It was really inspiring, and I think that got the ball rolling. I never really assisted many people. There were not so many people to assist at the time. I think that back then, you just picked yourself up and did it.

DAVID: When I was an assistant, I was enthralled watching certain people work and seeing how they constantly managed to create something. It was just like plucking something from thin air. It was an idea in somebody's mind, and then suddenly it became real, it was manifest, and we were watching that unfold and gather momentum to the point where it reached this sort of peak, gaining life out of its nascent phase and then turning into a page in a magazine.

LANA: How do you create an original image that might be remembered? What is the process like?

JANE: If I can manage to find a reference that I feel hasn't been so well used, then that starts the ball rolling. It is something I just latch onto, and then I build something new from that. I start building characters with the designer, art director, and photographer.
It is all in the details, taking from lots of different things. It is almost a soup. Everyone is inspired by what people have done in the past, but I think you try to avoid repeating that. You take bits from lots of different things, and for me, that's the only way forward—it has to be a soup. It is similar with images: you might take the body language from something, and you take the light from something else. You hope you come up with something that feels more unique.

DAVID: My answer to that is I have a fascination for faces. There's this sort of primordial force in everyone—it's just a question of how willing they are to let that show in the action of making a photograph. And I know when it's good because it happens without my involvement. I do not know if it's performative, or if it's natural, but there is a glee — for want of a better word—that I get, that I extract from that moment. The camera becomes essentially what it is: it's a mechanism to record, and I do not have to get too involved. All studios have a psychic atmosphere. It's sort of like the weather. Sometimes you have to be ready for all kinds of weather, but sometimes the sun just breaks through, and people glow, and I can just sit back and watch the picture being made. It's a really happy place for me.

EZRA: In our early days, the process of image-making was more time-consuming than it is today. You had more time to construct a creative direction. Today you need to be more intuitive and create in the moment. We are in a period where time and budgets have been compressed; mediums and assets have demultiplied.

DAVID: A kind of atrophy of our practice has happened as an outcome of the digital age, the post-information age. There is a vast amount of images that people have access to—or maybe don't see simply because of the sheer volume of them. So, things that are potentially of worth and have value just simply get missed in the crowd. Young people today are much more focused on having a career. People of our generation didn't have a strong focus on career aspirations because there was no pro forma for that. I was 12 years old when punk happened, and that iconoclastic slash-and-burn ideology around chaos as a creative force was implanted in our generation. And that was probably our abiding influence. We weren't adhering to the punk ethos, but we had definitely been fed on it. Creating pictures came from a place of just pure compulsion to create. It wasn't linked to an outcome objective, other than the picture itself. All art has to speak from the self, and we were able to do that because we didn't have a commercial appendage. We were not linked to selling—that did not affect our thinking at the time. I like to think that young people still have that.

JANE: There was a point early on when I actually never even shot any labels. We used to do whole stories that were just all vintage, and we never even thought about product placement.

LANA: Jane, you were one of the only people who told me that you still go to the library to research and Xerox books.

JANE: All the time, as much as I can, because for me, the Internet is just not interesting for research. I have to look at books, and I have to spend time. You have to go way back, further than the Internet, to come up with something new. In a way, you have to look back to look forward. I think that, to a degree, the past informs the future.

EZRA: In the process of image-making, how important is collaboration?

JANE: I prepare as much as possible before a shoot, but I always try to keep an open mind and think, "Okay, I could turn up, and this could not work, and something completely different will happen." And that's great, that's fine, and I don't feel like that's a problem. Someone on the team might bring something to the table that you never thought of. Somebody might do some hair or makeup, and it shifts the balance of what you were thinking, and I really love that. I think that's part of the process. I feel like that's the exciting bit: that things can change, things can develop. I often visualize something before a shoot, and I think, "That's how it's going to look," and it doesn't look that way in the end, and most of the time, you hope it's even better than what you expected.

DAVID: I'm a twin. I think that has afforded me the opportunity of having some fairly interesting adventures in the realm of codependency.

ON THE EARLY DAYS
A CONVERSATION WITH SUZANNE KOLLER

EZRA PETRONIO: When we started working together in the early 90s, it was a different context from today—it was pre-Colette, pre-Eurostar, pre-Web, and practically pre-everything. We were inspired by *The Face*, *i-D*, and *Dazed & Confused*. We had to go to the newsstand to get our information and the library to do our research. I also remember being in a rebellious mindset of "us-vs.-them" because our younger creative generation in France was neither supported nor even recognized.

SUZANNE KOLLER: We were just doing whatever we knew to make a place for ourselves in the establishment. Back then, it was not quite clear that an independent magazine could even succeed. Today, we have hundreds of independent magazines. Everyone is launching their magazines as self-promotion of their personal work. Back then, we would do a magazine to talk about our community and celebrate new talents.

EZRA: We would defend and support people.

SUZANNE: In the early 90s, there was an incredible creative crowd in Paris. "Paris was burning": the establishment was boring so we really had no other choice but to set up our own business.

EZRA: Yes, even if our freedom and independence meant designing annual reports, trade-show catalogs, or Disney brochures. There was never any ego.

SUZANNE: Even starting a company wasn't something I personally had envisioned. There was nothing exciting in Paris. Everything was happening in London back then: the great advertising agencies and magazines...

EZRA: Paris and France were so different from what they are today! There was no support system for anything progressive or creatively different and new. Even a lot of the new French house scene, led by Pedro Winter and Daft Punk, had to sell their albums at Rough Trade in London and seek recognition abroad. We soon realized that there was a raison d'être for *Self Service*. We started very organically by gathering our friends in different artistic fields. We had a good group of people around us who were all dreaming and creating.

SUZANNE: And everybody was participating in the magazine. Even Olivier Zahm, who had already launched *Purple Prose*, was writing for us. And Loïc Prigent, too.

EZRA: Sylvie Fleury was our beauty editor. Chloë Sevigny, Susan Cianciolo, Bernadette Corporation... Claude Closky was doing the horoscope. When you think of it, Xavier Veilhan and Philippe Parreno were contributing fun things. Everyone was involved. Even Jérôme Viger-Kohler, cofounder of Respect Parties who was also working with Christophe Vix at Radio FG, was part of our journey.

SUZANNE: Today, people think of *Self Service* as a fashion magazine, but it was more of a multicultural magazine at the beginning. Over time, we slowly evolved into focusing much more on the creativity in and of fashion.

EZRA: Fashion inspired us and allowed for a lot of creative freedom in image-making. Back then, it was a smaller industry that was also extremely modern and progressive. Fashion was the only industry that would financially support such a venture as ours.

SUZANNE: That was the only market that understood what we were doing back then. Nobody could really understand what *Self Service* was or even what the role of an independent magazine was.

EZRA: Everything was very segmented in France. You were either covering only music and would get music advertising, or you did an art magazine and would get art advertising. There weren't any cross-cultural, lifestyle, fashionable magazines like in London or New York.

SUZANNE: As we always said, Terry Jones [cofounder of *i-D Magazine*] was an inspiration and kind of our godfather in a way.

EZRA: And Nick Logan of *The Face* in another way, too. So, when the magazine was launched in 1994, it was clear to us that we would set out to celebrate and represent the creative minds and people around us in Paris.

SUZANNE: It also became a support for fashion and other creative industries. We were always talking about the people behind the scenes, and we had a lot of conversations. We wanted recorded and uncut conversations, rather than rewritten interviews.

EZRA: We offered support for the entire community and industry as a whole. We would feature the head designer but also the head of his design studio, or the stylist who worked with him, or the P.R. company who promoted his show, or his C.E.O. It has always been about celebrating all the players who work so hard to make our industry an exciting one. I think that issue 13, entitled "The Influence," was fundamental. We featured a long series of portraits photographed by Anuschka Blommers and Niels Schumm. It was of a group of designers and creative talent we were growing up with and we were close to: Raf Simons, Véronique Branquinho, Nicolas Ghesquière, Hedi Slimane, Hussein Chalayan...

SUZANNE: That's when we decided to put Nicolas and Véronique on the cover. Back then, nobody had ever put a designer on a cover, but we wanted to promote the talent rather than their creation. And it was very important for us to point out the new establishment in fashion. From the start, these portraits were shot for the cover. I remember when we called Nicolas to ask him if he would be comfortable about being on our next cover. He was surprised and hesitated but agreed finally.

EZRA: It has become iconic. We were becoming the new establishment. Those were such exciting times.

SUZANNE: I always asked myself—but I am not sure I ever asked you— why you wanted to start a magazine. It truly was your idea, and I always thought it was crazy. It seemed impossible to realize such a task back then, especially in France, where there was no culture of independent magazines like in the U.K. In England, they had independent magazines like *i-D* or *The Face*. I started to buy these magazines when I was 13 and was always so inspired by their imagery and graphic design, the creative people they featured, so different from everything else. What was personally driving you?

EZRA: It was the idea of pulling different people together, and my constant curiosity and desire to observe the energies unfolding and developing around me and just supporting that.

SUZANNE: For us, it was also an incredible opportunity or pretext to meet people we were interested in. The magazine gave us the space to involve all kinds of talents we met on our journey. Meeting all these talents, to share and document the encounters, made the magazine unique.

EZRA: I think it required a lot of humility to be able to say the magazine isn't about "me, myself, and I." I am not the center of the world. I am genuinely interested in putting the spotlight on all of the amazing talents who need to be appreciated for their unique vision and creative integrity. So, when you spend years on the road meeting and conversing with all types of creative minds—from curators, artists, fragrance noses, architects, composers, and dancers to the most innovative C.G.I. movie specialists—it is humbling and keeps you grounded and inspired.

SUZANNE: Today, the general motivation is very different. Social media is focused mainly on self-promotion. Everybody and everything seem disposable. Instead of talking about a community or promoting someone who is or has a great talent, social media gives everybody the opportunity to grow and get destroyed in a second.

EZRA: I want to go back to the time before we met. Were you always fascinated by fashion?

SUZANNE: I think my passion for fashion magazines started back when I was living and studying graphic design in Geneva. I bought *i-D Magazine*, *The Face*, and *Ray Gun* religiously every month. I was blown away by their imagery and the graphic design. I discovered French independent magazines like *Jill* on the newsstand back then. I believe the whole collection of my magazines must be in storage somewhere.

EZRA: When we met, we decided to work together as graphic designers, and then early on, you started styling a little.

SUZANNE: I never envisioned styling as an actual assignment. I hadn't assisted anybody—I just witnessed the other stylists on shoots. My feeling was that as a stylist, you could be more involved in the whole process of a fashion shoot. Starting to style for the magazine, from scratch, wasn't easy for me, but I think that the context of everything else—experimental and unpretentious—helped me a lot. As we were a very small team of three to four people, it was quite natural to switch around from graphic design, art direction, photography, or styling. My role models back then were stylists such as Jane How, Desiree Heiss, Melanie Ward, and Joe McKenna. I shared with them the same sensibility and approach to fashion. We always had a very strong point of view on women, their characters, the expression of those women...

EZRA: In the early days of the magazine, we constantly took risks. I was speaking with Joe McKenna the other day, and he was saying that he was just looking at all the old issues of *Self Service* and was amazed at how raw they were. In a good way.

SUZANNE: Raw in the sense of images being experimental and undiluted.

EZRA: Creativity had no limit back then. Image-making was rooted in the idea of constant exploration.

SUZANNE: Finding references and building upon them, or disrupting them by adding additional improbable layers.

EZRA: There was so much being thrown back and forth in this visual conversation, and back then, fashion was the perfect context to create unexpected images. We could come upon a picture of someone's legs with the sock mark still present on her skin, and we would build a whole story on this idea. Or we could walk out of an art gallery and then shoot a series of portraits inspired by the work of Thomas Ruff or initiate our group series inspired by Thomas Struth.

SUZANNE: That was the luxury of having your own magazine and not needing to report to anybody, just expressing yourself. We did whatever we thought was interesting and relevant at that moment. I think when you are passionate about something and you share it, the reaction can only be positive. We were totally instinctive and spontaneous about what or who we put in the magazine.

EZRA: We could decide to throw a big party in a studio or a nightclub, have every stylist we worked with dress people up, and have three photographers shoot us, and then run this as a story. Whatever was possible as long as we had fun.

SUZANNE: We believed in the things we were doing. We could drive to Antwerp with an entire team to shoot a story with Raf Simons on his latest collection.

EZRA: Or go to Amsterdam and shoot a hyper realistic story with Anuschka Blommers and Niels Schumm using their family members as our models. Shoot productions were simple, very D.I.Y. Mark Borthwick would tape a sheet of paper on a wall and shoot a cover, or Anders Edström, who at the time was working a lot with Martin Margiela, would spend a few hours with us to shoot a 10-page fashion story on two single rolls of film! Everyone was genuinely having a lot of fun, even if none of us was making much money.

SUZANNE: I think our natural curiosity would drive us to constantly create new imagery. At the time, a whole new generation of photographers couldn't necessarily work for the established magazines. *Self Service* was the ideal place to experiment for them—and for us, of course. We created images to say something different, to express a different way of looking at fashion. To reveal real characters, rather than a stereotype of models. It was all about the process and the experience of trying.

EZRA: Our initial fashion family started expanding quite rapidly. Inez & Vinoodh, Craig McDean, Jean-Baptiste Mondino, Nathaniel Goldberg, Terry Richardson, Anna Cockburn, Alister Mackie, Marcelo Krasilcic, Juergen Teller, David Sims, Luella Bartley, Katie Grand, Katy England... They were all very driven and ambitious and uncompromising in their creative ideologies.

SUZANNE: We had a lot of conversations about fashion and imagery.

EZRA: Absolutely, and that is exactly what I miss the most from our early days. It's the slowly eroding sense of engagement and conversation one could have with and within fashion. I miss the fact that in the 90s and 2000s, we would go to Milan or London to see the shows and still have the time to go to restaurants with a group of industry friends, journalists, and buyers, and have great critical and passionate conversations about what we were witnessing. Today you just consume fashion, whereas in the past, you really emotionally and critically engaged in it.

SUZANNE: The unfortunate thing today is the lack of time. You have to create faster, and everything has become disposable in a second. As soon as an image is out there, it becomes irrelevant, and there is the urge to create something new. That also explains the lack of quality in imagery or reflection. The creative brain doesn't have the appropriate time for reflection...

EZRA: We were all super ambitious. We all dreamed of one day sitting in the front row or shooting the cover of *Vogue*. But we also understood that it was something we would get based on merit. It was very difficult to fast-track your way up front or to the top back then. I remember one thing you faked: since we had one of the only color Xerox machines in Paris, you made us a fake Margiela invitation.

SUZANNE: Today, you don't need to make fake invitations for a fashion show anymore—you just go online. Everybody is invited to the party. Fashion and luxury become mainstream. I have the feeling there will be a natural reaction against that. Small, discreet, and confidential will be the new luxury. We are at the same point as in the early 90s, when fashion was over the top. At the end of the 80s, there was too much color, too much glam, too much everything, and as a reaction to that, you had Corinne Day, grunge, heroin chic... We are kind of in the same stage today: too much color, too much social media, too much of everything, I am quite sure the new "new establishment" will react to that, too.

EZRA: You and I stay relevant because we just keep on doing what we know how to do—that is, to help brands develop their image. We both do it differently, and we do it with the best of our ability and with passion.

initiated dialogs

How do you nurture and push your creativity, as well as preserve your personal ideology? How would you define the complexities of your creative process? Whether it be an advertising campaign or a brand identity, the end result is always a reflection of true collaborative excellence by a unique group of creative and strategic minds. Ezra Petronio invited the following people, drawn from his collaborative community and network, to reflect upon their own creative process and personal ideology. This outstanding congregation of remarkable individuals has greatly inspired Petronio in the ways in which they have continuously challenged conventions and maintained their creative integrity and independence in the face of conformity.

By Mert Alas, José Manuel Albesa, Emmanuelle Alt, Michael Amzalag & Mathias Augustyniak, Sarah Andelman, Fabien Baron, Victoria Beckham, Francesca Bellettini, Alexandre de Betak, Benjamin Bruno, Hussein Chalayan, Cédric Charbit, Christiaan, Roman Coppola, Piergiorgio Del Moro, Honey Dijon, Duffy, Franck Durand, Michel Gaubert, Paul Hanlon, Jane How, Inez & Vinoodh, Marc Jacobs, Simon Porte Jacquemus, Kim Jones, Darius Khondji, Glen Luchford, Hannah MacGibbon, Joe McKenna, Alastair McKimm, Alasdair McLellan, Aaron de Mey, Kate Moss, Pieter Mulier, Carlos Nazario, Hans Ulrich Obrist, Marta Ortega Pérez, Dick Page, Lucien Pagès, Peter Petronio, Peter Philips, Stefano Pilati, Miuccia Prada, Terry Richardson, Anja Rubik, Gustave Rudman, Floriane de Saint Pierre, Frédéric Sanchez, Jil Sander, Venetia Scott, Chloë Sevigny, Christopher Simmonds, Juergen Teller, Giovanni Testino, Ralph Toledano, Jean Touitou, Anthony Vaccarello, Ferdinando Verderi, Melanie Ward, and Pedro Winter.

INITIATED DIALOGS

Our view on creativity is that fashion thrives on the oscillation between nostalgia and newness, and it's precisely this constant remixing of memories that is at the start of every image we make. This can be just a feeling, an emotion, or a concrete image like a film still, a journalistic photograph, or a strong fashion image from any era that triggers our imagination and almost asks to be combined with something else—so that this remix becomes an entire new world on its own, full of references that will be understood by some and missed by others. This triggering of an old memory that becomes a new memory for the future is what keeps us going and excited!

INEZ & VINOODH, PHOTOGRAPHERS AND DIRECTORS

I love to work. My "process" is somewhat elusive and varies from project to project. Whatever work I'm entering into, I try to be as immersive as possible, be that through literature, film, or music—knowing my lines, communicating my ideas and desires with my fellow actors, the director, the cinematographer, and the people in charge of hair, makeup, and wardrobe. Always the most challenging aspect, which never seems to vary, is finding the strength and confidence inside myself to trust myself and my instincts and just go for it. Usually within a few days of working, that initial fear subsides, and I can settle in and enjoy the ride. Letting go of my ego and trusting myself and my collaborators—I suppose that's my process.

CHLOË SEVIGNY, ACTOR AND DIRECTOR

In order to preserve my personal, radical philosophy, I have endeavored to stay true to my core beliefs. As a makeup artist, I made bold choices early on in my career. I am fortunate to work with people who believe in my technique and trust my abilities. Thus, I am able to convey interesting and striking makeup that pushes the boundaries of convention, while working within a team to make only the best images possible. At *Self Service*, with its unique and free-spirited approach, I am set free to experiment with color, texture, and technique. It is this trust and these rare moments of freedom that allow the team and me the opportunity to create freely, without constraints, and to produce some truly great images.

AARON DE MEY, MAKEUP ARTIST

I feel it's important to occupy a creative mental space that allows one the freedom to explore ideas without setting any fixed parameters. This can often involve a research process that might include references from a variety of disciplines, such as art, architecture, cinema, and photography, as well as fashion. I then collate those references, let them breathe for a while, allowing connections or themes between the images to come to the fore naturally. It's important to not force an idea and to trust your instincts. I am constantly looking for visual stimulation. Usually what inspires me the most are images that feel unfamiliar or uncanny. This is where an intuition or desire to push myself and an idea outside of my comfort zone takes hold. Then, it becomes a process of elimination, whereby I start to isolate and hold onto specific elements of an idea and keep pushing it for as long as time and budget will allow.

JANE HOW, FASHION STYLIST AND CONSULTANT

I find that the best ideas often come from the most unexpected places and when you least expect them. I strongly feel that to bring emerging ideas to fruition and make them real—which, for me, is the true test of creativity—always takes teamwork and collaboration. It's impossible for any one individual to be the best at everything, so it's critical to better yourself by listening to one another and by working side by side. I never fail to be surprised about how one's perspective can be influenced by hearing about the experiences of others. Creative inspiration can be found in so many diverse forms and aspects of life. It is important to keep your eyes and mind open, keep your feet grounded, and stay close to your roots. I think anything done in a genuine, authentic way can allow creativity to shine through and therefore be excellent. Getting out of your comfort zone by traveling and exploring with an open mind and open heart always helps. Never say never!

MARTA ORTEGA PÉREZ, CHAIRPERSON, INDITEX

Concerning creativity, I try to constantly nourish my brain and sensibility. I read, I observe, I try to extend my knowledge to many different fields… I never had a problem to retain my ideas. Eventually I try to change them… I would not know how to define my process exactly. There is definitely a lot of thinking, and most of the time, I start with what I don't want to do. Probably the most complex part is to be receptive to the moment we're living in, with its vastness and complexity, and making it resonate into my work, whether in fashion or at the Fondazione Prada.

MIUCCIA PRADA

For me, it's really about being yourself completely, being true to what you have inside from the beginning and not playing around. You have to go deep inside yourself and find what represents who you really are. And you move, you change, and even if you're not the same person, there is something that stays very strong, that grounds you. For me, it's the discovery of the truth, the discovery of identity, of who you are creatively, but when I say "creatively," I mean who you are really. It's a search for an identity. I don't want to sound pedantic; it's simpler than that. I'm always looking at books. At the moment, I'm very into Robert Bresson. I'm always looking for something that is a basis for everything in an image: why do we put the camera here, how do we look at things…? It's all about the look, and what is the look? It's the image in itself, but it is always based on something. On a direction. I'm always on the search for something that is in a way the identity of things, the center of it all.

DARIUS KHONDJI, CINEMATOGRAPHER

I'M ALWAYS OPEN TO NEW IDEAS, BUT I ALWAYS REMAIN TRUE TO MY OWN TASTE.

KATE MOSS, MODEL AND FOUNDER OF KATE MOSS AGENCY AND COSMOSS BY KATE MOSS

My creativity shapes my being completely. I nurture it with a balanced state of mind and through physical activity. It is my whole well-being. I don't have any limit to my imagination. My curiosity, learning curve, and acknowledgment of the multiple possibilities that are available to me are all empowering my creativity and defining my choices. Together with my way of expressing them, they represent my personal way of pursuing a vision.

STEFANO PILATI, FASHION DESIGNER, RANDOM IDENTITIES

I push my creativity by keeping my eyes always open 360°. My mind is always in the "What? Where? Why? Which? Who?" mode. At the same time, eating history and drinking criticism. The backbone of a true personal ideology is the size of the emotional conviction with which it is held. It becomes innate. Before being conscious that there was a "creative" in me, I was aware that I had a "daring" streak in me. That streak became the seeds of my creative life. My motto became "never nothing, always something."

CHRISTIAAN, HAIR STYLIST

I have been living in a half-reality, half-fantasy world since I was a child. To be honest, I don't really do much work for my creativity. It comes from nowhere when it's least expected. My personal creative process begins with introverted, floating ideas that have no link to each other and arrive at discomforting speed. I dispose of thoughts and concepts and feelings like fast-forwarding a movie. Then a moment of decision comes along, with many questions of how and why! I submit to the concept and prepare key points and descriptive material so my team can follow the idea and be part of my world. I usually have a beginning, middle, and end to the "concept." Once I commit to the idea, then it's a free dance for me.

MERT ALAS, ARTIST

On any project I do, there needs to be an emotional connection to what the idea is. My emotional connections usually go back to my youth and the naivete and sense of wonder with which I embraced the world. However, I cannot be referential to the past forever. Increasingly I remember and act on the wise words of another creative director: to try and create something that feels new. Most important to my ethos is a sense of integrity in the work created and the collaborators who help me in this process. Sometimes we succeed, sometimes we fail miserably, but as long as the intention to move things forward is there, then it is a mission accomplished while acknowledging that everything is simply a "work in progress."

CHRISTOPHER SIMMONDS, ART DIRECTOR

For me, the only way to be creative is to walk away from fashion and distract myself with random pastimes or business adventures. The less I think about it, the more ideas I have. Sometimes, if it's really crunch time and a deadline is looming, I can self-isolate and try to focus, but I'm so easily distracted that I can only really do a flat 30 minutes before I lose focus. I don't really want to preserve any personal ideology because it's too restricting. I'd rather just flirt around willy-nilly and see where it takes me. Sometimes it's successful. My personal creative process is based on great teamwork. I love my team, and I lean on them heavily to mold things into shape. You have a kernel of an idea, and you push it out and listen to the reactions and feedback, and from there, you start the building blocks. The fun part is sitting in an office imagining some wonderful masterpiece, then it's all downhill and compromise from that point onward. My default setting is that everything I do is the worst thing that's ever been put on film, and if the reactions are okay, then I stop beating myself up.

GLEN LUCHFORD, PHOTOGRAPHER AND DIRECTOR

I have always believed that I am not a creative myself, but rather, dedicated to creativity. With Colette, I had the chance to plan hundreds of exhibitions, to curate countless windows, and to search constantly for new talents in fashion, design, publishing, and beyond. My curiosity is unlimited, and my excitement for The New impossible to stop... On my way, I met a handful of people who became pivotal to our story, and even fewer who became dear friends. Ezra Petronio has been both. I remember opening my first *Self Service* magazine and having this powerful revelation that this was a truly unique voice and vision, collecting and regrouping all the various artistic forms for which I, too, was so passionate. To then work with Ezra on evolving our store's brand identity and designing its music compilations was such a special experience. I love his consistency, his way of seeing things, and how he shares this perspective with us on each and every project.

SARAH ANDELMAN, FOUNDER, JUST AN IDEA

My creativity needs constant stimulation and provocation. It's important for me to be exposed to different forms of expression as well as different cultures, ways of life, personal stories, events, and challenges that make me feel uncomfortable. All that gets "filtered" through me—through my current state of mind and my emotions.

ANJA RUBIK, MODEL, SOCIAL ENTREPRENEUR, AND CREATIVE

> I don't care if people like what I do or not—I can only do what feels right for me. I want to wake up in the morning and feel that I'm proud of what I did the day before. It's just that.

ANTHONY VACCARELLO, CREATIVE DIRECTOR, SAINT LAURENT

I wouldn't want to speak of a personal ideology, since my principles are elastic and open to exceptions. I like to learn and work on my beliefs, through the observation of art, through reading, and through studying the world. Things change; the mood today is completely different from 10 years ago. So does our taste: right now, we look for larger dimensions, whether in shoes, in coats, or in cars. If you cultivate an ideology, creativity comes to a standstill. To keep it alive, one must stay naive enough to wonder and marvel at historical changes and to engage with new possibilities. Whenever I start a creative project, I get down to the elementary, to questions of space, proportion, and materials. I look at past solutions and ask myself why they no longer seem right. Fashion design is very complex. The cardinal aspects for me are functionality and a contemporary attractivity. I believe in sculpted clothes that move easily in three-dimensional space and convince from every angle. Furthermore, I am very conscious of changing proportions. I cherish the feel, the look, and the behavior of interesting new quality textiles. And I concentrate on sophisticated details, on workmanship, on perfect seams, on thought-out accessories. Colors and individual prints are essential for my work, and I put a lot of energy into their interaction. Most of all, I strive to make a collection relevant, to say something about the present and the near future by way of the decisions I make. I want every collection to be an answer to actual needs and desires. When I design a store or a fragrance, similar principles apply, especially my dislike of the superfluous. I want objects to stand by themselves as the laconic icons of what we are, made from the best-quality materials I can procure. I look for genuine contributors, masters in their field, to assist and challenge me. Since my beginnings, I have been a team person; my projects only succeed if the whole team is inspired and understands what we are heading for.

JIL SANDER, DESIGNER

> **Culture and knowledge help me develop my attention to weak signals, to contextualize today's society and develop critical thinking—hence creative ideas. The efficient ones come from vision, observation, intuition, and the obsession for finding solutions.**

FLORIANE DE SAINT PIERRE, FOUNDER AND C.E.O., FLORIANE DE SAINT PIERRE & ASSOCIÉS

> Creativity is a feeling, an emotion, an energy, an ultimate freedom that no one can take away from you—an honest, personal expression from the gut that cannot be forced; it is instinctual, authentic, human, transformational. It's a positive force, it's happiness, it's magic.

MELANIE WARD, STYLIST AND FASHION CONSULTANT

I do not see myself as a creative person, but rather, a person in love with creativity. What characterizes my way of working is deep respect for creative minds. I base my relationship with Anthony Vaccarello on that deep trust and respect. The proximity of Anthony's innate sensibility to the essence of Saint Laurent allows us to express the brand in full. It is almost impossible to distinguish one from the other. I really view us as partners who make his creative vision develop into a profitable business.

FRANCESCA BELLETTINI, PRESIDENT AND C.E.O., SAINT LAURENT

YOU JUST HAVE TO MAKE SURE YOU KEEP ON DOING YOUR OWN THINGS WITHIN EVERYTHING ELSE.

JUERGEN TELLER

My personal creative process is largely spontaneous and intuitive. I like to be well prepared in terms of the material requirements of a job, but I'm happiest when I can riff on a theme and play around with ideas. I imagine working with like-minded creative people in a largely visual field such as ours, to be like a musical jam session: figuring things out together, establishing form and content, and seeing where the ideas and feelings lead you. In this sense, my process is not complex at all—I love to make things up as I go and see what happens. It's as simple as that.

DICK PAGE, MAKEUP ARTIST

My creative process is all about character-building, putting together different facets of a woman's style and personality, like a jigsaw puzzle; it's when I am the most playful. I am always thinking about how I can make something better, looking for that finesse and elegance. Nature is a buffer between me and my often obsessive-compulsive creative thinking, tunnel vision, and the rawness of the world. I'm a curious observer. I love to people-watch—obsessed with faces and personal style idiosyncrasies— to observe how a passerby puts together small details and accessories, the mistakes and imperfection. I get a kick out of imagining how it's making them feel and how I can translate that into an idea or image. As I get older, energy, vitality, and vibrancy are the ultimate luxuries. That's what most inspires me, and I want to nurture that to be able to authentically express that image in my work— to capture a feeling and emotion, a *joie de vivre* that manifests in an image. This is the energy that excites me the most. Having a creative exchange and connection with the models, editors, art directors, and photographers—capturing a spontaneous moment, an attitude, a mistake—inspires and challenges my ideas and thought process. This is when the magic happens. I think we are all interconnected with this energy. Human connection. It's a magnetic field of energy.

HANNAH MACGIBBON, CREATIVE DIRECTOR

We are two very different characters who decided to work together over 30 years ago, so our creative process is both personal and collaborative. We have defined a space where intuition, conversation, tension, alignment, disagreement, interpretation, friction, and decision can take place and where egos are set aside. There are no preconceived notions of what we can or can't do. There is always the possibility for each of us to intervene in the other's work. It's an exploration where each of us can decide to get behind the wheel and drive where we want to go. There is always room for surprises and the possibility to make discoveries together along the way.

MICHAEL AMZALAG & MATHIAS AUGUSTYNIAK, FOUNDERS, M/M (PARIS)

I'm a believer in creative visualization to help bring all of my goals to fruition. I'm building a luxury fashion and beauty house of the future, and I take a different creative and strategic approach to achieve that. I am in control at every touchpoint of the business and creative process, down to the considered cuts of my dresses, the stitching on my leather goods, and even the specific size of the pearlescent pigments in my eyeliners. Everything I do is always considered—whether I'm designing a new product or simply getting dressed in the morning—and I approach every situation with positive energy. Collaboration is a vital part of my creative process: I like to work with smart people who can interpret my vision in a multifaceted way.

VICTORIA BECKHAM, CREATIVE DIRECTOR, VICTORIA BECKHAM

My personal creative process is largely instinctive because it is nearly impossible to strategize those deeply emotional or personal connections, which creativity at its core is rooted in.

CARLOS NAZARIO, FASHION EDITOR AND CREATIVE CONSULTANT

I find inspiration in beauty of all kinds—art, design, decorative art, architecture... For me, beauty goes beyond fashion. I stay on the watch of the contemporary art scene. Its creativity, its imagination, its power but mostly its infinite freedom. Artists create only what they care about, only what is essential to them. Not what we ask them. This freedom is vital to creation. With freedom, creation remains real. Antwerp, my city, is also at the heart of my creative process; it's a perpetual inspiration. I found in my Flemish roots an aspiration to a quest for beauty. From the Flemish Masters to the scene of creators when I started to work, I dive deep into an unlimited source of inspirations. Creation is a quest for the most genuine form of beauty. In nature, in art, in ourselves. Beauty will remain. Alaïa is much more than a brand—it's a home. A place where you can create without compromise. Where you can stay radical and rough. Where you can embrace all your paradoxes. The quest of beauty becomes a quest of perfection, pure lines, sculptural forms. A devotion to the gesture. That's why it's so difficult. You can't lie with a gesture. But when it's true and real, you can build timeless and revolutionary creations that will stand the test of time. And remain real. That's all I'm trying to do.

PIETER MULIER, CREATIVE DIRECTOR, ALAÏA

I push and nurse my creativity by observing the outside, seeing how people run and walk, and how they are all mixed up in the street. That is the way I absorb input for my creativity and build my ideology. From there, it goes to filters, references, memories, and experiences. Once I elaborate and reflect, I discuss and elaborate with my team. And that's when it becomes a full team process.

PIERGIORGIO DEL MORO, CASTING DIRECTOR

I'm an agent for artists in the commercial arena. This largely defines my process, so to speak, in that there are structures and boundaries for creativity in this business. I don't think that is negative or limiting, but it is certainly challenging. Those who can create meaningful work—work that moves and inspires within these parameters, within a brief or in service of a brand or a magazine— while still being true to their vision, and can do that consistently, are the ones who will shine in the industry and also often transcend these same boundaries. My role is to help find the right teams and platforms and opportunities that will foster this process for the artists I work with. Because of the nature of what I do for a living, I take a dual approach to my creativity and personal ideology. On one side, I read as much as I can daily on a variety of subjects and from completely opposite cultural points of view, as I think things are so polarized and, through algorithms, we are fed information that is too "one-sided," and one must always try to stretch one's mind and imagination. On the other side, I make a concerted effort to look at artists' work outside the main platforms, where there are no credits or "bragging rights" ... in the sense that I welcome seeing work without titles or brand logos. That way, I sharpen "my taste" in what I react to, without or with minimum outside influence. I think it is very important to be one's best point of reference for value, aesthetics, artistry, beauty, etc., regardless if it is shared or not by the people "in the know."

GIOVANNI TESTINO, FOUNDER, ART PARTNER

INITIATED DIALOGS

I have a natural curiosity to take in what's around me—it's a constant state for me. Whether it's a novel or poem I've been obsessing over, or a momentary experience when traveling, ideas can come from any direction, and it's their cross-pollination that excites me and gives me creative momentum.

KIM JONES, ARTISTIC DIRECTOR, DIOR MEN, FENDI WOMEN'S READY TO WEAR AND COUTURE

My creative process is a tension that must remain unresolved, in a way "uncomfortable." It is something that pushes me, not the other way around. It pushes my ideology rather than preserves it. I try to question my beliefs as much as I question my ideas. I challenge my conclusions, trying to make them clearer, ultimately simple, until the complexity disappears.

FERDINANDO VERDERI, CREATIVE DIRECTOR

The two ideals I try to live by are open-mindedness and willingness. They are the expression of my higher self, my connectivity, and my creativity.

ALASTAIR MCKIMM, EDITOR-IN-CHIEF, I-D MAGAZINE

1. Everything starts with curiosity and passion, the driving force of creativity. 2. Go beyond the fear of pooling knowledge. 3. Look for oxymorons. 4. Invent new rules of the game. 5. As J.G. Ballard told me, make new junctions.

HANS ULRICH OBRIST, ARTISTIC DIRECTOR, SERPENTINE GALLERIES

My creativity is always linked to that of my clients. I am not a creative myself in the classic sense. My clients are the creative source. I am just there to help them make their ideas as strong and elevated as possible, and to touch the chosen audience. When it comes to ideology, I try to preserve the authenticity and the humanity in every project. We are living in a material and corporate world, and I fight every day to maintain the human side at the center of discussions with major organizations. I advise; I do not judge any ideas—I just want them to be clear, right for the global vision of the brand, and powerful for the external world, not only for the insiders.

LUCIEN PAGÈS, FOUNDER, LUCIEN PAGÈS COMMUNICATION

My creative process can be complex as what I do can be obvious to me, but I have to translate it into an obvious proposal for those for whom I work. Traveling is very important to me as it heightens my senses and opens new doors. It also pushes me in more unknown territories. I absorb new sensations that I decipher through my own prism, and I put these into practice in my life and my work.

MICHEL GAUBERT, MUSIC SUPERVISOR

I manage to preserve and nourish my creative ideology without compromising because my team and I instinctively stay true to ourselves. I care a great deal. This is my passion. This is what I've always wanted to do. But sometimes, with all the stress and obstacles and life happening all the time, you ask, "Why am I doing this?" My shrink said something I love: "It's for those transcendent moments of joy." And they come. We could all be on the verge of just jumping out the window, and then the model puts on the jacket that we've been working on, and it looks really great. And we just think: "This is why we do it. That's just it."

MARC JACOBS, FOUNDER AND CREATIVE DIRECTOR, MARC JACOBS INTERNATIONAL

I love images—that's my passion. Since I was a child, I have been memorizing images in TV commercials, movies, and magazines. They remain the imagery in my head and my memories. I am very curious, and I have a stock of images in mind that I always try to reinterpret. These images obsess me, and they are always the starting point of my collections.

SIMON PORTE JACQUEMUS, CREATIVE DIRECTOR, JACQUEMUS

What I thrive on and drives me the most is creativity, especially when it becomes impactful and relevant from a societal and business standpoint. I have had the chance to work with some of the most talented creative minds in the industry, and I have learned a lot about the so-called "unmanageable" creative process. I prefer to manage for creativity, as opposed to managing creativity. It is also about vision and trust and making sure everyone has a voice, contributes, so the whole organization is part of it. This is important for creativity to remain at the center of the organization, not only at the top.

CÉDRIC CHARBIT, PRESIDENT AND C.E.O., BALENCIAGA

Nurturing my creativity and preserving my ideology go hand in hand. I carry many hats in what I do: creating products that end up on someone's lips or eyes demands respect for that individual; creating catwalk looks demands respect for the designer's vision; creating looks for an editorial demands respect for the teamwork process. Keeping a right balance between the excitement of the creative process and the concept of "respect" is how I keep going. One of the complexities is when you have to start thinking rationally to make sure that your creative project will be manageable and can be executed.

PETER PHILIPS, CREATIVE AND IMAGE DIRECTOR, CHRISTIAN DIOR MAKEUP

I nurture my creativity by always tackling the subject matter that I explore, while simultaneously creating a new perspective on what I am working on. This means that I am making a new statement each time and learning something new. My personal ideology has been formed by many years of accumulating ideas, which have formed the backbone for everything I do. My personal approach to my creative process is a continuation or a contraction of whatever I was working on before. I am always taking risks and thrive on each new project, thus generating a new experience. It will be exciting to see new generations taking more risks…

HUSSEIN CHALAYAN, DESIGNER AND ARTIST

For me, it's all about passion and enthusiasm. The eternal interest and love for photography and fashion. And to appreciate still every day how lucky we are to produce images, to transform any dreamy idea into a concrete image.

EMMANUELLE ALT, STYLIST

Differentiation is the most important parameter in brand equity, as it is the key factor of long-term development. Therefore, in my partnership with designers, I have also put, front and center, creativity and respect of the brand D.N.A. The main mission of a C.E.O. is to make sure operations and marketing are run so rigorously that creativity can be expressed freely and totally.

RALPH TOLEDANO, CHAIRMAN, VICTORIA BECKHAM, AND SENIOR PARTNER, NEO INVESTMENT

I believe that my gut has always guided me. I have a very primal, almost vital relationship with creativity. It keeps me alive, it haunts me, it excites me, it fills me with dread, it makes me go through darkness, it makes me gauge how I feel about existence and measure if the psychological material that I have within me is good enough to be translated into creative substance. It's a very sadomasochistic relationship with myself, fueled by a devouring yet exhilarating quest for cathartic perfectionism. Whatever I put out there needs to have mastery in it, whatever that means to me. And each time, it's always as if my whole mind and body were being "fed" to the lions of creativity. I cannot not have that visceral experience. And I acknowledge that it is extreme.

BENJAMIN BRUNO, CREATIVE CONSULTANT, IMAGE-MAKER, AND STYLIST

I am happiest when I can push the limits and break the rules. For me, the thrill of creating has always been about discovering the new. When the problem has been solved, it's no longer interesting. So, I am always challenging myself to go the extra mile and push it even further. How can this be improved, how can I take it to another level? So, in a way, the search for newness defines my personal ideology, but only when it means something and says something that ultimately transcends time.

FABIEN BARON, FOUNDER AND CHIEF CREATIVE OFFICER, BARON & BARON

I always think that your own life experiences shape you not only as a person but also as an image-maker. I always draw from my past, whether that's recreating moments from memories that have happened or recreating moments from memories that I wish had happened. All of this is important, whether the memories are real or not. It's also a world that no one else really has access to.

ALASDAIR MCLELLAN, PHOTOGRAPHER AND DIRECTOR

My creative process is undefined. It is always ongoing and never finished. I personally feel most confident when I'm prepared and very organized ahead of any project. I have found my best work happens spontaneously and fluidly through the process of discovery on each project. Regardless of the level of preparation, the surprises that occur on set or backstage inevitably force me out of my prepared mindset and planned direction, and that's when my hands and mind begin to connect unconsciously and flow, leading to something surprising and unexpected.

PAUL HANLON, HAIR STYLIST

WHEN IT COMES TO MY PERSONAL CREATIVE PROCESS, WHERE I START ISN'T USUALLY WHERE I FINISH.

JOE MCKENNA, FASHION STYLIST

Someone gave me a word for my work: they called it "experiential," and I realized I had a unique story and path, and that no one could tell that story but me. And so, there was no other way for me to be someone else because no one was able to see the things that I saw and live the life that I lived, so I always stay focused on my work. I just did a T-shirt that's coming out called "Mind Your Business." "Mind Your Business" is really just to stop comparing your work to others, and really to focus on and excel in what you do, and that is how you have longevity: you find your audience, you build your audience, and you can't be everything to everyone. It's more important to focus on your own work and to know what's going on, but your story is unique, and if you try to water it down or change it for someone else to accept it, you've lost the point of your art.

HONEY DIJON, ARTIST AND MUSICIAN

My process usually starts with a character, real or imagined. Once I have a subject in mind, I start to build a profile. I surround myself with magnetic boards and fill them with images. The studio starts to look like a criminal investigation. Where do they live? What do they like to do? What do they wear? Their attitude? Hair? Makeup? The fragments start piecing together. I'm conscious not to fit them together too tightly so that elements can come in on the shoot day and enhance where I thought I was going.

VENETIA SCOTT, PHOTOGRAPHER AND STYLIST

I guess you are the product of a certain kind of ideology, which you manufactured yourself, and the life you've been through. In my case, it is Marxism (more on the Marcusian side by my mid-20s) mixed with my father's bankruptcy, mixed with a certain taste for unattainable beauty, by all means. To put that into simple words, I will say: between revolt and measure, when do you choose to call or not call on your superego authorities? It's all about that, especially in one-dimensional global thinking. Everything and everybody push us to have a one-track mind. I try to stay away from that, while not spreading chaos at the same time. Because we all know that sometimes we stop ourselves from doing things that could be bad for others, including ourselves.

For me, the process of creativity is a collective one; it's like a seed that needs water, sunlight, and soil to flourish. Each of us plays our part.

DUFFY, HAIR STYLIST

My creative process is complex in that I base my process on maintaining a fully open mind while always trying to twist it all my way. I never learned by studying or working for someone else before starting my own endeavors, therefore I have no prejudice, no rules, and no limits.

ALEXANDRE DE BETAK, FOUNDER AND CREATIVE DIRECTOR, BUREAU BETAK

Creativity is where I found my freedom, where music can replace words, and where visuals look like melodies. For a child of the 80s, pop culture offered us the best and the worst. As part of the history of French electronic music from the 90s, we had the responsibility to offer a new hope to our generation. We witnessed the changes, the transition of the old world to our Wi-Fi life, from E.T. who desperately tried to "call home" to the year of 2023, where high-speed communication became natural. As a music label, we had to digest all this, and our goal is to create a new form. Major labels can't fight digital and social networks; independent labels are free and are the only ones capable of reinventing themselves. This is the freedom I told you about in my process of creation.

PEDRO WINTER, HEAD OF ED BANGER RECORDS

Music exists through listening. My creative process is one of listening, with radical honesty, to the answer that comes when I ask myself: "Who am I? What do I really feel?" I don't see compromise as an option. If I did, I simply wouldn't be inspired, so I feel the choice is made for me, in that sense. I don't feel like I compose the music, but rather, that it is given to me by a higher power, in proportion to the truth and sincerity of my intentions. I may navigate different worlds, but ultimately, it's a spiritual process for me, and that's what protects me.

GUSTAVE RUDMAN, COMPOSER

My creative process is based on making interesting, unexpected connections. Combining things that have never been placed together in the same way is the fundamental core of my creativity. Often, really good ideas come when you are faced with a challenge or impediment. I'm a believer in embracing limitations, whether they are a budgetary restriction, a time constriction, or a practical issue.

ROMAN COPPOLA, FILMMAKER

The complexity of my creative process lies in finding the thread I am going to pull. I would rather be in front of a white page and let my emotions speak than look elsewhere. It makes it more personal. I have learned that what I want and feel is most important in my creative concepts. There is something mental and sensitive in this way of proceeding that preserves the poetry.

FRÉDÉRIC SANCHEZ, SOUND ILLUSTRATOR

I nurture and push my creative process by believing in my intuition and having a clear vision of where I want each brand to go. Curating a house of meaningful "Love Brands" is a passion for me. Working very closely with diverse talents of all ages, nationalities, and cultures is very enriching; listening constantly to others' opinions, visions, and thoughts is always super inspiring for me. Our main force is a fearless spirit, passion, and a daring attitude to do things with a different approach.

JOSÉ MANUEL ALBESA, PRESIDENT, PUIG BEAUTY AND FASHION

When reflecting on the creative process, I have often said that the idea comes in the first 15 minutes or the last 15 minutes. The rest of the time is a waste of time. My creative process is structured and linear. I begin by understanding the competitive and social environment, the brand's culture, and the mindset, personality, vision, and aspirations of the C.E.O. When I have absorbed all of this information, I become so intimate with the brand that, in my mind, I become the client. Once you have reached this stage of understanding, you have nobody to convince but yourself.

PETER PETRONIO, ART DIRECTOR, DESIGNER, AND ENTREPRENEUR

I've always tried to remain curious and be inspired by what I've experienced in my life. I feel it's about being spontaneous and capturing the energy in the moment. It's not about the technique: it's about the mystique.

TERRY RICHARDSON, PHOTOGRAPHER

I never made a career plan. All I have managed to do is by feeling a conviction that even the simplest of things can affect me. Beauty can be found everywhere, if only we choose to see it. It is my way of feeling free and ultimately dependent upon little else.

FRANCK DURAND, CREATIVE DIRECTOR, ATELIER FRANCK DURAND

THE UNEDITED

ADIDAS_IN MAG1.jpg | ALAIA_SF22_INVITATION.jpg | ALAIA_BLACK_DRESSES_2.jpg | ALAIA_PICASSO_LAYOUT_4.jpg | ALAIA DP LAYOUT GAGOSIAN DIGITAL3.jpg | ALAIA DP SF22 1.jpg

APC_FW13_INMAG4.jpg | APC_25YEARS_INVITATION3.JPG | APC_SS11_POSTER 2.jpg | APC_TRANSMISSION_BOOK 1.jpg | APC_WEBSITE 2.jpg | APC_TRANSMISSION_POSTER.jpg

CHANEL_NOIR OBSCUR_LAYOUT DPS4.jpg | CHANEL_PRINTEMPS_LAYOUT SP1.jpg | CHANEL_SUBLIMAGE_LAYOUT DPS1.jpg | CHANEL_WHITENING_DPS2.jpg | CHANEL_ALLURE_HOMME_SPORT_DPS1.jpg | CHANEL_CRISTALLE_EAU_VERTE_SP.jpg

CHLOE_EAU DE FLEURS 6.jpg | CHLOE_LOVE 4.jpg | CHLOE_FRAGRANCE_PACKAGING 1.jpg | CHLOE_EAU DE CHLOE_LAYOUT DPS 1.jpg | CHLOE_EAU DE FLEURS_LAYOUT SP1.jpg | CHLOE_SIGNATURE_LAYOUT SP2.jpg

   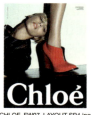  

CHLOE_LOOKBOOK_3.jpg | CHLOE_SS04_LAYOUT SP1.jpg | CHLOE_FW05_LAYOUT DPS2.jpg | CHLOE_FW07_LAYOUT SP4.jpg | CHLOE_FW08_LAYOUT SP1.jpg | CHLOE_FW10_LAYOUT SP3.jpg

COLETTE_LIMITED_TSHIRT_1 | CDG_POSTER 6.jpg | CDG_POSTER 4.jpg | CDG_ODEUR71_4.jpg | CDG_HAPPY VALENTINES_2.jpg | CDG_SERIES_2_RED_3.jpg

DIOR ROUGE_4.jpg | DSQUARED2_POTION_LAYOUT_DPS.jpg | DSQUARED2_POTION 2.jpg | DSQUARED2_POTION 10.JPG | DUNHILL_FW17_LAYOUT DPS 5.jpg | FENDI_PALAZZIO_LAYOUT_DPS1.jpg

GLOSSIER PLAY_MAKEUP 5.jpg | GUCCI_25H_IDRIS_ELBA_IG_FEED_5.jpg | GUCCI_25H_IDRIS_ELBA_IG_FEED_4.jpg | GUCCI_25H_JESSICA_CHASTAIN_DPS_1.jpg | GUCCI_HJ_LAYOUT_ALTERNATIVE_SP_1.jpg | GUCCI_HJ_LAYOUT_DPS_3.jpg

THE UNEDITED

ALAIA_WS23_CAMPAIGN_SP3.jpg

ALAIA_WS23_CAMPAIGN_DPS2.jpg

ALINE_CD.jpg

APC_XMAS 2010 BAG_04.jpg

APC_SS11_POSTER 1.jpg

APC_FW11_POSTER 2.jpg

APC_KANYE_LAYOUT_DPS1.jpg

ART_PARTNER_LOGO.eps

BETTTER_LOGO.eps

CACHAREL_INVITATION FW2002.jpg

CACHAREL_FW02_LAYOUT 1.eps

CHANEL_NOIR OBSCUR_LAYOUT DPS3.jpg

CHANEL_MONTRE PREMIERE_LAYOUT 1.jpg

CHANEL_2C_5.jpg

CHANEL_2C_7.jpg

CHLOE_LOVE_PRESS KIT 2.jpg

CHLOE_SIGNATURE_PRESS KIT 6.jpg

CHLOE_EAU DE CHLOE 1.jpg

CHLOE_SIGNATURE_LAYOUT SP3.jpg

CHLOE_SIGNATURE_STILL LIFE_SP1.jpg

CHLOE_SIGNATURE_STILL LIFE_SP3.jpg

CHLOE_FW20_INVITATION_2.jpg

CHLOE_SIGNATURE2_LAYOUT SP2.jpg

CHLOE_SIGNATURE2_LAYOUT DPS1.jpg

CHLOE_SS12_LAYOUT_SP_1.jpg

CHLOE KIDS_SS11_LAYOUT SP1.jpg

SEE BY CHLOE_FW07_LAYOUT SP1.jpg

CHLOE_FW07_OUTDOORS 10.jpg

COLETTE_CD HOUSE OF COLETTE_2.jpg

COLETTE_PAPER SLEEVE 3.jpg

CDG_LE_PETIT_BONHOMME_ROUGE_1.jpg

CDG_TSHIRT XMAS 2.jpg

CDG_TSHIRT ROSE 2.jpg

COSTA_BRAZIL_LAYOUT_DPS_3.jpg

DELABEL_BAG.jpg

DIOR ADDICT_1.jpg

FREDERIC SANCHEZ BAG.jpg

GIBO_BAG_1.jpg

GIORGIO_ARMANI_LA_PRIMA_SP_8.jpg

GIORGIO_ARMANI_LA_PRIMA_SP_2.jpg

GLOSSIER PLAY_LOGO.eps

GLOSSIER PLAY_MAKEUP 2.jpg

GUERLAIN_BOTTLE_2.jpg

HELMUT LANG_LAYOUT_DPS2.jpg

HELMUT LANG_LAYOUT_DPS.jpg

HELMUT LANG_CATALOG3.jpg

HENNESSY_2012_DPS2.jpg

HUSSEIN CHALAYAN_FW2002_DPS1.jpg

THE UNEDITED

 HUSSEIN CHALAYAN_INVITATION.jpg
 HUSSEIN CHALAYAN_AS FOUR.jpg
 H&M_LAYOUT_1.jpeg
 H&M_LAYOUT_5.jpeg
 JEAN PAUL GAULTIER_CATALOG.jpg
 JEAN PAUL GAULTIER_FRAGILE.jpg

 JIL SANDER_FW14_DPS2.jpg
 JIL SANDER_FW14_DPS6.jpg
 JIL SANDER SS13 INVITATION_01.JPG
 JIL SANDER_SPORT 11.jpg
 JIL SANDER_SPORT 1.jpg
 JIL SANDER_STYLE 2.jpg

 LBR_MONOGRAM.jpg
 LBR_LIPSTICK_2.jpg
 LANVIN_LOGO.eps
 LANVIN_BAGS 1.jpg
 LANVIN_INVITATIONS GROUP 2.jpg
 LANVIN_FW19_LAYOUT DPS3.jpg

 LBM_2013_LAYOUT 11.jpg
 LBM_2014_LAYOUT 6.jpg
 LBM_2014_LAYOUT 10.jpg
 LBM_2014_LAYOUT 9.jpg
 LBM_2014_LAYOUT 12.jpg
 LBM_CATALOG_FOOD 9.jpg

 LMF_WEBSITE 1 IN BROWSER.png
 LOUIS VUITTON_01.jpg
 LOUIS VUITTON_02.jpg
 LOUIS VUITTON_05.jpg
 MANGO_FW19_LAYOUT_DPS1.jpg
 MANGO_SS20_LAYOUT_DPS2.jpg

 MDS_LAYOUT_DPS_1.jpg
 MIUMIU_SITE_LANDING2.png
 MIUMIU_FW06_INVITATION3.jpg
 MIUMIU_INVITATION_MACAU.jpg
 MIUMIU_LOOKBOOK1 CROP.jpg
 MIUMIU_FW05_LOOKBOOK1.jpg

 MIUMIU_FW05_LAYOUT DPS2.jpg
 MIUMIU_FW06_LAYOUT DPS2.jpg
 MIUMIU_FW08_LAYOUT DPS1.jpg
 MIUMIU_SS09_LAYOUT DPS3.jpg
 MIUMIU_SS07_OUTDOOR1.JPG

 NANUSHKA_LOGO.jpg

 PRADA_STORE_SNIPE POSTERS 8.jpg
 PRADA_STORE_SNIPE POSTERS 1.jpg
 PRADA_AOYAMA_STORE.jpg
PRADA_AOYAMA_WWD 2.jpg
PRADA_EXCLUSIVE_SCENTS_LAYOUT SP2.jpg
 PRADA_ORANGER_LAYOUT DPS1.jpg

THE UNEDITED

JEAN PAUL GAULTIER_LE MALE_IN MAG.jpg   JEROME DREYFUSS FW15_LOOKBOOK1.jpg   JEROME DREYFUSS_POSTER.jpg   JIL SANDER_SPORT 8.jpg   JIL SANDER_SS13_DPS1.jpg   JIL SANDER_SS14_SP10.jpg

JOHNNY HALLYDAY_ALBUM 1.jpg   JOHNNY HALLYDAY_LIMITED EDITION 9   LBR_LOGO.eps   LBR_HENRICK_LAYOUT SP1.jpg   LBR_EZRA_LAYOUT SP1.png   LBR_COLOR CASE COLLECTION_1.jpg

LANVIN_SS20_OUTDOOR 4.jpg   LANVIN_FW20_IN MAG_1.jpg   LANVIN_SS21_LAYOUT_DP_1.jpg   LANVIN_FW21_LAYOUT_SP_1.jpg   LANVIN_FW21_LAYOUT_SP_6.jpg   LBM_2012_OUTDOOR 8.JPG

LBM_NEWSPAPER_L'HOMME 16.jpg   LBM_NEWSPAPER_L'HOMME 9.jpg   LBM_CATALOG_KIDS 5.jpg   LBM_NEWSPAPER_LES TBM 2.jpg   LBM_NEWSPAPER_LES TBM 8.jpg   LMF_BOX 01.jpg

MANSUR GAVRIEL_BAG & BOX.jpg   MANSUR GAVRIEL_INVITATION 9.jpg   MANSUR GAVRIEL_SS17_WILDPOSTING 1.jpg   MASSIMO_DUTTI_FW22_LAYOUT_DPS_2.jpg   MASSIMO_DUTTI_FW22_LAYOUT_DPS_6.jpg   MDS_LAYOUT_DPS_5.jpg

MIUMIU_FW05_LOOKBOOK2.jpg   MIUMIU_FW06_LOOKBOOK2.jpg   MIUMIU_FW06_LOOKBOOK3.jpg   MIUMIU_FW07_LOOKBOOK2.jpg   MIUMIU_LOOKBOOKS.jpg   MIUMIU_SHOWSET 5.JPEG

NINA RICCI_SS11 DPS 1.jpg   NINA RICCI BAG 2.JPG   NORDSTROM SS12 1.JPG   PARCELS_OVERNIGHT 1.jpg   PRADA DOUBLE LOGO.jpg   PRADA_TIEDYE 1.jpg

PRADA_IRIS HOMME_LAYOUT DPS2.jpg   PRADA_IRIS FEMME_IN MAG1.jpg   PRADA_IRIS FEMME_LAYOUT SP3   PRADA_IRIS FEMME PURSE SPRAY_DPS1.jpg   PRADA_AMBER 1.jpg   PRADA_FRAGRANCE_GROUP 6.jpg

THE UNEDITED

PRADA_ORANGER 4.jpg | PRADA_ORANGER 2.jpg | PRADA_IRIS HOMME_5.jpg | PRADA_INFUSION IRIS 2.jpg | PRADA_ROSA 4.jpg | PRADA_LES INFUSIONS 1.jpg

PUCCI_ALL LOOKBOOKS 1.jpg | PUCCI_BOX 1.jpg | PUCCI_SS04_1.jpg | PUCCI_FW04_INEZ.tif | PUCCI_FW06_LOOKBOOK.jpg | PUCCI_FW07_LOOKBOOK.jpg

DAFT CLUB_VIP_PASS.jpg | ROCHAS_BAG 1.jpg | SLRD_LOGO.eps | SLRD_LOGO_STORE.jpg | SLRD_MANIFESTO_1.jpg | SL_COLETTE_NEON LIGHT IN STORE 2.png

SLRD_WEBSITE 1.png | SLRDxSS_STICKERPACK_3.jpg | SLRDxSS_STICKERS_1.jpg | SLRDxSS_STICKERS_POLA_3.jpg | SALVATORE_FERRAGAMO_EMOZIONE_DPS1.jpg | SALVATORE_FERRAGAMO_SIGNORINA_DPS1.jpg

SOLID & STRIPED_LOGO.eps | SOLID & STRIPED_BAGS.jpg | SOLID & STRIPED_SUNCARE_1.jpg | SONY ERICSSON_LAYOUT_DPS7.jpg | SPORTMAX_SS18_DPS2.jpg | SPORTMAX_FW18_DPS3.jpg

VANESSA SEWARD_BAGS_01.jpg | VANESSA SEWARD_STATIONARY_01.jpg | VERONIQUE BRANQUINHO_F/W02_1.jpg | VERONIQUE BRANQUINHO_F/W02_2.jpg | VB_LOGO.eps | VB_BEAUTY_2.jpg

YS ARMY_FW18_SP8.jpg | YSL_FW08_MANIFESTO 1.jpg | YSL_FW08_MANIFESTO 2.jpg | YSL_FW08_MANIFESTO BTS 3.jpg | YSL_SS09_LAYOUT_DPS6.jpg | YSL_SS09_MANIFESTO STICKER 2.jpg

YSL MENS_SS09 1.jpg | YSL_IDENTITY 2.jpg | YSL_EDITION 24_IDENTITY 1.jpg | ZARA KIDS_AW17_LAYOUT 6.jpeg | ZARA KIDS_AW17_LAYOUT 10.jpeg | ZARA KIDS_SS18_LAYOUT 1.jpg

THE UNEDITED

PRADA_PURPLE RAIN 1.jpg | PRADA BEAUTY_PACKAGING 2.jpg | PRADA BEAUTY_PACKAGING 5.jpg | PRADA BEAUTY_PACKAGING 3.jpg | PRADA BEAUTY_PACKAGING 11.jpg | PRADA BEAUTY_STORE1.jpg

PUCCI_SS09_POSTER.eps | PUCCI_SS05_2.JPG | PUCCI_FW16_IN MAG 3.jpg | REPOSSI_SS13 IN MAG3.jpg | RESPECT_CHEERS_INVITATION_1.jpg | RESPECT_VARIOUS_2.jpg

SLRD_STORE_PALETTES.jpg | SLRD_BAGS.jpg | SLRD_STATIONARY_LA 2.png | SLRD_EDITIONS_1.jpg | SLRD_KATE_MOSS_TSHIRT 3.jpg | SLRD_PAPERWEIGHT_1.jpg

     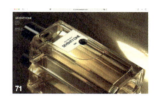

SALVATORE_FERRAGAMO_SIGNORINA_SP3.jpg | SS_THE_VINTAGE_YOU_COVER.jpg | SELF SERVICE TSHIRT_1.jpg | SEVENTY ONE GIN_LOGO.eps | SEVENTY ONE GIN_PACKAGING_6.jpg | SEVENTY ONE GIN_WEBSITE_2.png

SPORTMAX_SS19_DPS3.jpg | SPORTMAX_FW19_DPS3.jpg | STUDY_MAGAZINE_POSTER_2.jpg | THE_WEBSTER_BAGS_2.jpg | TORY_BURCH_LOVE RELENTLESSLY_SP1.jpg | VANESSA SEWARD_INVITATION_03.jpg

VB_BEAUTY_1.jpg | VB_BEAUTY_36.jpg | VB_PACKAGING AND LOGO_34.jpg | VB_BODY_LOGOTYPE.eps | VIRGIN LETTERHEAD 2.jpg | YS ARMY_LOGO.eps

YSL_FW09_LAYOUT_DPS11.jpg | YSL_FW09_OUTDOOR 2.jpg | YSL_FW09_MANIFESTO TOTE BAG 3.jpg | YSL_SS10_LAYOUT_DPS1.jpg | YSL_FW10_008.jpg | YSL_SS11_LAYOUT_DPS5.jpg

 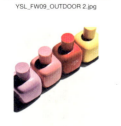   

ZARA XMAS 20_BOX.jpg | ZARA_FRAGRANCE_WEEKEND 12.jpg | ZARA_OLFACTIVE_CITIES 4.jpg | ZARA_FRAGRANCE_DENIM 1.jpg | ZARA_OLFACTIVE_CITIES SET 1.jpg | ZARA_FRAGRANCE_MEN 3.jpg

1. With my spiritual godfather, Swami Satchidananda. N.Y.C., 1969. 2. Photo booth with my parents, Peter and Sarah. Geneva, 1971. 3. My mother with her dance partner and mentor, Jimmy Slyde, rehearsing in Paris. 4. On set with director Tony Scott during an ad commercial art-directed by my father. Seychelles, mid-70s. 5. Young me photographed by my father for the cover of my school paper on its 100th anniversary. 6. My first set of drums. 7. With my sister, Leela, jamming in a studio in N.Y.C. 8. Me and my sister as tap-dancing bunnies for French icon Chantal Goya. Palais des Congrès, Paris, early 80s. 9. Summer studies at Rhode Island School of Design, 1985. 10. On the way to rehearsal, Paris, 80s. 11. Cover for the high-school newspaper, of which I was editor-in-chief and founder. Lycée Montaigne, 1986. 12. Various covers for the Parsons School of Design paper, of which I was editor-in-chief. N.Y.C., 1990. 13. Performing at a jazz festival with my sister and mother. Virginia, late 80s. 14. Album of local Paris bands, including mine, produced by New Rose label, mid-80s. 15. With my first Mac Classic during Parsons college years in N.Y.C. 16. Among photo printers at Picto during my internship. Photo by Josef Koudelka. 17. Linotype catalog left to me as an

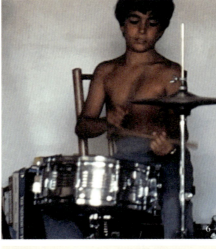
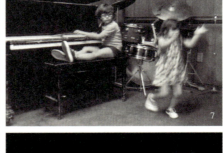

VISUAL BIOGRAPHY

inheritance by my father, which was gifted to him by his father, a Linotype machinist and union leader in N.Y.C. 18. During my graduation year at Parsons, at Henry Wolf's studio. 19. My first-ever business card, silk-screened on wood. 20. My third office in Paris. Faubourg Saint-Denis, early 2000s. 21. My teacher, mentor, and friend, Henry Wolf. 22. With Suzanne Koller in our early years. 23. *Self Service*'s first issue on stands, 1995. 24. Business cards for *Self Service* and our first agency, Work in Progress. 25. Printer sheet of first Comme des Garçons project, early 90s. 26. Invitation to first launch party for *Self Service*. 27. Low-tech production of Chloë Sevigny shot by Mark Borthwick, 1995. 28. Jam session with Jean Touitou and Terry Richardson. A.P.C. headquarters, Paris. 29. Staff picture, mid 90s. Left to right: Christopher Niquet, Marie Chaix, Catherine Mollanger, Skye Parrott, Katariina Lamberg, Patrick Li, me, Suzanne Koller, Carina Frey, Ed Brachfeld, Camille Bidault-Waddington, and Otto Diekgerdes. 30-31. A random day in the office, 2008. 32. A.P.C. party, D.J. warm-up for 2 Many DJ's. 33. Walking for Yohji Yamamoto with Christopher Niquet, Spring/Summer 1999.

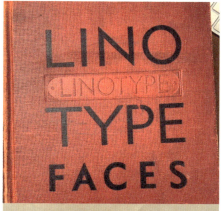

1. Irving Penn's sketch for the Prada *Infusion d'Iris* fragrance campaign. 2-3. Rue Debelleyme offices designed by Gonzalez Haase. 4. Raquel and Shalom with Inez & Vinoodh for *Self Service*. 5. Photographing Jefferson Hack at Nick Knight's SHOWstudio, 2004. 6. James Chinlund trying to wrap Tenerife island. Malgosia and Carmen on set for Chloé, 2004. 7. My son, Aaron, with Malgosia. 8. On set with Raquel for Chloé's first made-to-measure digital campaign. Photography by Mario Sorrenti. Spring/Summer 2010. 9. Outtake from Chloé campaign by Inez & Vinoodh. 10. Photographing Carmen for *Self Service* at Bryan Adams's Paris pied-à-terre. 11. With Juergen Teller photographing Malgosia for Pucci. Sicily, 2007. 12. In my Chanel office, next to the wall painting commissioned to Sylvie Fleury. Neuilly, 2008. 13. Photographing Anja Rubik. 14. Hannah MacGibbon with my daughter, Tess. 15. Conversation with Wes Anderson, Marc Jacobs, and Jarvis Cocker. Photography by Katja Rahlwes. 16-17. My first photography solo exhibition at the Dallas Contemporary museum, 2011. 18. *Bold & Beautiful*, published by Karl Lagerfeld and Steidl. 19. Me photographed by Vinoodh while scouting for a YSL campaign location on the Hollywood Hills. 20. Johnny Hallyday book, published by Flammarion and Galerie 213.

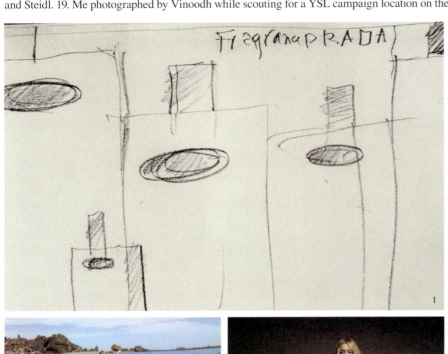

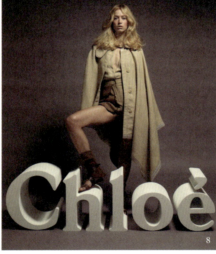

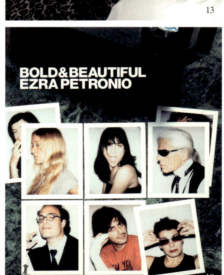

VISUAL BIOGRAPHY

21. My cameras, customized by Sage Elsesser and the Supreme team. 22. On stage with Johnny Hallyday, photographing his concert in Nîmes, 2016. 23. Show catalog for the *Stylistics* exhibition at Galerie Gmurzynska, Zürich, 2021. 24. My creative partner, Lana Petrusevych. 25. With Juergen Teller setting up, one assistant short. London, 2022. 26. On stage with Lana, shooting Johnny Hallyday concert. Nîmes, 2016. 27. Shooting Johnny Hallyday. Bercy, Paris, 2016. 28. My photo team: Nicolas Despis, Mathieu Boutang, Stefano Poli, during an AR shoot for Zara. Inria, Grenoble, 2018. 29. Remotely shooting Paris Hilton for Lanvin while in confinement, 2020. 30. *25 Years of Fashion, People and Ideas Reconsidered. Self Service* exhibition at Dallas Contemporary, 2019. 31. Shooting Kylian Mbappé. Paris, 2021. 32. Working with my father at the office. 33. Shooting Kate Moss for the cover of *Self Service* with Mert Alas, Marcus Piggott, Emmanuelle Alt, and Lana. 34. My photograph of Kate Moss on a scarf for Saint Laurent. 35. My son, Aaron, photographed by my daughter, Tess. 36. Idris Elba rehearsing his "It's Gucci Time" line. 37. *Self Service 1994-2022, The Ads,* published by IDEA. 38-41. *Stylistics* exhibition at Galerie Gmurzynska, Zürich, 2021.

ACKNOWLEDGMENTS

Creative direction
with Lana Petrusevych

Fragrance, Beauty, Skincare,
Jewelry, and Watches in-house
art direction for Chanel
Photography by Sølve Sundsbø
Hair by Stephane Lancien
Makeup by Peter Philips
Model: Malgosia Bela

Saint Laurent Rive Droite
by Anthony Vaccarello
Photography by Bryan Liston
Styling by Vero Didry
Hair by Marion Anée
Makeup by Marion Robine
Model: Jamie Bochert
Creative direction with Lana Petrusevych

Creative direction
with Lana Petrusevych

Photography by Philippe Lacombe

Photography by Mert Alas
and Marcus Piggott
Hair by Paul Hanlon
Makeup by Val Garland
Model: Kate Moss
Creative direction with Lana Petrusevych

Creative direction
with Lana Petrusevych

Yves Saint Laurent by Stefano Pilati
Photography by Inez & Vinoodh
Styling by Melanie Ward
Hair by Luigi Murenu
Makeup by Tom Pecheux
Model: Claudia Schiffer
Creative direction with Suzanne Koller

Gucci by Alessandro Michele
Photography by Mert Alas
and Marcus Piggott
Styling by Jane How
Hair by Christian Wood
Makeup by Mary Greenwell
Talent: Jessica Chastain
Creative direction with Lana Petrusevych

Photography by Juergen Teller
Styling by Jane How
Hair by Christiaan
Makeup by Dick Page
Model: Malgosia Bela
Creative direction with Suzanne Koller

Gucci by Alessandro Michele
Photography by Mert Alas
and Marcus Piggott
Styling by Ibrahim Kamara
and Cheryl Konteh
Hair by Riaze Foster
Grooming by Jojo Williams
Talent: Idris Elba
Creative direction with Lana Petrusevych

Photography by David Sims
Styling by Joe McKenna
Hair by Guido Palau
Makeup by Diane Kendal
Model: Édie Campbell

Pirelli Calendar 2006
Photography by Inez & Vinoodh
Styling by Joe McKenna
Hair by Luigi Murenu
Makeup by Peter Philips
Model: Lou Doillon
Creative direction with Suzanne Koller

Photography by Steven Meisel
Styling by Fabio Zambernardi
Hair by Jimmy Paul
Makeup by Pat McGrath
Model: Sasha Pivovarova

Creative direction
with Suzanne Koller

Photography by Inez & Vinoodh
Styling by Suzanne Koller
Hair by Christiaan
Makeup by Dick Page
Models: Shalom Harlow and
Raquel Zimmermann

Photography by Inez & Vinoodh
Hair by Luigi Murenu
Makeup by Tom Pecheux
Model: Anja Rubik
Creative direction with Suzanne Koller

Alaïa by Pieter Mulier
Photography by Tyrone Lebon
Hair by Anthony Turner
Makeup by Lucia Pica
Model: Kaia Gerber
Creative direction with Lana Petrusevych

Photography by Richard Burbridge
and Thomas Lagrange
Creative direction with Suzanne Koller

Photography by Philippe Lacombe

Photography by Thomas Lagrange

Photography by Daniel Jackson
Styling by Marie Chaix
Hair by Samantha Hillerby
Makeup by Alex Box
Model: Heather Bratton

Creative direction
with Suzanne Koller

Chloé by Phoebe Philo
Photography by Inez & Vinoodh
Creative direction with Suzanne Koller

Photography by Henry Leutwyler
Creative direction with Lana Petrusevych

Creative direction with
Suzanne Koller and Patrick Li

Photography by Inez & Vinoodh
Styling by Joe McKenna
Hair by Luigi Murenu
Makeup by Lisa Butler
Model: Raquel Zimmermann
Creative direction with Suzanne Koller

Yves Saint Laurent by Stefano Pilati
Photography by Inez & Vinoodh
Styling by Joe McKenna
Hair by Christiaan
Makeup by Tom Pecheux
Model: Natalia Vodianova
Creative direction with Suzanne Koller

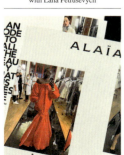

Creative direction
with Lana Petrusevych

Photography by Ezra Petronio
Styling by Fiona Hicks
Hair by Marion Anée
Makeup by Giulio Panciera
Model: Loulou Robert

Yves Saint Laurent by Stefano Pilati
Photography by Inez & Vinoodh
Styling by Camilla Nickerson
Hair by Luigi Murenu
Makeup by Tom Pecheux
Model: Naomi Campbell
Creative direction with Suzanne Koller

Creative direction
with Lana Petrusevych

Photography by Craig McDean
Styling by Alastair McKimm
Hair by Shay Ashual
Makeup by Francelle Daly
Model: Binx Walton

Yves Saint Laurent by Stefano Pilati
Photography by Inez & Vinoodh
Styling by Melanie Ward
Hair by Luigi Murenu
Makeup by Tom Pecheux
Model: Christy Turlington
Creative direction with Suzanne Koller

Repossi by Gaia Repossi
Photography by David Sims
Styling by Joe McKenna
Hair by Paul Hanlon
Makeup by Diane Kendal
Model: Iselin Steiro
Creative direction with Suzanne Koller

Photography by Liz Collins
Creative direction with Suzanne Koller

Photography by Glen Luchford
Styling by Jane How
Hair by Anthony Turner
Makeup by Yadim
Model: Suzi Leenaars

Creative direction with Suzanne Koller

ACKNOWLEDGMENTS

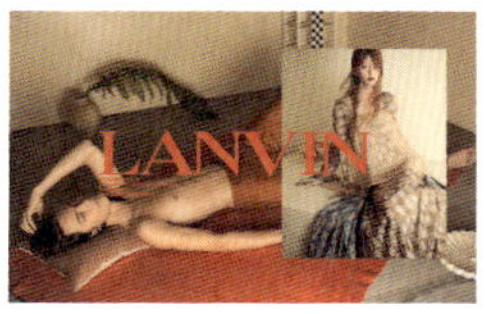

Lanvin by Bruno Sialelli
Photography by Glen Luchford
Styling by Carlos Nazario
Hair by Paul Hanlon
Makeup by Lucia Pieroni
Models: Freek Iven
and Sara Grace Wallerstedt
Creative direction with Lana Petrusevych

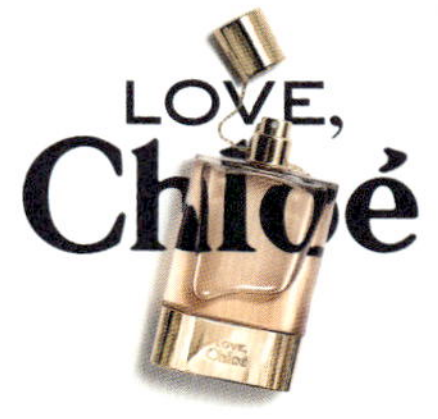

Photography by Philippe Lacombe
Creative direction with Suzanne Koller

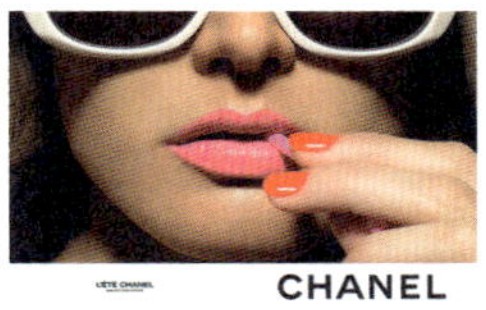

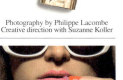

Photography by Sølve Sundsbø
Styling by Suzanne Koller
Hair by Stephane Lancien
Makeup by Peter Philips
Model: Malgosia Bela

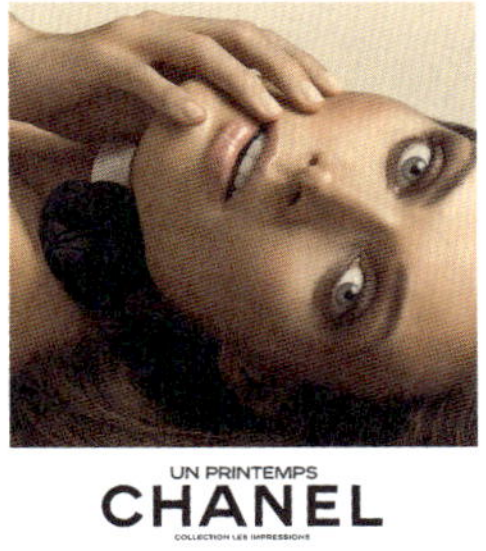

Photography by Inez & Vinoodh
Styling by Suzanne Koller
Hair by Eugene Souleiman
Makeup by Peter Philips
Model: Malgosia Bela

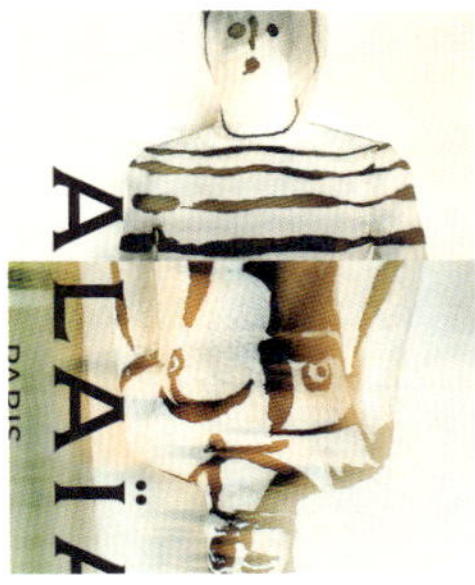

Photography by Ronan Gallagher
Creative direction with Lana Petrusevych

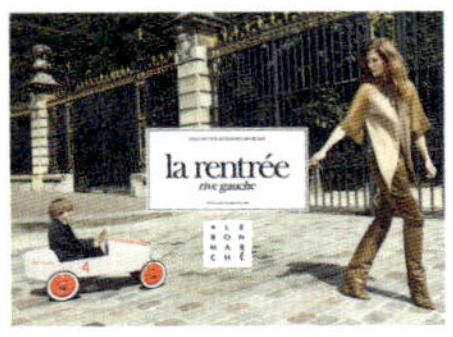

Photography by Glen Luchford
Hair by Anthony Turner
Makeup by Lucia Pica
Model: Malgosia Bela
Creative direction with Suzanne Koller

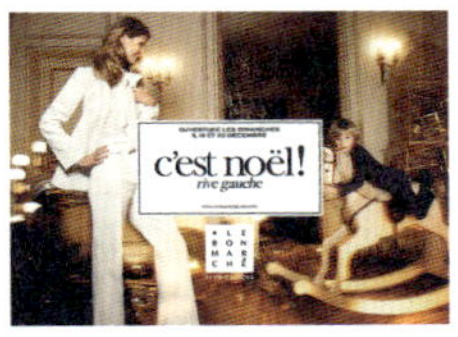

Photography by Glen Luchford
Hair by Akki Shirakawa
Makeup by Lucia Pica
Model: Malgosia Bela
Creative direction with Suzanne Koller

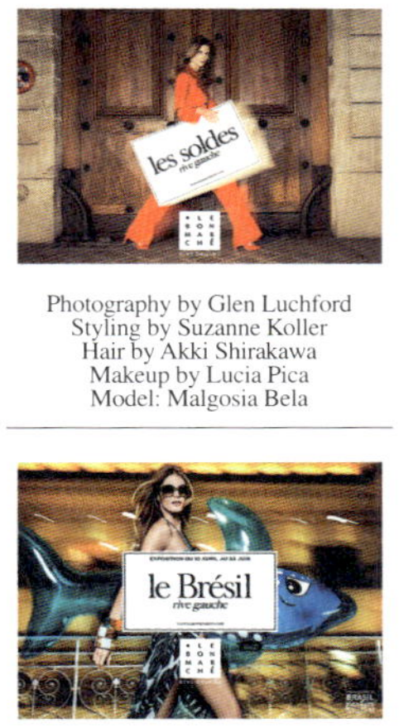

Photography by Glen Luchford
Styling by Suzanne Koller
Hair by Akki Shirakawa
Makeup by Lucia Pica
Model: Malgosia Bela

Photography by Mario Sorrenti
Styling by Suzanne Koller
Hair by Anthony Turner
Makeup by Karim Rahman
Model: Malgosia Bela

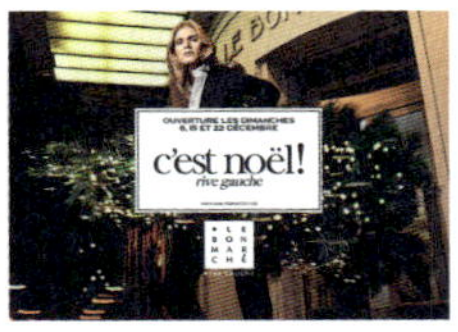

Photography by Mario Sorrenti
Styling by Suzanne Koller
Hair by James Pecis
Makeup by Lucia Pica
Model: Malgosia Bela

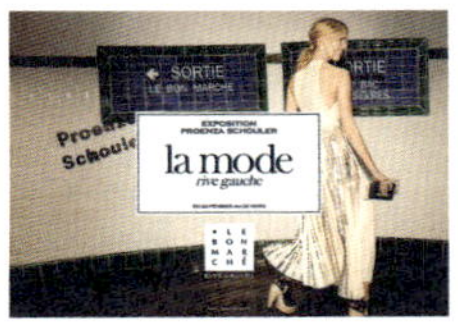

Photography by Glen Luchford
Styling by Antje Winter
Hair by Marion Anée
Makeup by Karim Rahman
Model: Iselin Steiro
Creative direction with Suzanne Koller

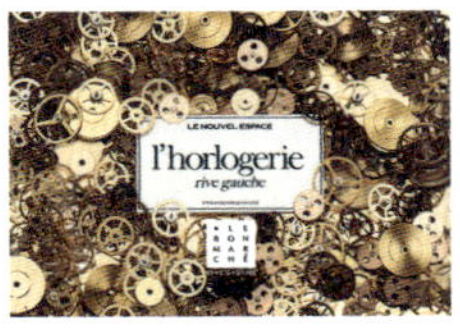

Photography by Thomas Lagrange

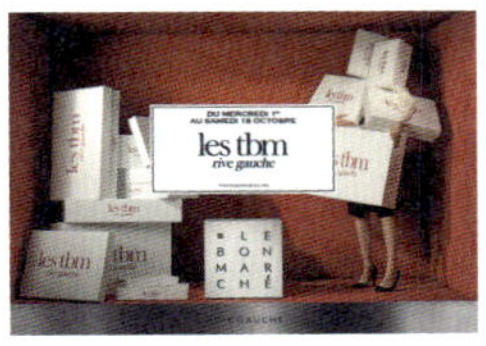

Photography by Ezra Petronio
Styling by Antje Winter
Hair by Marion Anée
Makeup by Karim Rahman
Model: Manon Leloup

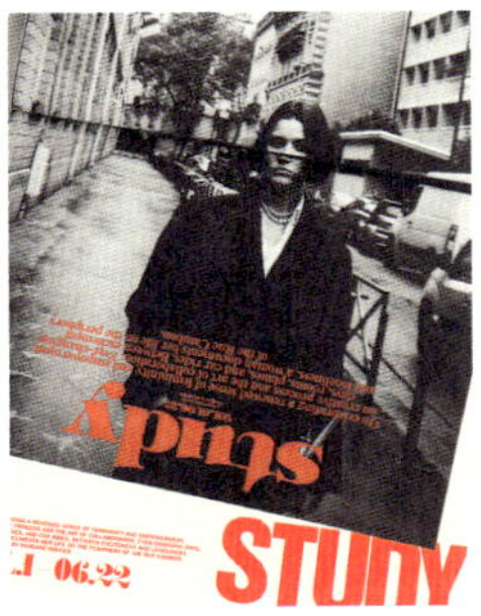

Photography by Vivienne Rohner
Creative direction with Lana Petrusevych

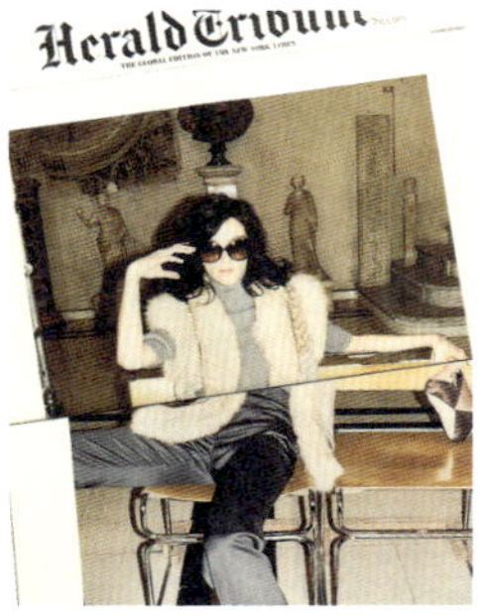

Photography by Juergen Teller
Styling by Jane How
Hair by Christiaan
Makeup by Dick Page
Model: Mariacarla Boscono
Creative direction with Suzanne Koller

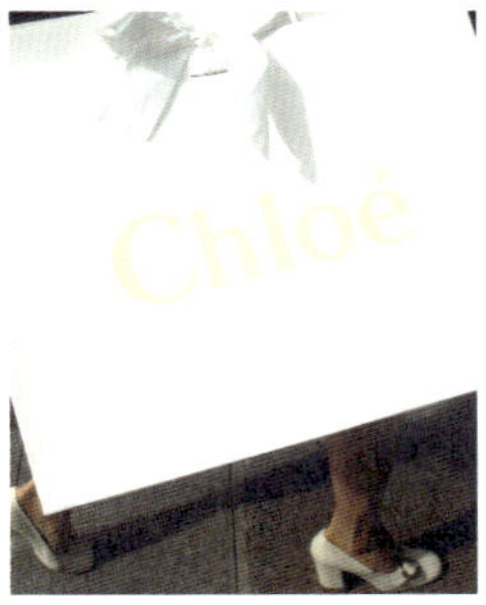

Creative direction
with Suzanne Koller

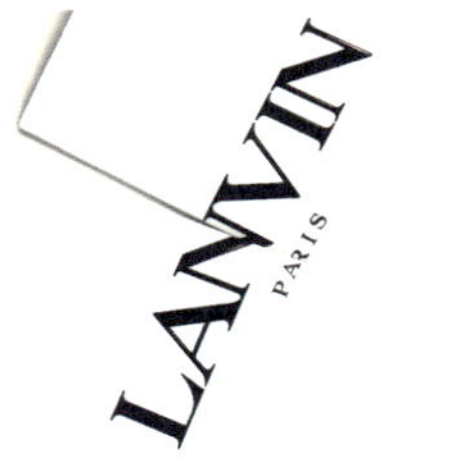

Creative direction
with Lana Petrusevych

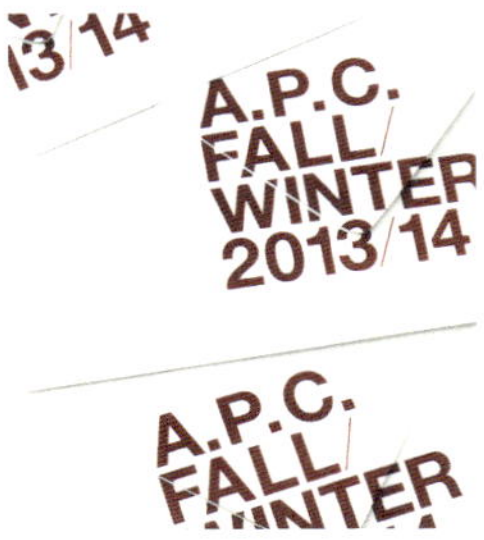

Creative direction
with Suzanne Koller

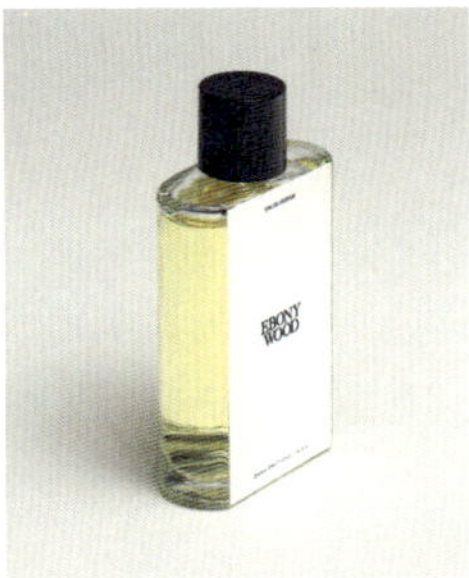

Photography by Philippe Lacombe
Creative direction with Lana Petrusevych

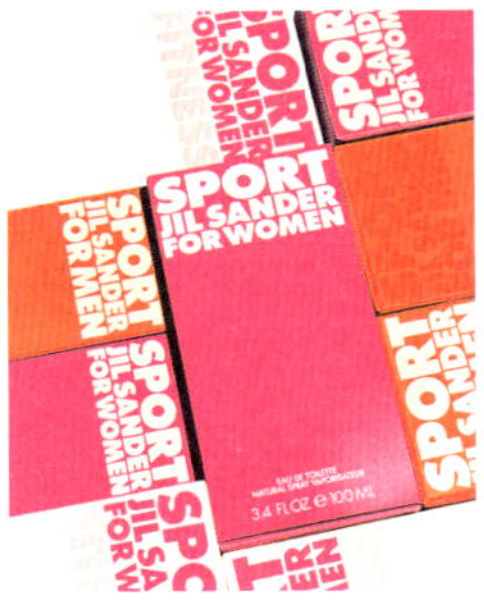

Creative direction
with Suzanne Koller

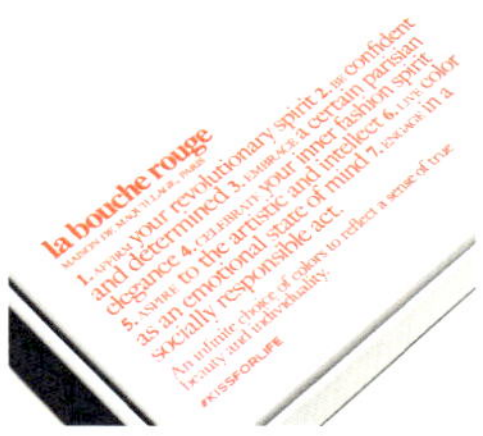

Creative direction
with Lana Petrusevych

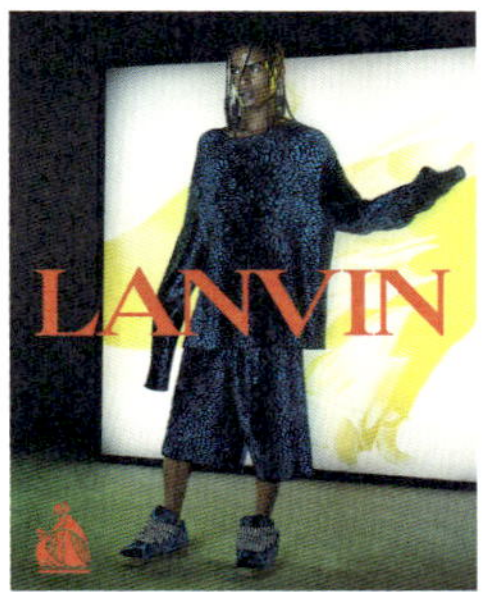

Lanvin by Bruno Sialelli
Photography by Mert Alas
and Marcus Piggott
Styling by Carlos Nazario
Hair by Jawara
Makeup by Cécile Paravina
Model: Luv Resval
Creative direction with Lana Petrusevych

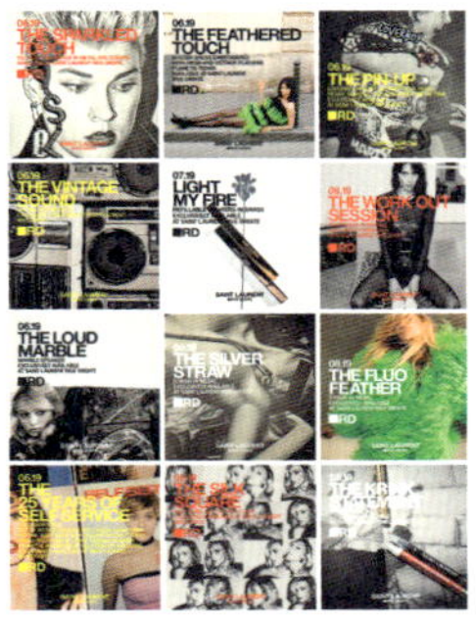

Creative direction
with Lana Petrusevych

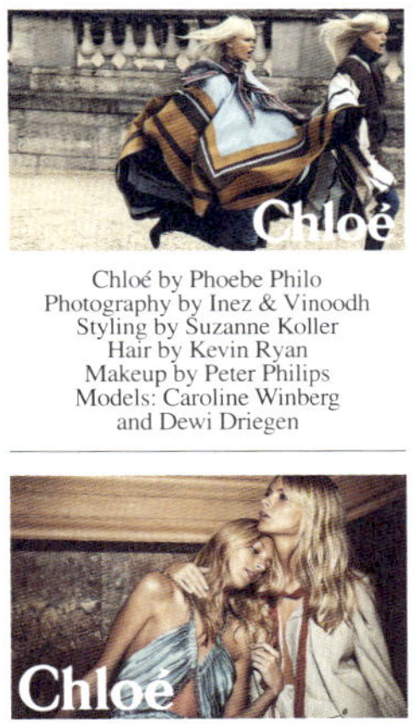

Chloé by Phoebe Philo
Photography by Inez & Vinoodh
Styling by Suzanne Koller
Hair by Kevin Ryan
Makeup by Peter Philips
Models: Caroline Winberg
and Dewi Driegen

Chloé by Phoebe Philo
Photography by Inez & Vinoodh
Styling by Suzanne Koller
Hair by Eugene Souleiman
Makeup by Peter Philips
Models: Anja Rubik and Julia Stegner

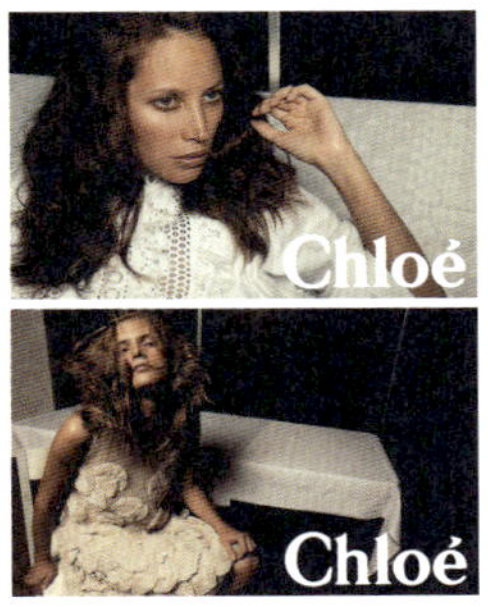

Chloé by Phoebe Philo
Photography by Inez & Vinoodh
Styling by Suzanne Koller
Hair by Luigi Murenu
Makeup by Lisa Butler
Models: Christy Turlington
and Malgosia Bela

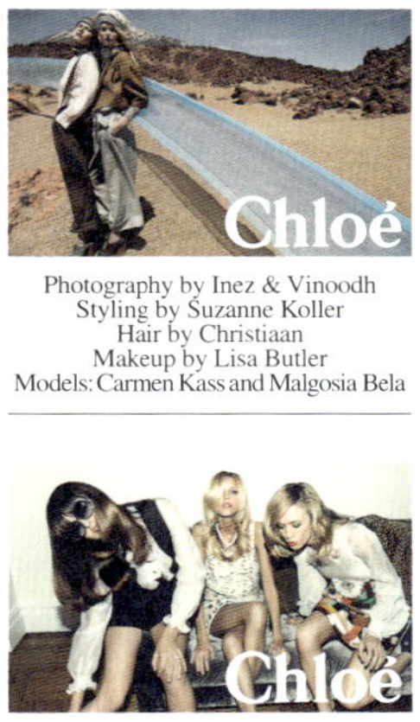

Photography by Inez & Vinoodh
Styling by Suzanne Koller
Hair by Christiaan
Makeup by Lisa Butler
Models: Carmen Kass and Malgosia Bela

Chloé by Yvan Mispelaere
Photography by Inez & Vinoodh
Styling by Suzanne Koller
Hair by Christiaan
Makeup by Lisa Butler
Models: Trish Goff, Anja Rubik,
and Raquel Zimmermann

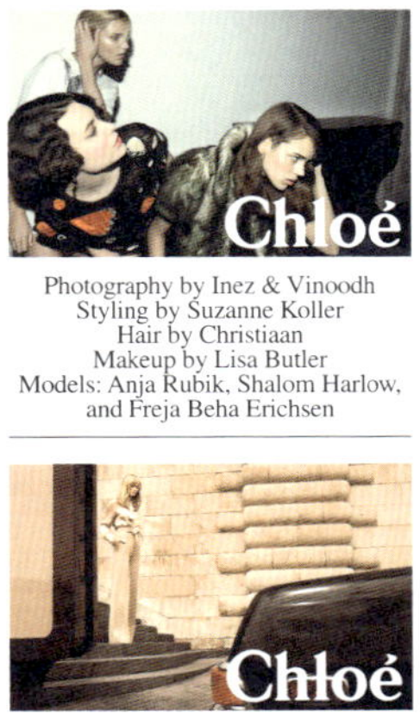

Photography by Inez & Vinoodh
Styling by Suzanne Koller
Hair by Christiaan
Makeup by Lisa Butler
Models: Anja Rubik, Shalom Harlow,
and Freja Beha Erichsen

Chloé by Hannah MacGibbon
Photography by Inez & Vinoodh
Styling by Suzanne Koller
Hair by Christiaan
Model: Raquel Zimmermann

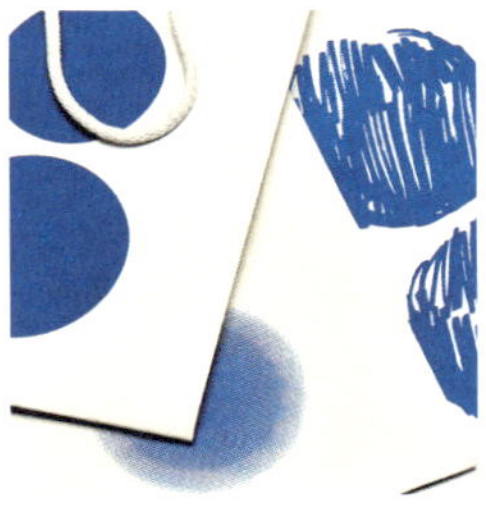

Creative direction
with Suzanne Koller

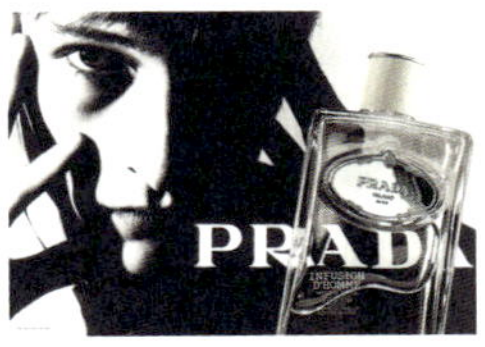

Photography by Steven Meisel
Styling by Fabio Zambernardi
Hair by Guido Palau
Makeup by Pat McGrath
Model: Rogier Bosschaart

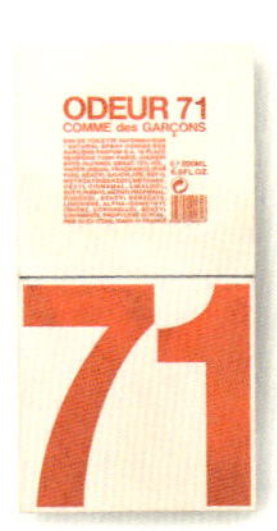

Creative direction
with Suzanne Koller

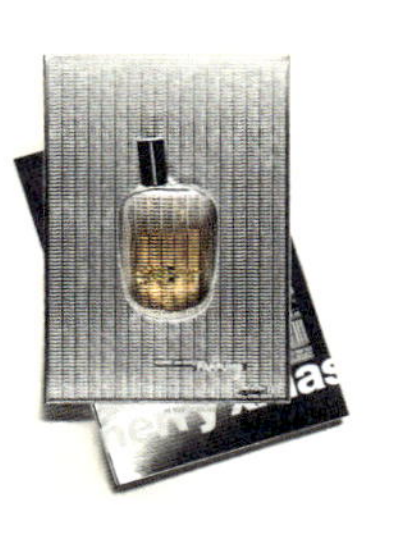

Creative direction
with Suzanne Koller

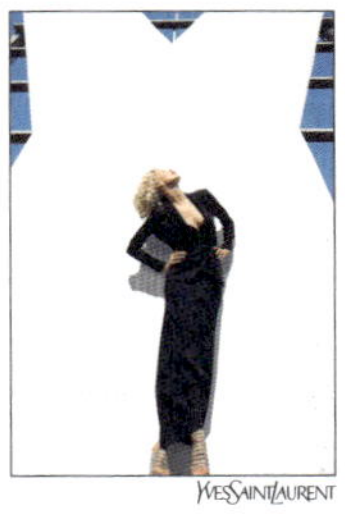

Yves Saint Laurent by Stefano Pilati
Photography by Inez & Vinoodh
Styling by Melanie Ward
Hair by Luigi Murenu
Makeup by Tom Pecheux
Model: Claudia Schiffer
Creative direction with Suzanne Koller

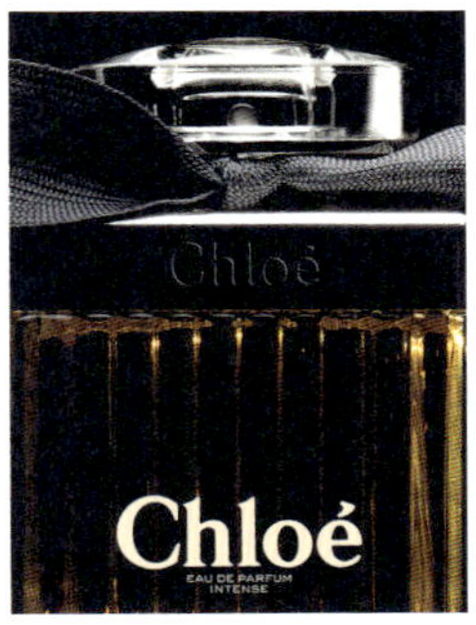

Photography by Thomas Lagrange
Creative direction with Suzanne Koller

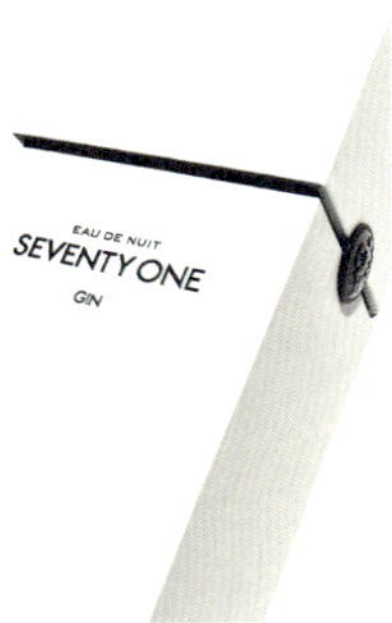

Creative direction
with Lana Petrusevych

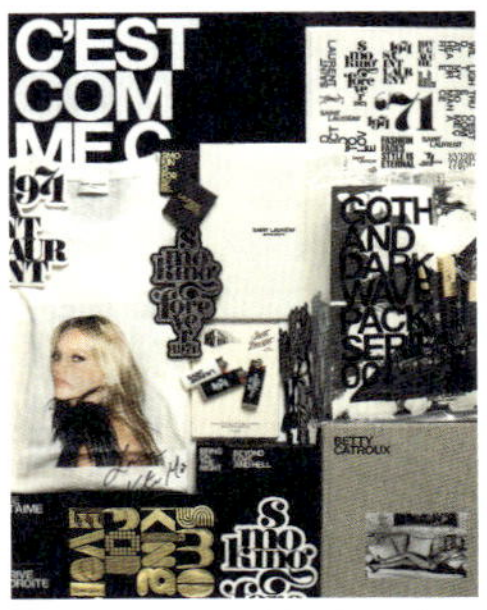

Photography by Philippe Lacombe
Creative direction with Lana Petrusevych

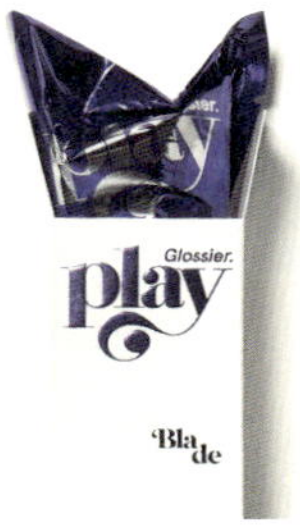

Creative direction
with Lana Petrusevych

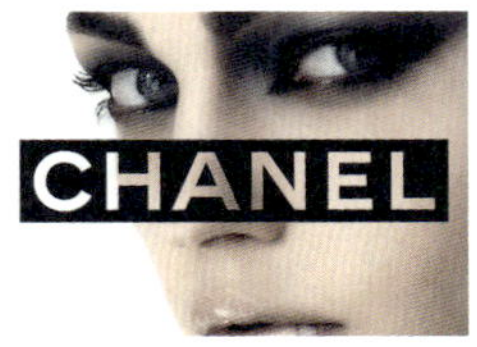

Photography by Karl Lagerfeld
Makeup by Peter Philips
Model: Sasha Pivovarova

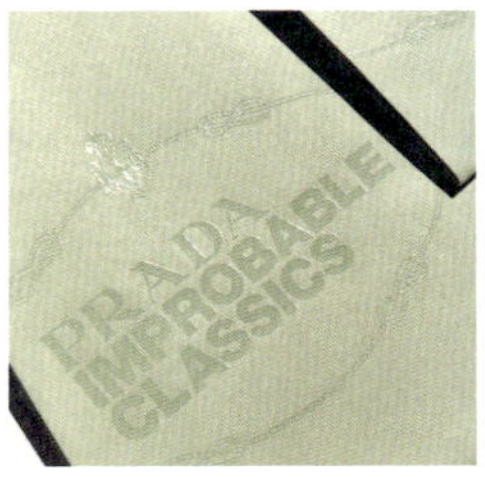

Creative direction
with Suzanne Koller

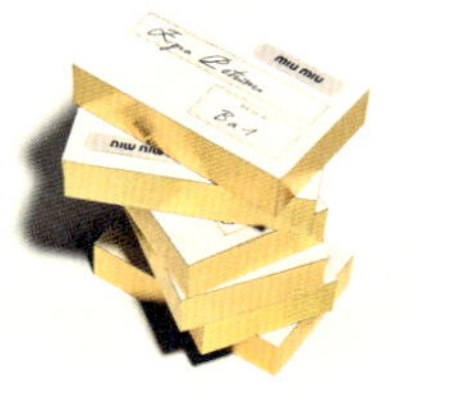

Creative direction
with Suzanne Koller

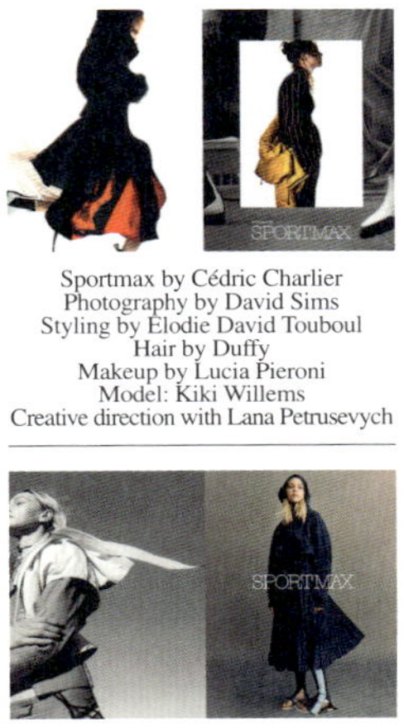

Sportmax by Cédric Charlier
Photography by David Sims
Styling by Elodie David Touboul
Hair by Duffy
Makeup by Lucia Pieroni
Model: Kiki Willems
Creative direction with Lana Petrusevych

Sportmax by Cédric Charlier
Photography by Jamie Hawkesworth
Styling by Elodie David Touboul
Hair by Jimmy Paul
Makeup by Dick Page
Model: Sasha Pivovarova
Creative direction with Lana Petrusevych

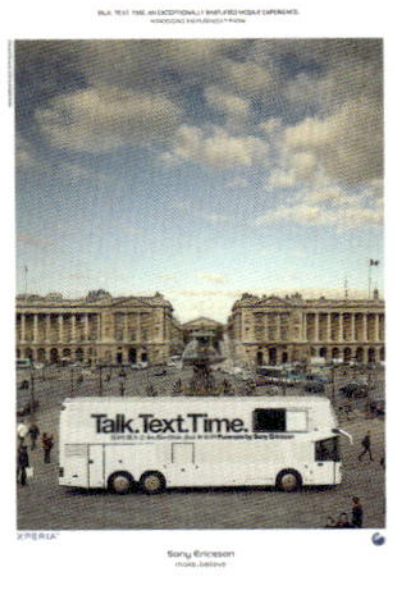

Photography by Jonathan de Villiers
Creative direction with Suzanne Koller

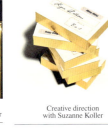

ACKNOWLEDGMENTS

Creative direction
with Lana Petrusevych

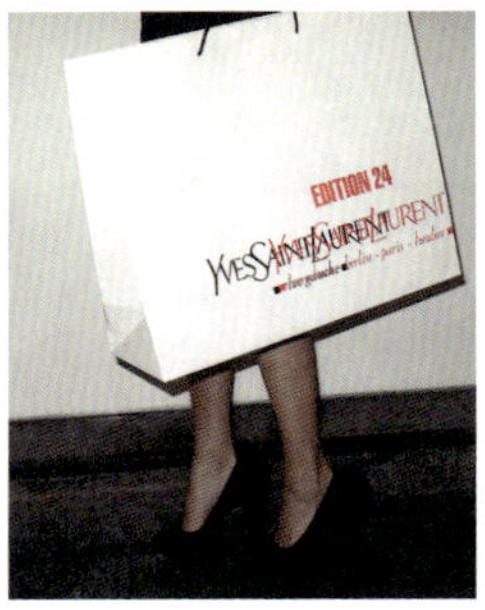

Creative direction
with Suzanne Koller

Photography by Philippe Lacombe
Creative direction with Lana Petrusevych

Photography by Ezra Petronio
and Juergen Teller
Models: Simona Kust and Anja Rubik
Creative direction
with Lana Petrusevych

Photography by Juergen Teller
Styling by Jane How
Hair by Christiaan
Makeup by Dick Page
Model: Stella Tennant
Creative direction with Suzanne Koller

Photography by Inez & Vinoodh
Styling by Suzanne Koller
Hair by Jeff Francis
Makeup by Peter Philips
Model: Carmen Kass

Yves Saint Laurent by Stefano Pilati
Photography by Inez & Vinoodh
Styling by Camilla Nickerson
Hair by Luigi Murenu
Makeup by Tom Pecheux
Model: Naomi Campbell
Creative direction with Suzanne Koller

Photography by Thomas Lagrange
Creative direction with Suzanne Koller

Photography by Guido Mocafico

Creative direction
with Suzanne Koller

Chloé by Hannah MacGibbon
Photography by Mario Sorrenti
Styling by Marie-Amélie Sauvé
Hair by Bob Recine
Makeup by Aaron de Mey
Models: Raquel Zimmermann
and Malgosia Bela
Creative direction with Suzanne Koller

Chloé by Hannah MacGibbon
Photography by David Sims
Styling by Marie-Amélie Sauvé
Hair by Guido Palau
Makeup by Diane Kendal
Models: Iselin Steiro and Malgosia Bela
Creative direction with Suzanne Koller

Chloé by Hannah MacGibbon
Photography by David Sims
Styling by Suzanne Koller
Hair by Guido Palau
Makeup by Diane Kendal
Models: Sigrid Agren and Zuzanna Bijoch

Chloé by Natacha Ramsay-Levi
Photography by David Sims
Styling by Camille Bidault-Waddington
Hair by Duffy
Makeup by Lucia Pieroni
Models: Mona Tougaard,
Rebecca Leigh Longendyke, and
Felice Nova Noordhoff
Creative direction with Lana Petrusevych

Chloé by Natacha Ramsay-Levi
Photography by David Sims
Styling by Camille Bidault-Waddington
Hair by Duffy
Makeup by Lucia Pieroni
Models: Lous and the Yakuza,
Anna Brewster, and Lola Nicon
Creative direction
with Lana Petrusevych

Creative direction
with Suzanne Koller

Creative direction
with Suzanne Koller

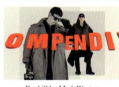

Dunhill by Mark Weston
Directed by Ezra Petronio
Photography by Mark Kean
Hair by Matt Mulhall
Makeup by Wendy Rowe
Creative direction
with Lana Petrusevych

Yves Saint Laurent by Stefano Pilati
Edition 24
Directed by Ezra Petronio
Styled by Joe McKenna
Model: Ginta Lapina
Creative direction with Suzanne Koller

Nike x Riccardo Tisci
Directed by Ezra Petronio
Creative direction
with Lana Petrusevych

Zara Improbable
Directed by Bryan Liston
Styling by Elodie David Touboul
Hair by Kevin Ryan
Model: Lily Vogt
Creative direction with Lana Petrusevych

A.P.C., FW11
Creative direction with Suzanne Koller

Alaïa by Pieter Mulier,
WS23 Show Film
Directed by Ezra Petronio
and Shayne Laverdiere
Hair by Duffy
Makeup by Pat McGrath
Creative direction with Lana Petrusevych

Photography by Venetia Scott
Styling by Suzanne Koller
Hair by Sébastien Richard
Makeup by Stephanie Kunz
Model: Eniko Mihalik

Costa Brazil
Photography by Luis Alberto
Rodríguez
Hair by Syd Hayes
Makeup by Marion Robine
Model: Jordan Barrett
Creative direction with Lana Petrusevych

Alaïa by Pieter Mulier
Photography by Paolo Roversi
Hair by Odile Gilbert
Makeup by Lauren Parsons
Model: Lilli Zoe
Creative direction with Lana Petrusevych

Saint Laurent by Anthony Vaccarello
Photography by Ezra Petronio
Hair by Akki Shirakawa
Makeup by Georgi Sandev
Model: Anja Rubik
Creative direction with Lana Petrusevych

Yves Saint Laurent by Stefano Pilati
Photography by Inez & Vinoodh
Styling by Joe McKenna
Hair by Luigi Murenu
Makeup by Tom Pecheux
Model: Daria Werbowy
Creative direction with Suzanne Koller

Yves Saint Laurent by Stefano Pilati
Photography by Inez & Vinoodh
Styling by Joe McKenna
Hair by Christiaan
Makeup by Lisa Butler
Model: Arizona Muse
Creative direction with Suzanne Koller

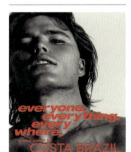

Gucci by Alessandro Michele
Photography by Thomas Lagrange
Creative direction
with Lana Petrusevych

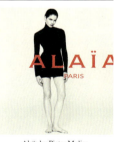

Gucci by Alessandro Michele
Directed by Mert Alas
and Marcus Piggott
Styling by Jane How
Hair by Christian Wood
Makeup by Mary Greenwell
Talent: Jessica Chastain
Creative direction with Lana Petrusevych

Chloé, Love
Directed by Roman Coppola
Styling by Joe McKenna
Hair by Luigi Murenu
Makeup by Lisa Butler
Talents: Kim Basinger and
Camilla Belle

Photography by Emilio Montero
Creative direction
with Lana Petrusevych

Alaïa by Pieter Mulier
Photography by Willy Vanderperre
Styling by Olivier Rizzo
Hair by Duffy
Makeup by Karin Westerlund
Models: Mona Tougaard,
Mirthe Dijk, and Victoria Fawole

Photography by Marion Parez
Creative direction
with Lana Petrusevych

Photography by Mert Alas
and Marcus Piggott
Styling by Joe McKenna
Hair by Luigi Murenu
Makeup by Lucia Pieroni
Talent: Kirsten Dunst
Creative direction
with Suzanne Koller

Photography by Mert Alas and Marcus
Piggott
Styling by Joe McKenna
Hair by Jane How
Makeup by Lucia Pieroni
Talent: Vanessa Paradis
Creative direction with Suzanne Koller

Photography by Mert Alas
and Marcus Piggott
Styling by Joe McKenna
Hair by Luigi Murenu
Makeup by Charlotte Tilbury
Talent: Laetitia Casta
Creative direction with Suzanne Koller

Photography by Mert Alas
and Marcus Piggott
Styling by Joe McKenna
Hair by Luigi Murenu
Makeup by Charlotte Tilbury
Talent: Lindsay Lohan
Creative direction with Suzanne Koller

Photography by Inez & Vinoodh
Styling by Suzanne Koller
Hair by Luigi Murenu
Makeup by Dick Page
Talents: Selma Blair, Lou Doillon, and
Evan Rachel Wood

Photography by Inez & Vinoodh
Styling by Carine Roitfeld
Hair by Luigi Murenu
Makeup by Peter Philips
Models: Zhou Xun,
Rina Ohta, and Dong Jie
Creative direction with Suzanne Koller

Chloé, L'Eau de Chloé
Directed by Mario Sorrenti
Styling by Jane How
Makeup by Aaron de Mey
Hair by Bob Recine
Model: Camille Rowe
Creative direction with Suzanne Koller

ACKNOWLEDGMENTS

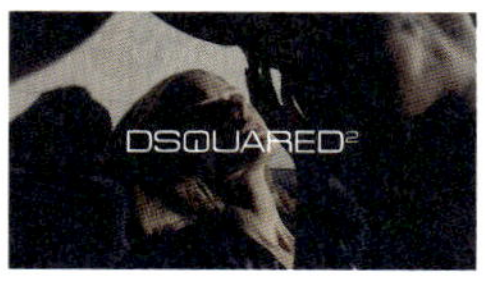

DSquared2, Potion
Directed by Mario Sorrenti
Styling by Dean & Dan Caten
Hair by Luigi Murenu
Makeup by Stéphane Marais
Models: Malgosia Bela
and Diego Miguel
Creative direction
with Suzanne Koller

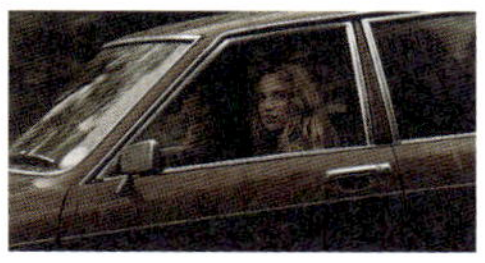

Mango, FW19
Directed by Glen Luchford
Styling by Elodie David Touboul
Hair by Anthony Turner
Makeup by Lucia Pieroni
Models: Anna Ewers, Rebecca Leigh
Longendyke, Kaya Wilkins, Mathias
Lauridsen, and Hugo Sauzay
Creative direction
with Lana Petrusevych

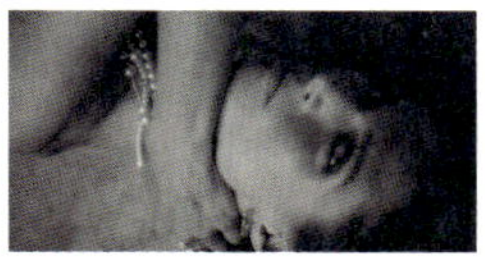

Salvatore Ferragamo, Emozione
Directed by Mert Alas
and Marcus Piggott
Styling by Alex White
Hair by Angelo Seminara
Makeup by Lisa Eldridge
Model: Malgosia Bela

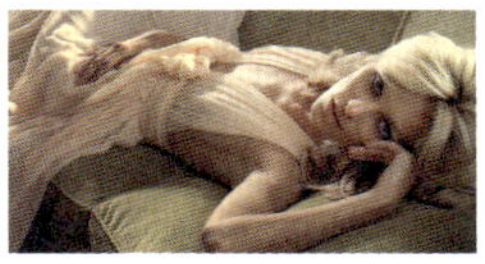

Salvatore Ferragamo, Signorina
Directed by Mario Sorrenti
Styling by Camilla Nickerson
Hair by Bob Recine
Makeup by Aaron de Mey
Model: Anja Rubik

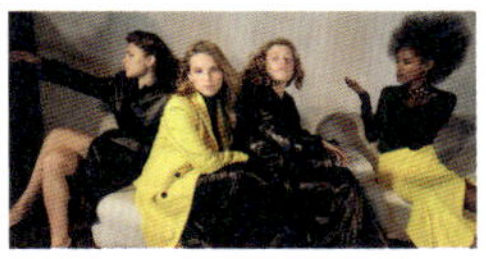

Massimo Dutti, FW22
Directed by Oliver Hadlee Pearch
Styling by Emmanuelle Alt
Hair by Marc Lopez
Makeup by Christelle Cocquet
Models: Rebecca Leigh Longendyke,
Malika Louback, Adele Aldighieri,
and Mariam de Vinzelle
Creative direction
with Lana Petrusevych

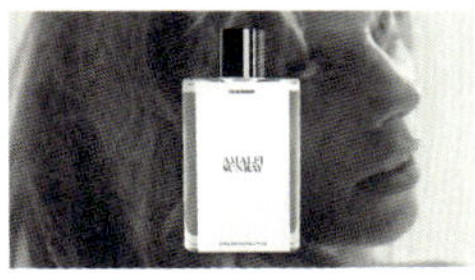

Zara, Emotions
Directed by David Sims
Styling by Jane How
Makeup by Duffy
Hair by Lucia Pieroni
Models: Lexi Boling, Maartje
Verhoef, Klara Kristin, Blésnya
Minher, Moon Kyu Lee,
Mijo Mihaljcic, and Sacha Quenby
Creative direction
with Lana Petrusevych

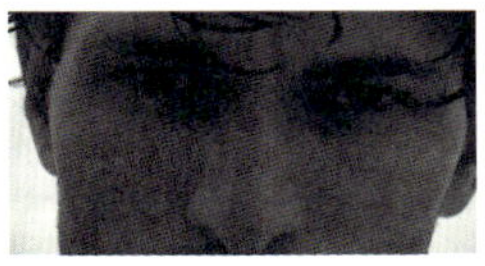

Chanel, Allure Homme Sport
Directed by Bruce Weber
Styling by Joe McKenna
Hair by Didier Malige
Talent: Andrés Velencoso Segura

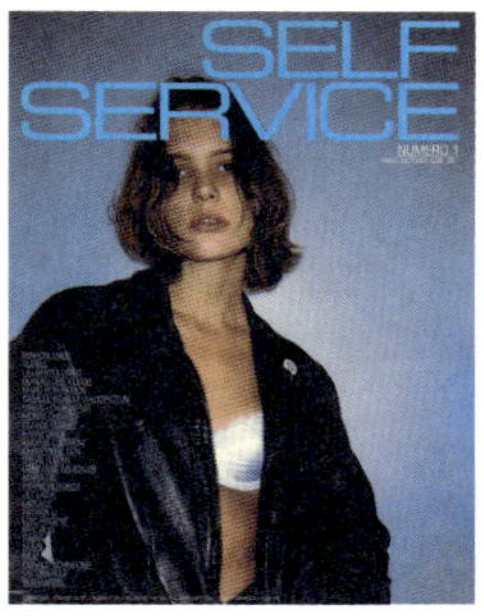

Photography by Mark Borthwick
Styling by Jane How
Model: Hélène Fillières

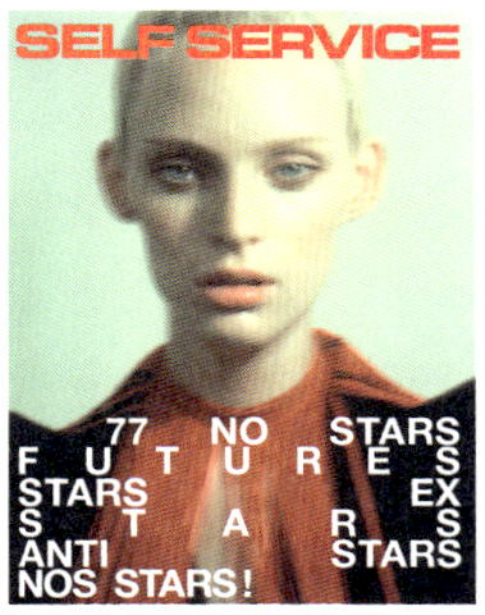

Photography by Mark Borthwick
Styling by Jane How
Model: Amy Wesson

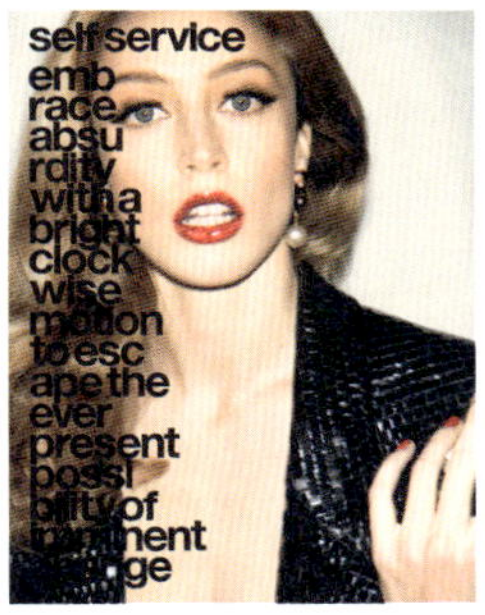

Photography by Ezra Petronio
Styling by Suzanne Koller
Hair by Sébastien Richard
Makeup by Lucia Pica
Model: Raquel Zimmermann

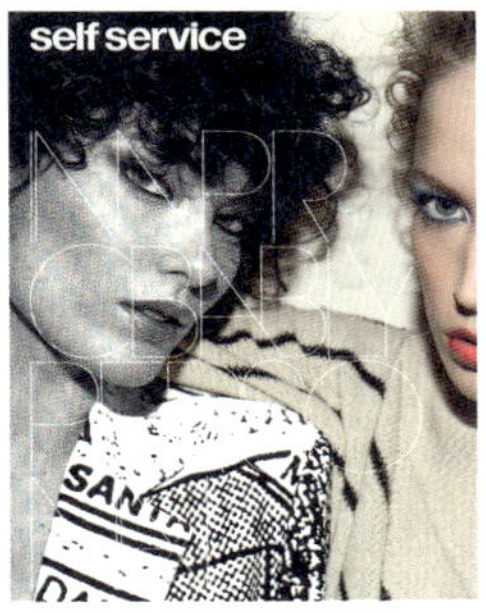

Photography by Inez & Vinoodh
Styling by Suzanne Koller
Hair by Christiaan
Makeup by Dick Page
Models: Shalom Harlow
and Raquel Zimmermann

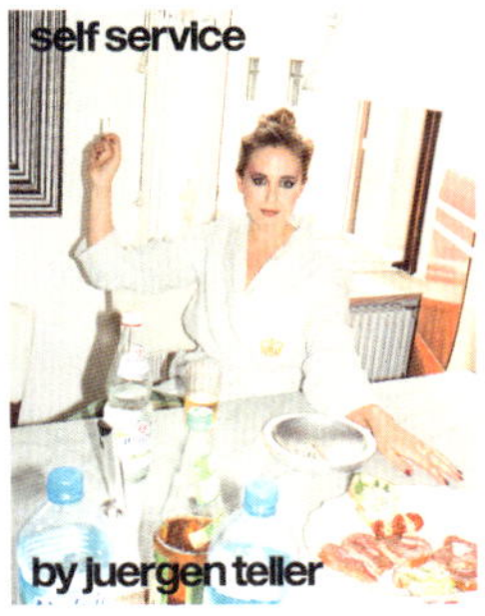

Photography by Juergen Teller
Styling by Duro Olowu
Hair by Christiaan
Makeup by Dick Page
Model: Elisabeth von Thurn
und Taxis

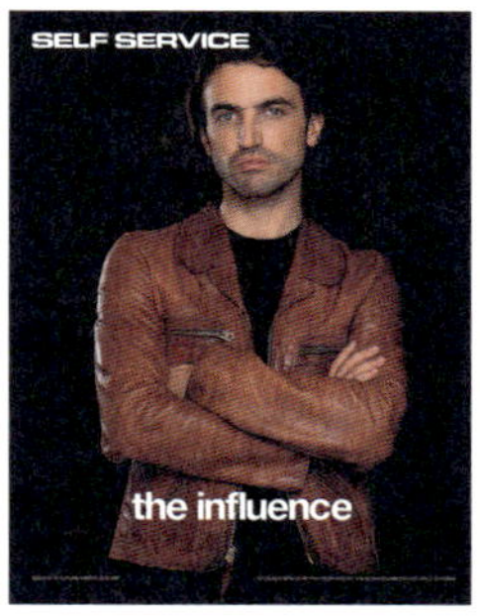

Photography by Anuschka Blommers
and Niels Schumm
Hair by Marion Anée
Makeup by Karim Rahman
Model: Nicolas Ghesquière

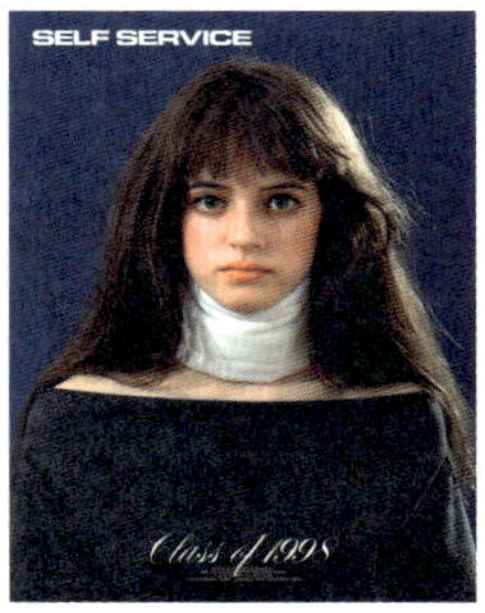

Photography by Anuschka Blommers
and Niels Schumm
Styling by Suzanne Koller
Hair by Eugene for Toni&Guy
Makeup by Lisa Butler
Model: Ciara Nuguet

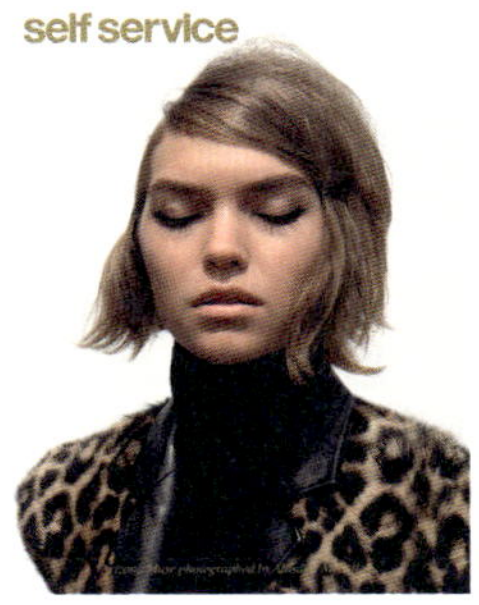

Photography by Alasdair McLellan
Styling by Suzanne Koller
Hair by Anthony Turner
Makeup by Lucia Pica
Model: Arizona Muse

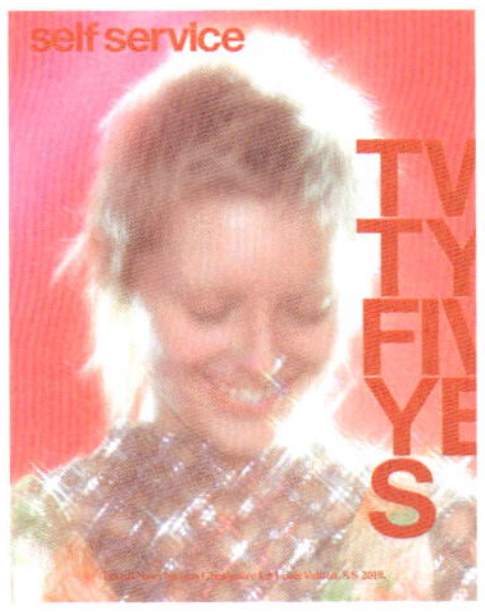

Photography by David Sims
Styling by Joe McKenna
Hair by Duffy
Makeup by Lucia Pieroni
Model: Florence Hutchings

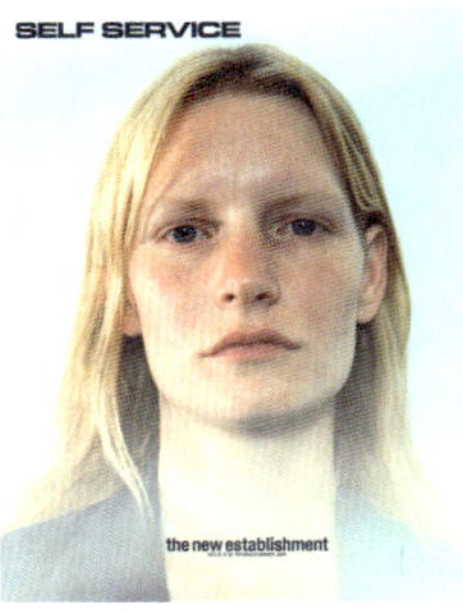

Photography by Mark Borthwick
Styling by Suzanne Koller
Model: Kirsten Owen

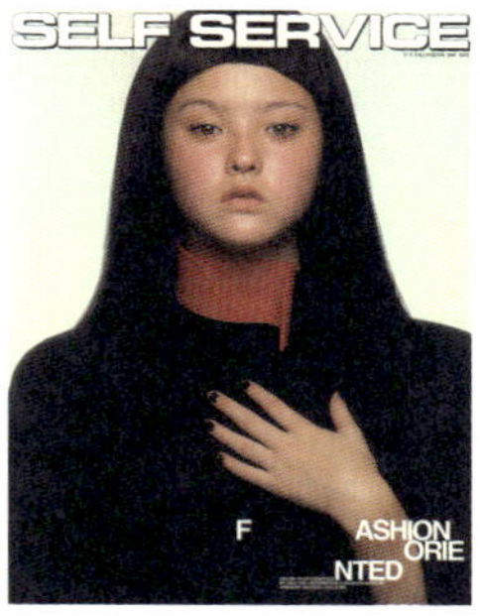

Photography by Inez & Vinoodh
Styling by Nancy Rohde
Hair by Eugene Souleiman
Makeup by Lisa Butler
Model: Devon Aoki

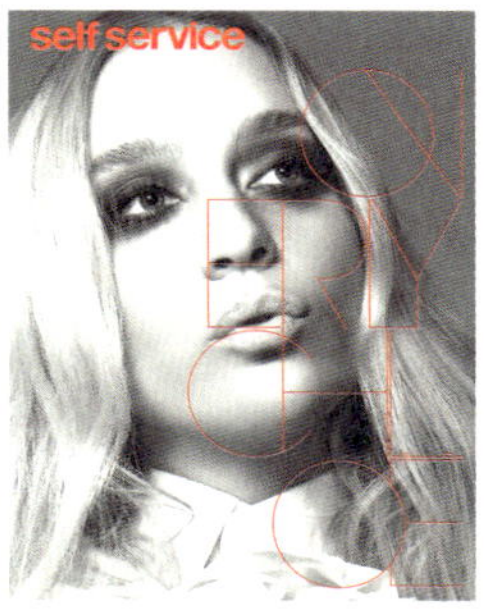

Photography by David Sims
Styling by Joe McKenna
Hair by Paul Hanlon
Makeup by Lucia Pieroni
Talent: Chloë Sevigny

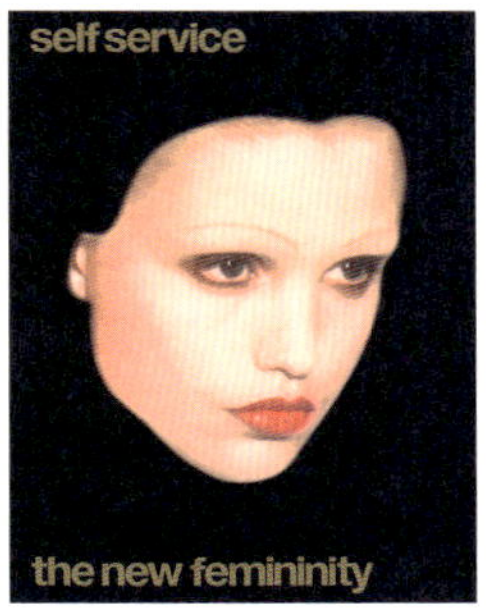

Photography by David Sims
Styling by Joe McKenna
Hair by Duffy
Makeup by Lauren Parsons
Model: Luna Bijl

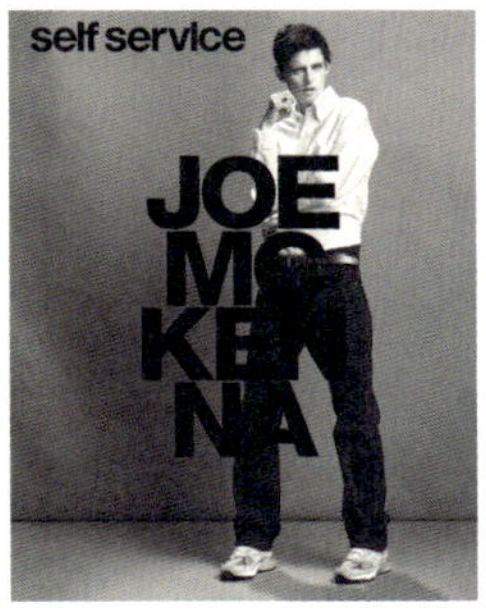

Styling by Joe McKenna
Hair by Christiaan
Makeup by Lisa Butler
Model: Stella Tennant

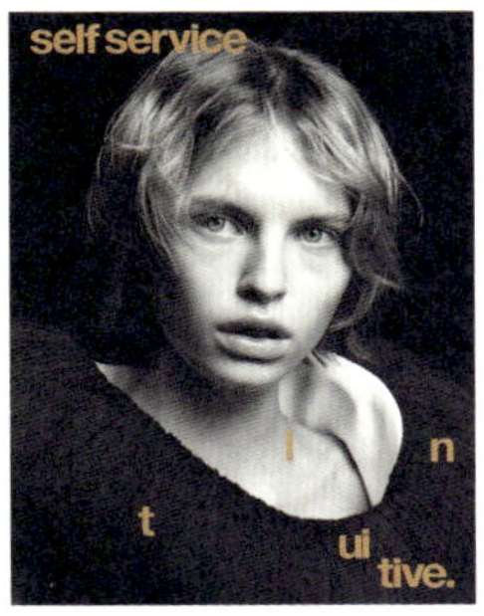

Photography by David Sims
Styling by Joe McKenna
Hair by Duffy
Makeup by Hiromi Ueda
Model: Karolina Spakowski

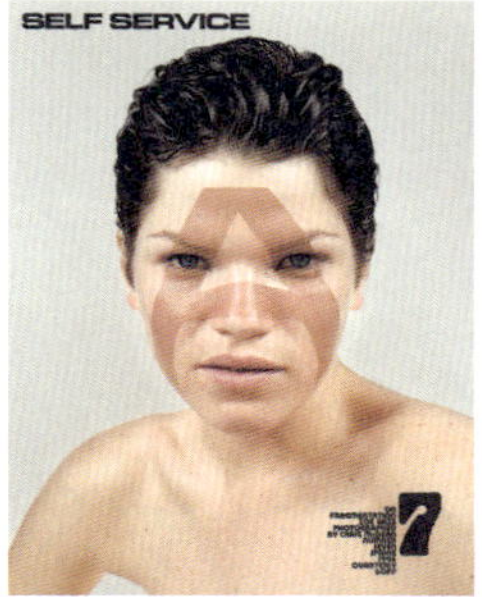

Photography by Craig McDean
Hair by Eugene Souleiman
Makeup by Pat McGrath
Model: Zoe Gaze

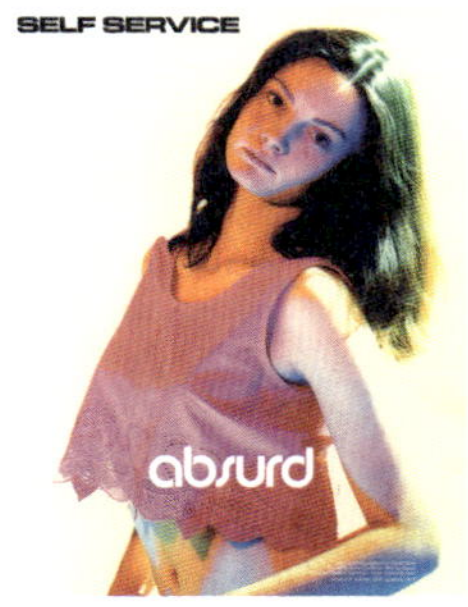

Photography by David Sims
Styling by Anna Cockburn
Hair by Guido
Makeup by Lauren Parsons
Model: Laura Foster

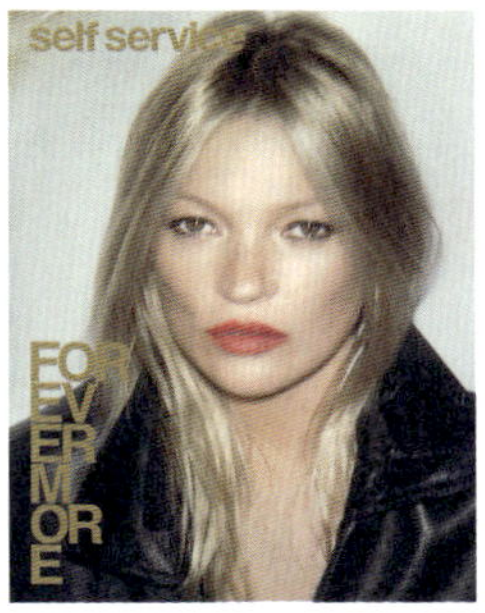

Photography by Ezra Petronio
Styling by Alastair McKimm
Hair by Duffy
Makeup by Mark Carrasquillo
Model: Kate Moss

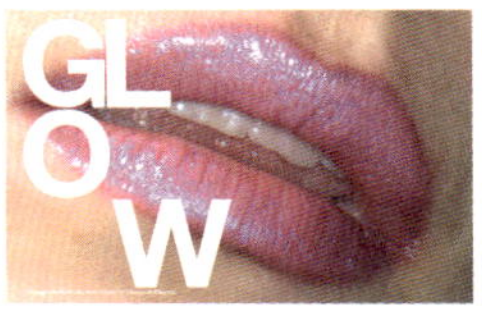

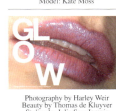

Photography by Harley Weir
Beauty by Thomas de Kluyver
Styling by Julia Sarr-Jamois
Model: Antonia Sell

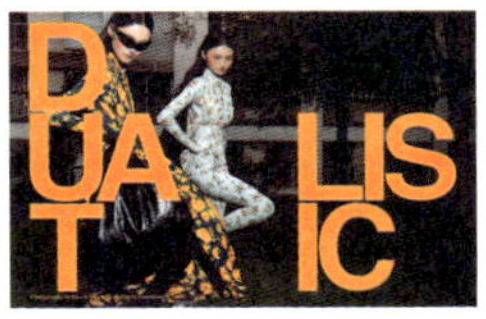

Photography by Inez & Vinoodh
Styling by Emmanuelle Alt
Hair by James Pecis
Makeup by Lisa Butler
Model: He Cong

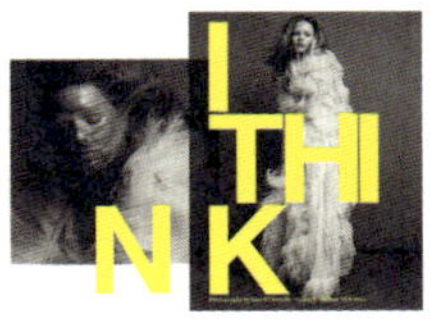

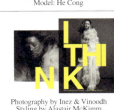

Photography by Inez & Vinoodh
Styling by Alastair McKimm
Hair by Ward
Makeup by Yadim
Model: Anna Ewers

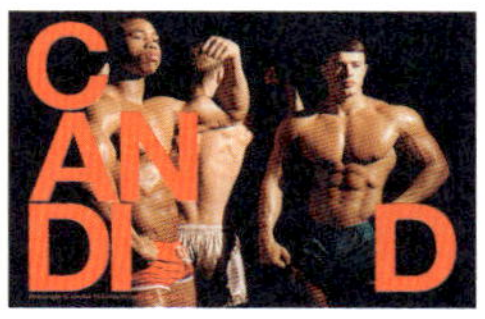

Photography by Alasdair McLellan
Styling by Benjamin Bruno
Hair by Anthony Turner
Makeup by Lynsey Alexander
Models: Moziah Pinder, David Carter,
and Ben Bray

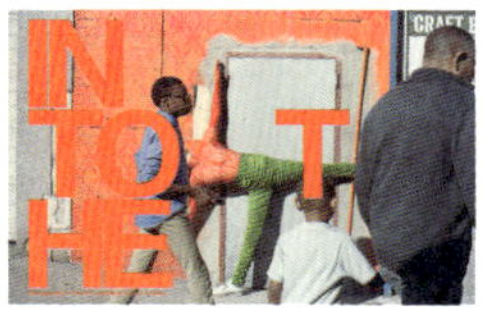

Photography by Cass Bird
Styling by Ondine Azoulay
Hair by Esther Langham
Makeup by Hannah Murray
Model: Raquel Zimmermann

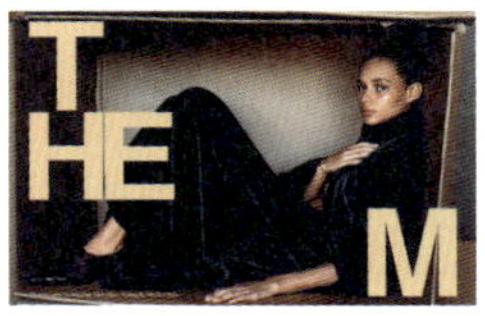

Photography by Alasdair McLellan
Styling by Marie Chaix
Hair by James Pecis
Makeup by Lauren Parsons
Model: Binx Walton

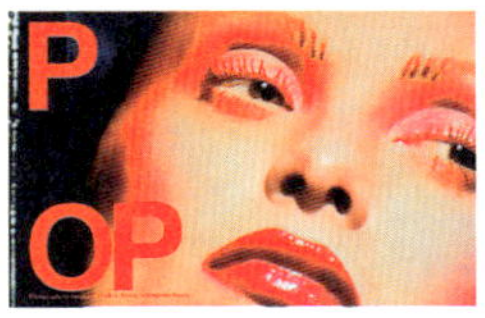

Photography by Alasdair McLellan
Styling by Benjamin Bruno
Hair by Anthony Turner
Makeup by Lynsey Alexander
Model: Karen Elson

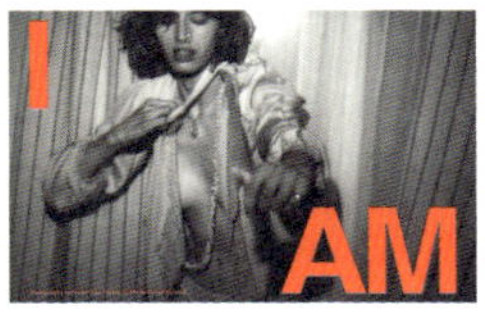

Photography by David Sims
Styling by Elodie David Touboul
Hair by Duffy
Makeup by Lucia Pieroni
Model: Daisy

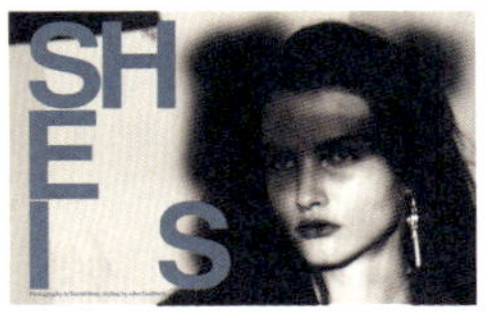

Photography by David Sims
Styling by Alice Goddard
Hair by Duffy
Makeup by Hiromi Ueda
Model: Hilal Ata

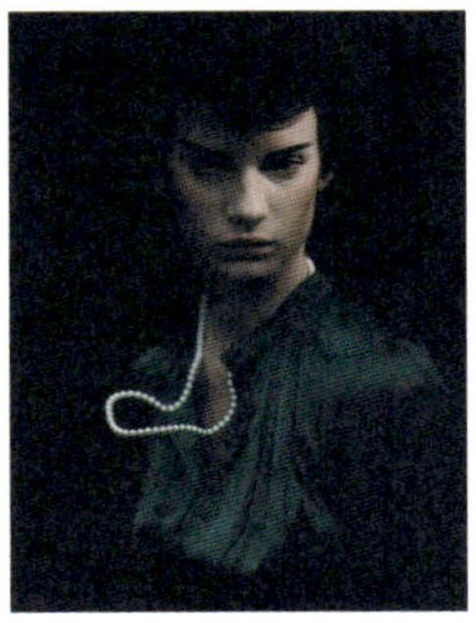

Photography by Paolo Roversi
Styling by Jane How
Hair by Eugene Souleiman
Makeup by Val Garland
Model: Querelle Jansen

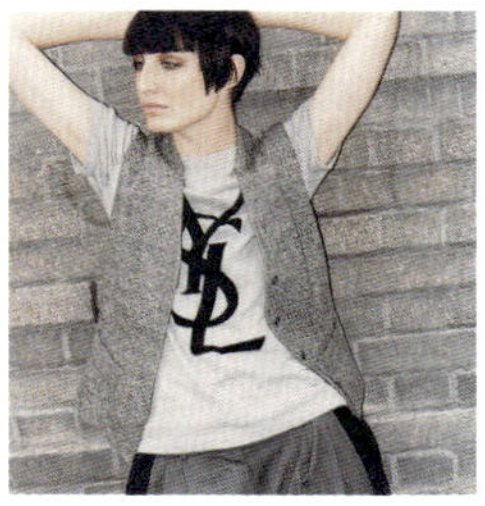

Photography by Magnus Unnar
Styling by Bay Garnett
Hair by Jimo Salako
Makeup by Kirstin Piggott
Model: Erin O'Connor

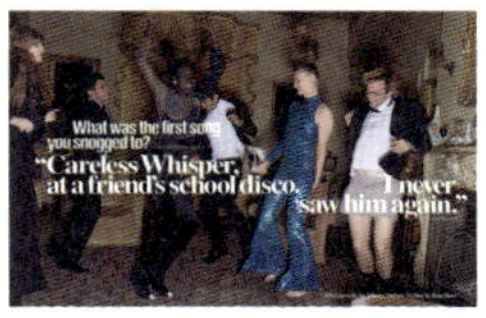

Photography by Johnny Dufort
Styling by Jane How
Hair by Cyndia Harvey
Makeup by Thomas de Kluyver
Models: Adit Priscilla and Alice Cooper

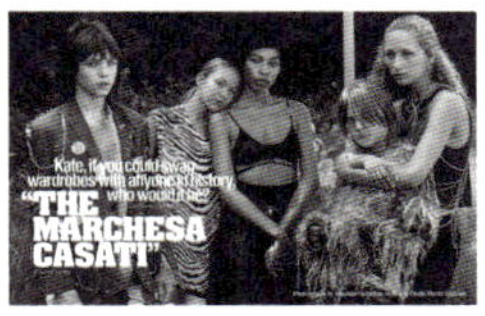

Photography by Alasdair McLellan
Styling by Elodie David Touboul
Hair by Anthony Turner
Makeup by Lynsey Alexander
Models: Vinnie Rockins, Lila Moss,
Tora-i, Lenny Rockins, and Elfie Reigate

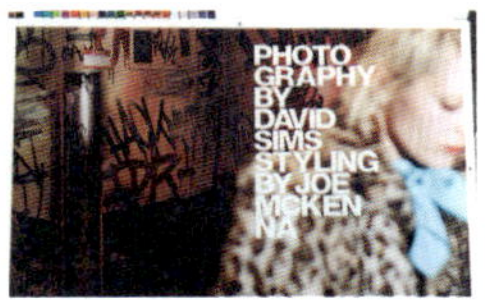

Photography by David Sims
Styling by Joe McKenna
Hair by Duffy
Makeup by Lucia Pieroni
Model: Florence Hutchins

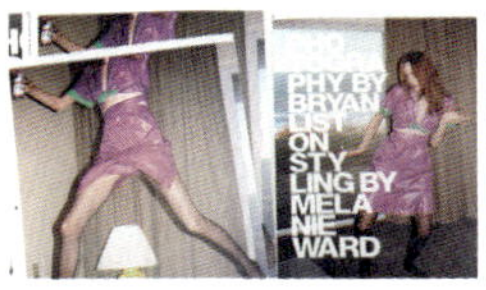

Photography by Bryan Liston
Styling by Melanie Ward
Hair by Kevin Ryan
Makeup by Emi Kaneko
Model: Kiki Willems

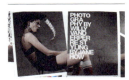

Photography by Willy Vanderperre
Styling by Jane How
Hair by Paul Hanlon
Makeup by Sally Branka
Model: Anabela Belikova

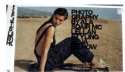

Photography by Alasdair McLellan
Styling by Jane How
Hair by Kevin Ryan
Makeup by Miranda Joyce
Model: Kasia Struss

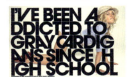

Photography by Terry Richardson
Styling by Camille Bidault-
Waddington
Hair by Christian Eberhard
Makeup by Frank B
Talent: Chloë Sevigny

ACKNOWLEDGMENTS

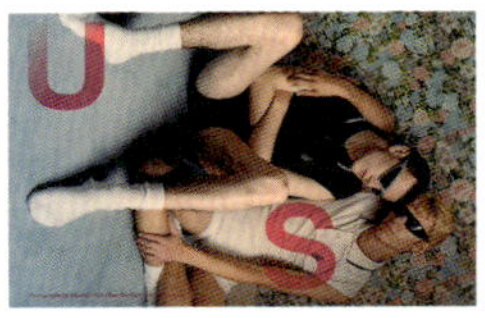

Photography by Alasdair McLellan
Styling by Max Pearmain
Hair by Anthony Turner
Makeup by Lynsey Alexander
Models: Tom Davison and Finn Morgan-Murrell

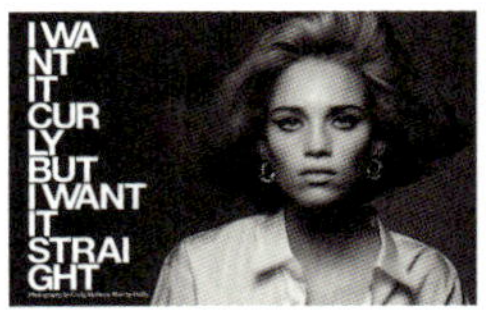

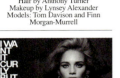

Photography by Craig McDean
Styling by Stella Greenspan
Hair by Duffy
Makeup by Diane Kendal
Model: Rebecca Leigh Longendyke

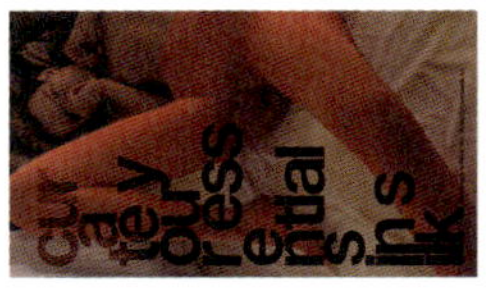

Photography by David Sims
Styling by Emmanuelle Alt
Hair by Duffy
Makeup by Lucia Pieroni
Model: Maaike Klaasen

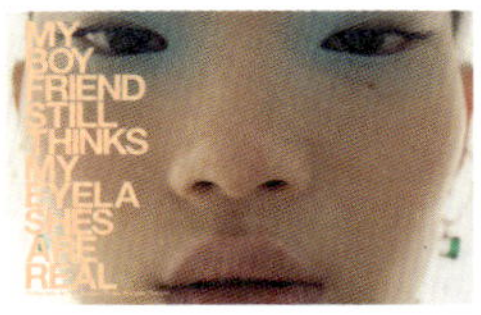

Photography by Zoë Ghertner
Styling by Carlos Nazario
Hair by Jimmy Paul
Makeup by Diane Kendal
Model: HyunJi Shin

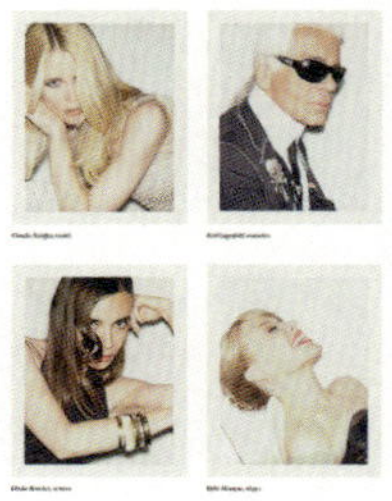

Photography by Ezra Petronio

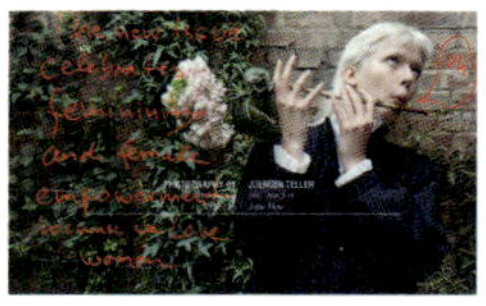

Photography by Juergen Teller
Styling by Jane How
Hair by Anthony Turner
Model: Suzi Leenaars

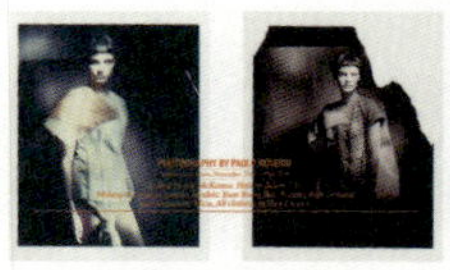

Photography by Paolo Roversi
Styling by Joe McKenna
Hair by Julien d'Ys
Makeup by Linda Cantello
Models: Faretta and Kris Grikaite

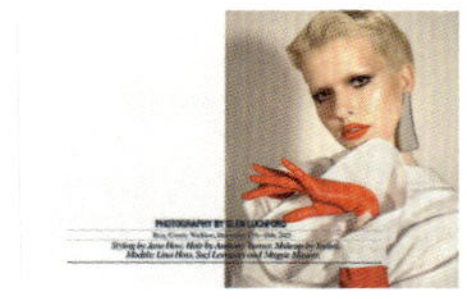

Photography by Glen Luchford
Styling by Jane How
Hair by Anthony Turner
Makeup by Yadim
Model: Suzi Leenaars

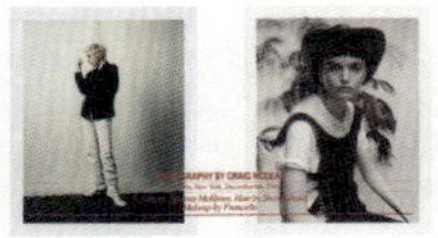

Photography by Craig McDean
Styling by Alastair McKimm
Hair by Shay Ashual
Makeup by Francelle Daly
Models: Julia Cumming and Ruth Bell

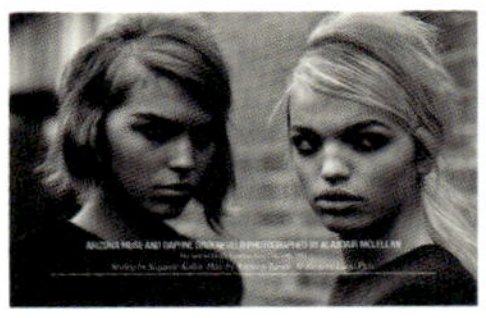

Photography by Alasdair McLellan
Styling by Suzanne Koller
Hair by Anthony Turner
Makeup by Lucia Pica
Models: Arizona Muse and Daphne Groeneveld

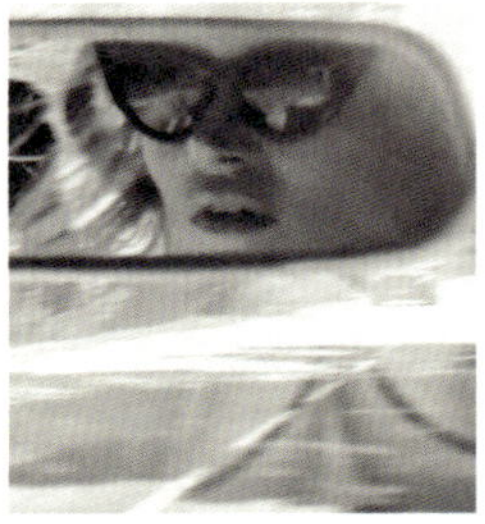

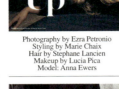

Photography by Mario Testino
Model: Kate Moss

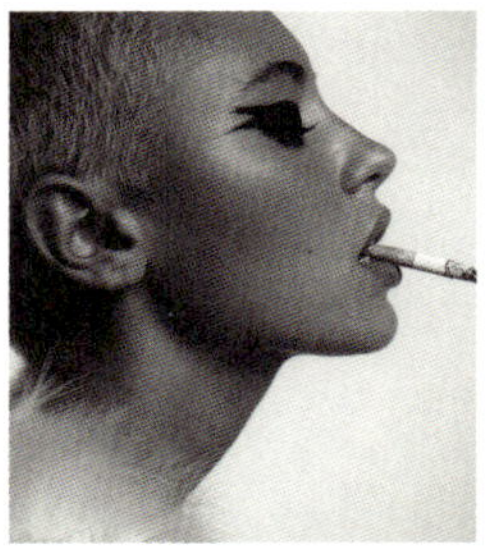

Photography by Robin Galiegue
Styling by Elodie David Touboul
Hair by Laurent Philippon
Makeup by Petros Petrohilos
Model: Iris Law

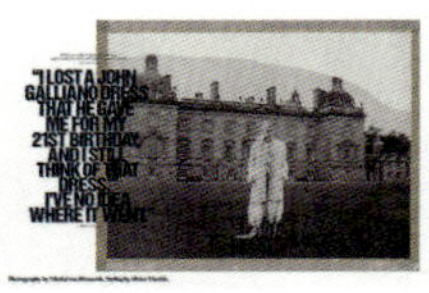

Photography by Nikolai von Bismarck
Styling by Alister Mackie
Hair by Matt Mulhall
Makeup by Anne Sophie Costa
Model: Angel Prost

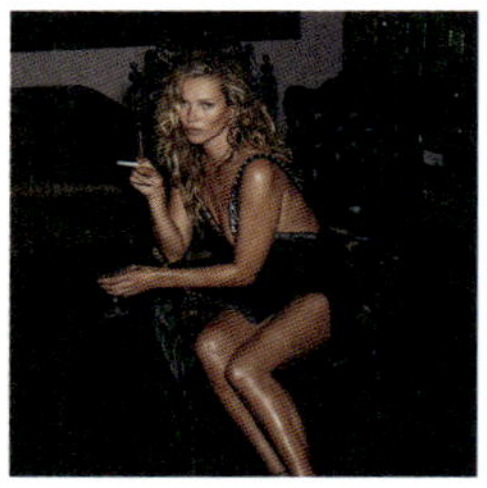

Photography by Mert Alas
and Marcus Piggott
Styling by Emmanuelle Alt
Hair by Paul Hanlon
Makeup by Val Garland
Model: Kate Moss

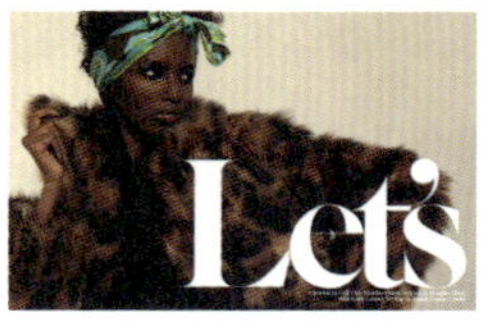

Photography by Call This Number
(Steve Mackey and Douglas Hart)
with Katie Grand
Styling by Jeanie Annan-Lewin
Hair by Syd Hayes
Makeup by Rebecca Wordingham
Model: Bibi Abdulkadir

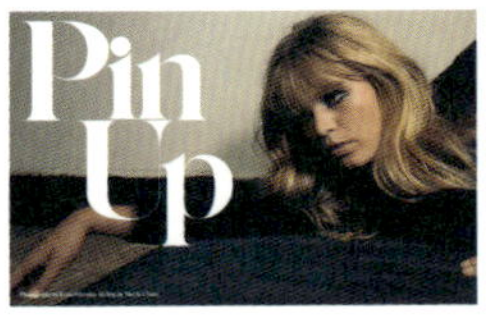

Photography by Ezra Petronio
Styling by Marie Chaix
Hair by Stephane Lancien
Makeup by Lucia Pica
Model: Anna Ewers

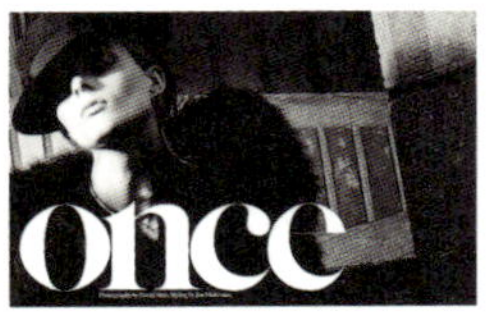

Photography by David Sims
Styling by Joe McKenna
Hair by Paul Hanlon
Makeup by Lucia Pieroni
Model: Aylah Peterson

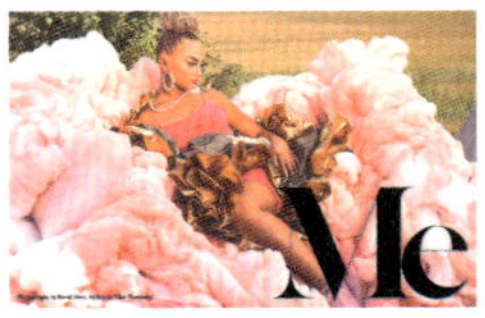

Photography by David Sims
Styling by Max Pearmain
Model: Fabiola

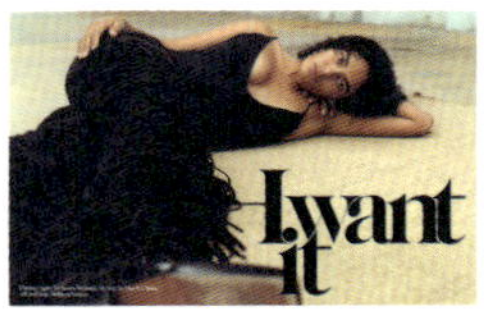

Photography by Senta Simond
Styling by Marie Chaix
Hair by Akemi Kishida
Model: Ylang Messenguiral

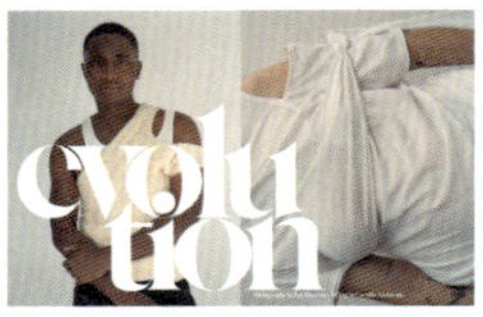

Photography by Zoë Ghertner
Styling by Camilla Nickerson
Models: Chi Ossé and Izzy Adams

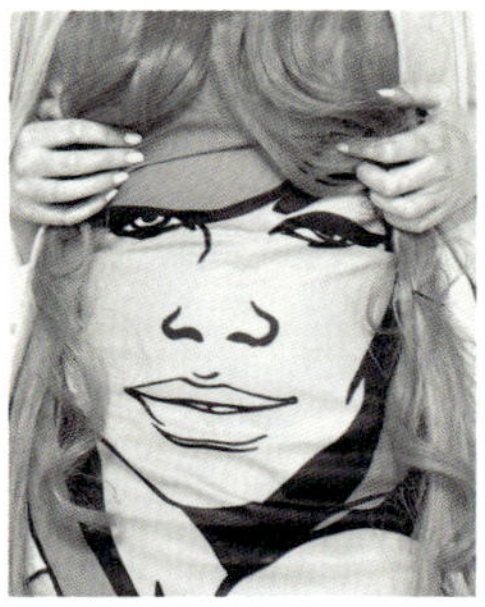

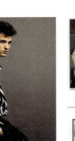

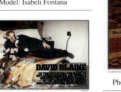

Photography by Dirk Seiden Schwan
Styling by Andre Walker
Hair by Sebastien Bascle
Makeup by Michelle Rainer
Model: Kristina S.

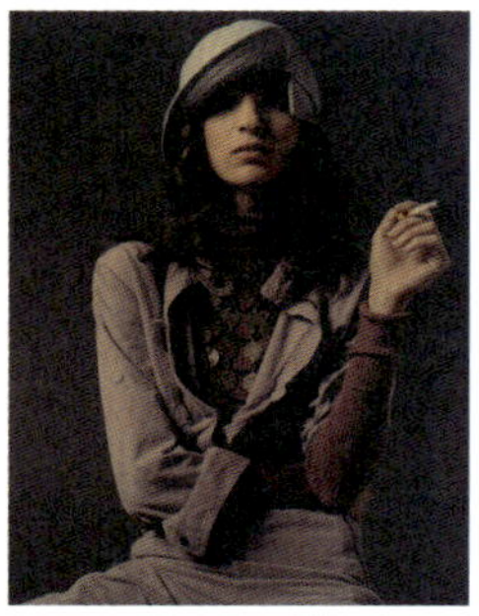

Photography by Karen Collins
Styling by Camille Bidault-Waddington
Hair by Alain Pichon
Makeup by Miranda Joyce
Model: Mariacarla Boscono

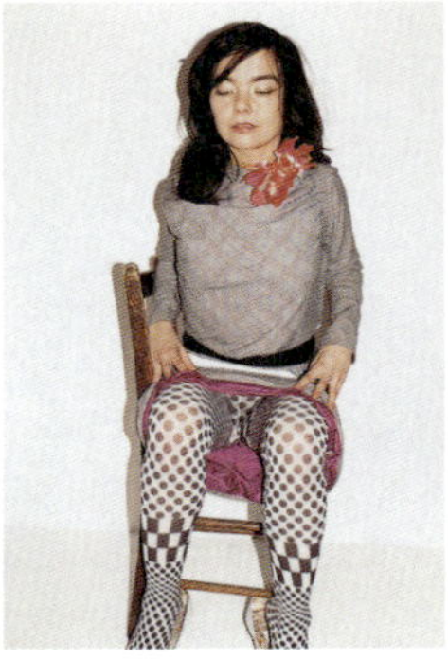

Photography by Juergen Teller
Styling by Venetia Scott
Hair by Eugene Souleiman
Makeup by Dick Page
Talent: Björk

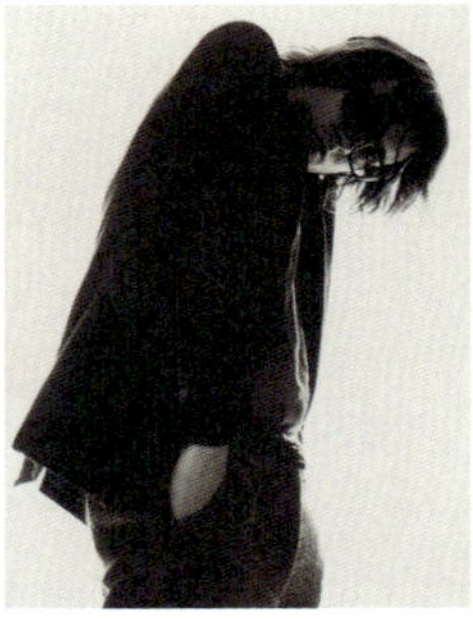

Photography by David Sims
Styling by Elodie David Touboul
Hair by Luke Hersheson
Makeup by Karen Alder
Talent: Jarvis Cocker

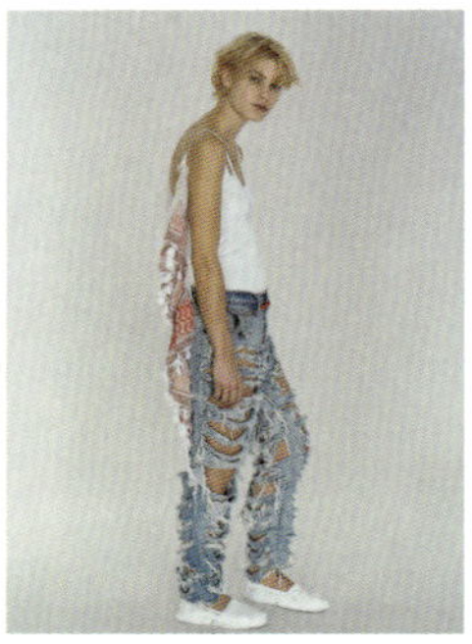

Photography by Corinne Day
Styling by Jane How
Hair by Neil Moodie
Makeup by Inge Grognard
Model: Delfine Bafort

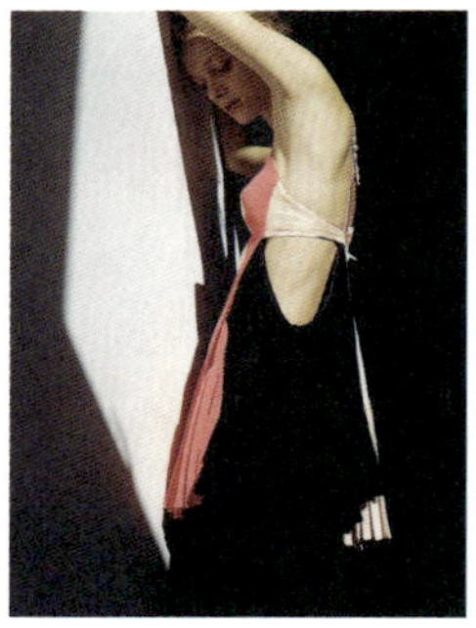

Photography by David Armstrong
Styling by Panos Yiapanis
Hair by Rudi
Makeup by Inge Grognard
Model: Lisa Davies

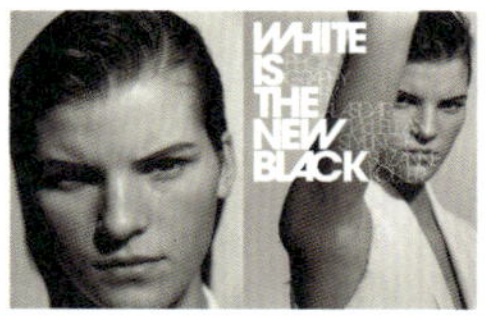

Photography by Alasdair McLellan
Styling by Suzanne Koller
Hair by Luke Hersheson
Makeup by Mack
Model: Madeleine Blomberg

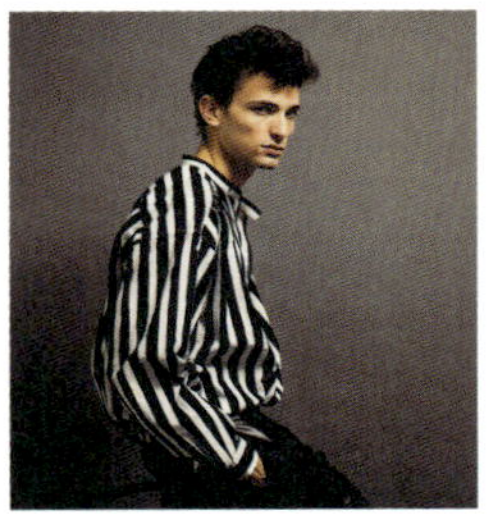

Photography by Suzanne Koller
Styling by Suzanne Koller
Hair by Marion Anée
Model: Christopher Niquet

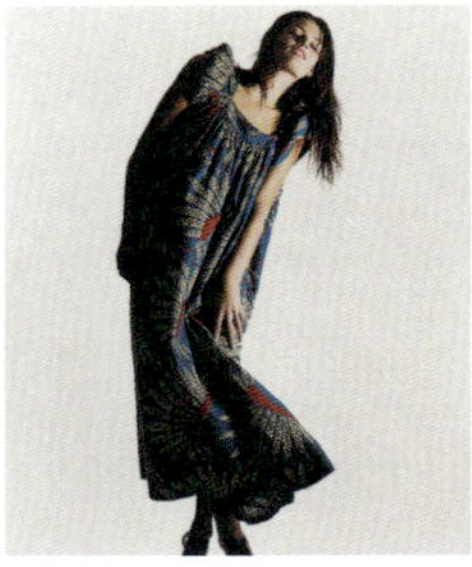

Photography by David Sims
Styling by Anna Cockburn
Hair by Eugene Souleiman
Makeup by Val Garland
Model: Isabeli Fontana

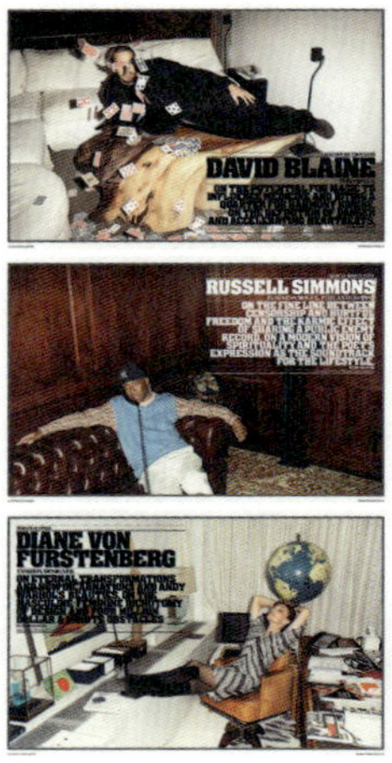

Photography by Maciek Kobielski

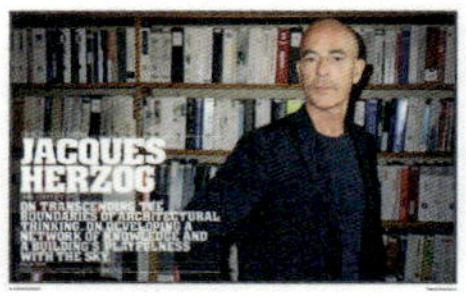

Photography by Ami Sioux

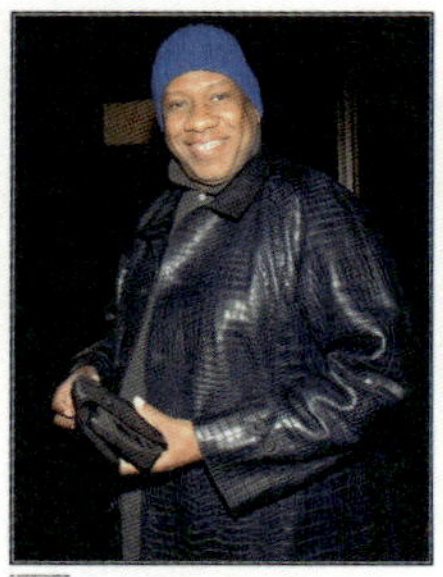

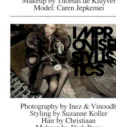

Photography by Patrick McMullan

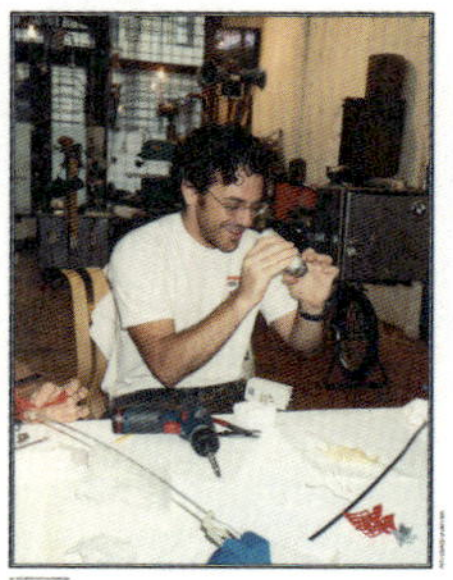

Photography by KT Auleta

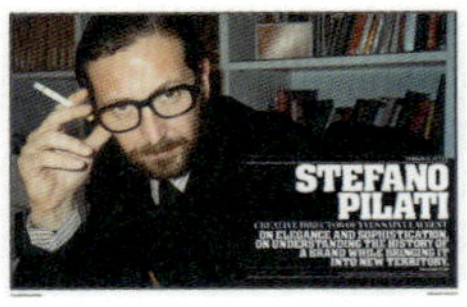

Photography by Katja Rahlwes

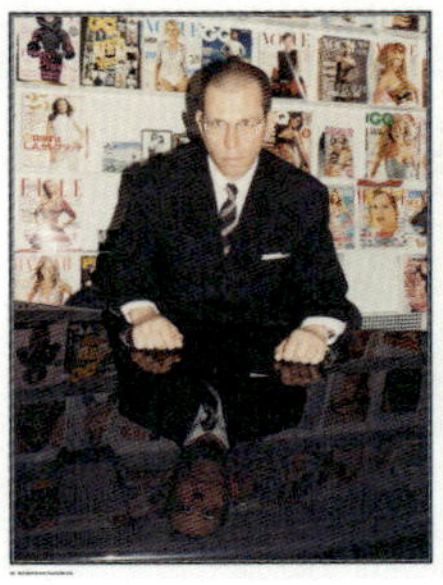

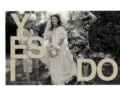

Photography by Juergen Teller

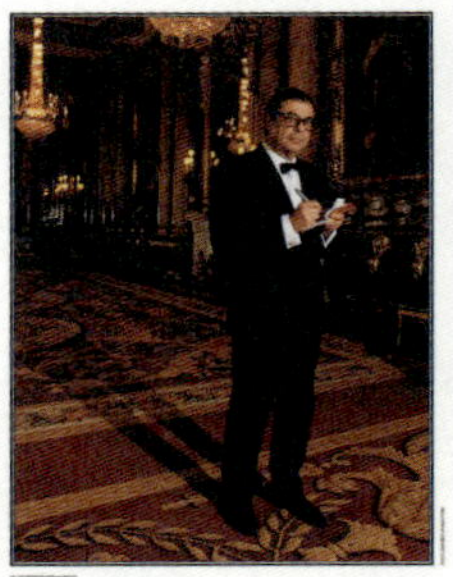

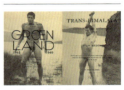

Photography by Jonathan Becker

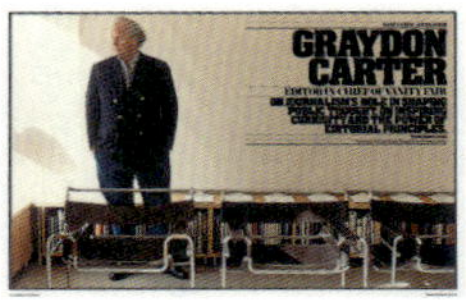

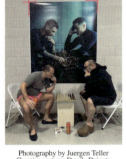

Photography by Christopher Sturman

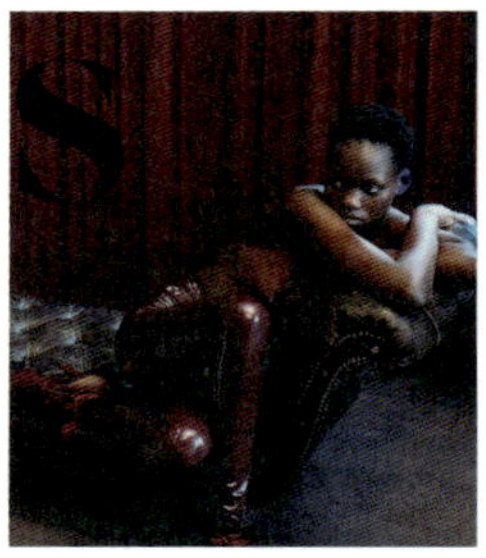

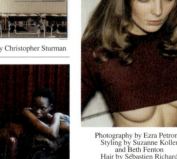

Photography by Mert Alas
and Marcus Piggott
Styling by Jane How
Hair by Anthony Turner
Makeup by Thomas de Kluyver
Model: Caren Jepkemei

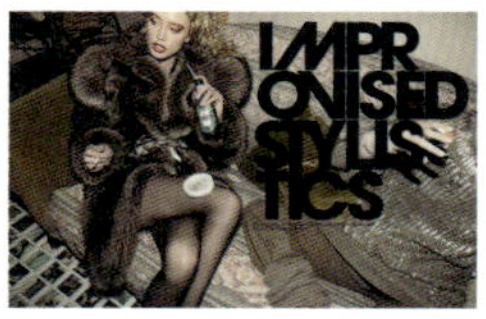

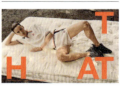

Photography by Inez & Vinoodh
Styling by Suzanne Koller
Hair by Christiaan
Makeup by Dick Page
Models: Shalom Harlow and Raquel Zimmermann

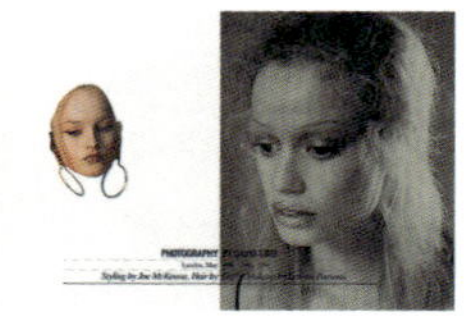

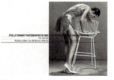

Photography by David Sims
Styling by Joe McKenna
Hair by Duffy
Makeup by Lauren Parsons
Models: Jean Campbell and Abby

Photography by Glen Luchford
Styling by Jane How
Hair by Soichi Inagaki
Makeup by Lucia Pica
Models: Toni Bagley, Edwina Preston, and extras

Photography by Bruce Weber

Photography by Juergen Teller
Creative partner: Dovile Drizyte
Styling by Jane How
Hair by Kei Terada
Makeup by Sunao Takahashi
and Pia Gartner
Talents: Juergen Teller, Ezra Petronio, Lana Petrusevych, and Dovile Drizyte

Photography by Ezra Petronio
Styling by Suzanne Koller
and Beth Fenton
Hair by Sébastien Richard
Makeup by Lucia Pica
Models: Raquel Zimmermann, Eniko Mihalik, Lara Stone, and Dree Hemingway

Photography by Alasdair McLellan
Styling by Benjamin Bruno
Hair by Anthony Turner
Makeup by Lynsey Alexander
Model: Anne-Catherine Lacroix

Photography by Inez & Vinoodh
Styling by Joe McKenna
Hair by Christiaan
Makeup by Lisa Butler
Model: Stella Tennant

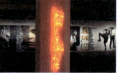

Photography by Mathieu Boutang
and Lana Petrusevych

ACKNOWLEDGMENTS

I WISH TO EXPRESS MY GRATITUDE TO THE FOLLOWING

A.P.C.
Adidas
Alaïa
Ash
Bettter
BLESS
BPI
Bureau Betak
Cacharel
Carolina Herrera
Carven
Chanel
Chloé
Christian Lacroix
Claudie Pierlot
Colette
Comme des Garçons
Costa Brazil
Coty
Delabel
Dior
Dsquared2
Dunhill
Ed Banger
Emilio Pucci
Estée Lauder
Evian
Fendi
Fischerspooner
Gibo
Giorgio Armani
Givaudan
Glossier
Gucci
Guerlain
H&M
Helmut Lang
Hennessy
Hermès
Hussein Chalayan
Iro
Jacquemus
Jean Paul Gaultier
Jérôme Dreyfuss
Jil Sander
Kitsuné
La Bouche Rouge
Lacoste
Lanvin
Le Bon Marché
Lemaire

Lisa Marie Fernandez
Loewe
L'Oréal
Louis Vuitton
Mango
Mansur Gavriel
Massimo Dutti
Miu Miu
Nanushka
Nike
Nina Ricci
Nordstrom
Parcels
Pirelli
Prada
Profirst
Puig
Repossi
Revlon
Rochas
Saint Laurent
Salvatore Ferragamo
Seventy One Gin
Solid & Striped
Sonia Rykiel
Sony Ericsson
Sportmax
Study Magazine
The Society Management
The Webster
Tommy Hilfiger
Tory Burch
Uniqlo
Vanessa Seward
Veronique Branquinho
Victoria Beckham
Villa Moda
Virgin
Yves Salomon
Zara

1972 Agency
Aaron de Mey
Aaron Petronio
Aaron Rose
Adélaïde d'Orléans
Adrian Joffe
Afif Baroudi
Agnès B.
Airport Agency
Akki Shirakawa
Alain Wertheimer
Alasdair McLellan

Alastair McKimm
Alber Elbaz
Alessandro Michele
Alexandre Calogeropoulos
Alexandre de Betak
Alexandre Thumerelle
Alister Mackie
Alix Browne
Amber Olson
Amber Richards
Anastasia Barbieri
Anders Edström
André Saraiva
Andre Walker
Andres Guarrido
Angela Neal
Ángela Picon
Angelo Flaccavento
Anita Bitton
Anja Rubik
Ann D'Ovidio
Anna Ewers
Anne-Gael Senic
Annika McVeigh
Anoushka Borghesi
Anthony Seklaoui
Anthony Turner
Anthony Vaccarello
Antoine Arnault
Anuschka Blommers
Anya Yiapanis
Arnaud Michaux
Art + Commerce
Artlist
Ashley Brokaw
Aude Delerue
Audrey Houssin
Audrey Marnay
Aurélie Bidermann
Ayesha Arefin
Aymeric Delaroche-Vernet
Bastien Daguzan
Ben Grimes
Bénédicte Fournier
Benjamin Bornazzini
Benjamin Bruno
Bob Recine
Brachfeld/
Brianne Almeida
Brigitte Sondag
Bruce Weber
Bruno Pani
Bruno Pavlovsky

Bruno Sialelli
Cadence Image
Calliste Agency
Camilla Nickerson
Camilla Thomas
Camille Bidault-Waddington
Camille de Vaumas
Camille Vincent
Candice Marks
Carina Frey
Carlos Nazario
Carmen Kass
Carolina Queirós
Caroline Bun
Caroline de Maigret
Caroline Deroche Pasquier
Caroline Javoy
Casey Spooner
Catherine Mollanger
Cédric Charbit
Cédric Charlier
Charles Hardouin
Charlotte Beauvisage
Charlotte Cotton
Charlotte Tilbury
Chateau Marmont
Chiltern Firehouse
Chloë Sevigny
Christelle Cocquet
Christiaan
Christian Astuguevieille
Christian Lacroix
Christine Godard
Christophe Eon
Christophe Lemaire
Christopher Michael
Christopher Niquet
Christopher Simmonds
Cierra Sherwin
Clara 3000
Clara Jane Matteucci
Clare Waight Keller
Claude Closky
Colin Dodgson
Collier Schorr
Covadonga Alonso
Craig McDean
Cyril Cabellos
Daft Punk
Dallas Contemporary
Damien Boissinot
Dan Caten
Daniela Andrier

ACKNOWLEDGMENTS

Darius Khondji
David Blot
David Owen
David Sims
Dean Caten
Deborah Aaronson
Delphine Mollanger
Demna Gvasalia
Desiree Heiss
Diane Kendal
Dick Page
Didier Malige
DigitArt
Dirk Seiden Schwan
Dovile Drizyte
Drieke Leenknegt
Duan Duan Wu
Duc Liao
Duffy
Edward Brachfeld
Edy Gassmann
Eleni Gatsou
Eliza Conlon
Elizabeth Sulcer
Elliott Smedley
Elodie David Touboul
Emilio Montero
Emily Weiss
Emmaline Saito
Emmanuel de Buretel
Emmanuelle Alt
Emmanuelle Mayer
Éric Troncy
Eugene Souleiman
Eva Moreau Ikidbachian
Eve Lacheteau
Fabien Baron
Fabio Zambernardi
Fabiola Barzan
Fallon Castella
Fei Gwee
Felipe Oliveira Baptista
Ferdinando Verderi
Floriana Gavriel
Floriane de Saint Pierre
FOT Imprimeurs
Francesca Bellettini
Francis Vandenbussche
Francisco Costa
Franck Durand
François Bouchara
François du Chatenet
Fred Woodward

Frédéric Appaire
Frédéric Sanchez
Gaia Repossi
Galerie Gmurzynska
Geoffroy de La Bourdonnaye
Gérard Issert
Gerard Santos
Gerhard Steidl
Gideon Ponte
Gildas Loaëc
Gilles Andrier
Giorgina Jolly
Giorgio Armani
Giovanna Martial
Giovanni Testino
Giulia DiGiuseppe
Glen Luchford
Granon Digital
Gregory Spencer
Guido Mocafico
Guido Palau
Guillaume Gellusseau
Guillaume Salomon
Guillaume Troncy
Gustave Rudman
Haider Ackermann
Hami Delimi
Hannah MacGibbon
Hans Ulrich Obrist
Happy Massee
Harley Weir
Harriet Quick
Hedi Slimane
Helmut Lang
Henry Leutwyler
Henry Wolf
Hiromi Ueda
Honey Dijon
Horst Diekgerdes
Hussein Chalayan
Imprimerie du Marais
Inacio Ribeiro
Ines Kaag
Inez Van Lamsweerde
Inge Grognard
Isaac Ross
Isabelle Bscher
Isabelle Des Garets
Jack Dahl
Jackson Tenessee
James Chinlund
James Gilchrist
James Pecis

Jamie Hawkesworth
Jan Rivera Bosch
Jane How
Janvier
Jarvis Cocker
Jawara
Jay Choi
Jean-Baptiste Dupuis
Jean-Baptiste Mondino
Jean Bousquet
Jean Colonna
Jean Paul Gaultier
Jean-Pierre Blanc
Jean Touitou
Jefferson Hack
Jérôme Dreyfuss
Jérôme Viger-Kohler
Jil Sander
Jimmy Paul
JN Production
Joan Braun
João Rebelo
Joe McKenna
Johann Rupert
John Demsey
Johnny Dufort
Johnny Hallyday
Jonathan de Villiers
Jonathan Ros
José Manuel Albesa
Joseph Toledano
Judith Touitou
Juergen Teller
Julia Hackel
Julia Lange
Julie Pelipas
Justinian Kfoury
Karen Quek
Karim Rahman
Karim Sadli
Karl Lagerfeld
Karla Otto
Katariina Lamberg
Kate Moss
Katia Beauchamp
Katia Hakko
Katie Barker
Katie Grand
Katie Hillier
Katja Rahlwes
Katy England
KCD
Kevin Rosa

Khoa Dodinh
Kim Chapiron
Kim Jones
Kim Laidlaw
Kim Sion
Kozue Tokuda
Kristina Bui
Laeticia Hallyday
Lana Petrusevych
Larissa Hofmann
Laudomia Pucci
Laure Hériard-Dubreuil
Lauren Parsons
Laurence Touitou
Laurie Castilloux-Bouchard
Leela Petronio
Leslie David
Lionel Vermeil
Lisa Butler
Lisa Marie Fernandez
Liz Collins
Liz Goldwyn
Loïc Prigent
Lotta Volkova
Lottie Walsh
Louise Meylan
Louise Wilson
Lucia Pica
Lucia Pieroni
Lucie Cluzeau
Lucien Pagès
Lucy Baxter
Luigi Murenu
Lynsey Alexander
Magdalena Frackowiak
Maggie Chamoun
Magnus Unnar
Maida Gregori Boina
Malcolm Edwards
Malgosia Bela
Malina Joseph Gilchrist
Mandarine
Marc Jacobs
Marc Puig
Marco Bizzarri
Marcus Piggott
Maria Elena Cima
Marie Chaix
Marie Fioriti
Marie Jacoupy
Marie Tantet
Marieke Liewehr
Marine Molinario

ACKNOWLEDGMENTS

Mario Sorrenti
Marion Anée
Marion Lepori
Marion Robine
Marion Zaphirato
Mark Borthwick
Mark Carrasquillo
Mark Holgate
Mark Kean
Mark Levy
Mark Weston
Marta Ortega Pérez
Martine Sitbon
Mary Komasa
Maryline Jost-Kiehl
Masha Novoselova
Masha Orlov
Mathias Augustyniak
Mathias Rastorfer
Mathieu Boutang
Maureen Chiquet
Maxime Plescia-Büchi
Melanie Ward
Mélina Brossard
Mert Alas
Michael Amzalag
Michel Gaubert
Michela Tafuri
Miuccia Prada
Myriam Obadia
Myriam Serrano
Nadège Winter
Nadine Fonta
Natacha Ramsay-Levi
Nathalie Canguilhem
Nathalie Ours
New-Tone
Nicolas Breton
Nicolas Despis
Nicolas Gerlier
Nicolas Ghesquière
Nicolas Trembley
Niels Schumm
Nightshift
Nikolai von Bismarck
Norman Lemay
North Six
Ola Rindal
Oliver Hadlee Pearch
Oliver Ress
Olivier Bialobos
Olivier Theyskens
Olivier Zahm
Ondine Azoulay
Osana Ekue
Paco Raynal
Panos Yiapanis
Paola Bicci
Paola Vanin
Paolo Roversi
Partner Films
Pascal Dangin
Pat McGrath
Patrice Wagner
Patrick Li
Patrick McMullan
Patrizio Bertelli
Paul Deneve
Paul Hanlon
Paul Sevigny
Pauline Vandenbussche
Pedro Winter
Penelope Caillet
Peter Baldaszti
Peter Copping
Peter Doroshenko
Peter Petronio
Peter Philips
Philip Andelman
Philippe Contini
Philippe Lacombe
Philippe Miro
Phoebe Philo
Picto
Piergiorgio Del Moro
Pierre Consorti
Pierre Gassmann
Pierre-Olivier Agostini
Pierre Rougier
Pieter Mulier
Poppy Bartlett
PR Consulting
Quentin De Briey
Rachel Chandler
Rachel Mansur
Raf Simons
Ralph Toledano
Raquel Zimmermann
Ray Tetauira
Rebecca Leigh Longendyke
Reed Krakoff
Rei Kawakubo
Riccardo Bellini
Riccardo Tisci
Richard Buckley
Richard Burbridge
Richard Phillips
Robin Derrick
Robin Galiegue
Roman Coppola
Rory Satran
Rosco Production
Ruba Abu-Nimah
Rudi Lewis
Sabrina Marshall
Saif Mahdhi
Sam Rock
Samuel Ellis Scheinman
Sandra Purificato
Sandra Sándor
Sandrine Macé Krabal
Sarah Andelman
Sarah Creal
Sarah Dawes
Sarah Mower
Sarah Petronio
Sébastien Richard
Sebastien Bascle
Second Name Agency
Senta Simond
Serge Brunschwig
Shalom Harlow
Shay Ashual
Siddhartha Shukla
Silvia Galfo
Simon Holloway
Simon Porte Jacquemus
Sissy Vian
Skye Parrott
Sølve Sundsbø
Sophia Kokosalaki
Sophie Boilley
Sophie Hodgkin
Spike Jonze
Stan Kosyakovskiy
Stefano Pilati
Stefano Poli
Stephane Lancien
Stéphane Marais
Stephanie Kunz
Stéphanie Moisdon
Stéphanie Morel
Steve Mackey
Steven Meisel
Stewart Searle
Streeters
Susan Cianciolo
Susanne Deeken
Suzanne Clements
Suzanne Koller
Sylvie Fleury
Tamara Taichman
Tasso de Góes Ferreira
Terry Richardson
Tess Petronio
Thaddaeus Ropac
The Mercer Hotel
Thea Barkoff
Theo Wenner
Thomas Butkiewicz
Thomas de Kluyver
Thomas Lagrange
Tim Blanks
Tom Pecheux
Tomaso Galli
Tory Burch
Total Management
Trouble Management
Tyler Mitchell
Val Garland
Valeria Herklotz
Valerie Duport
Valerie Hermann
Valerie Weill
Vanessa Seward
Venetia Scott
Verde Visconti
Véronique Branquinho
Vick Mihaci
Vieson Guevara
Victoire Nicodème
Victoria Beckham
Vincent Olivieri
Vincent Thilloy
Vincent Viard
Vinoodh Matadin
Violeta Lopez
Virgil Abloh
Virginie Viard
Vito Saccaro
Walter Schupfer
Ward
Wendy Rowe
Wes Anderson
Wilson Oryema
Wladimir Schall
Xavier Encinas
Yadim
Yann Gauthier
Yves Salomon
Zachary Ohlman
Zoë Ghertner

FUTURE PROJECTS
SCAN THE ABOVE QR CODE TO EXPLORE PROJECTS AND WORKS
COMPLETED IN THE YEARS FOLLOWING THE PUBLISHING OF THIS BOOK.

E-SHOP SPACE
SCAN THE ABOVE QR CODE TO ACCESS AN E-SHOP
SPACE EXCLUSIVELY AVAILABLE THROUGH THIS BOOK.

EZRA PETRONIO
VISUAL THINKING & IMAGE-MAKING

Phaidon Press
2 Cooperage Yard
London E15 2QR

Phaidon Press Inc.
65 Bleecker Street
New York NY 10012

phaidon.com

First published 2023
© 2023 Phaidon Press Limited

ISBN 978 1 83866 712 2

A CIP catalog record for this book is available from the British Library and the Library of Congress.

All rights reserved. No part of this publication may be reproduced, stored in a retrieval system or transmitted, in any form or by any means, electronic, mechanical, photocopying, recording or otherwise, without the express written permission of Phaidon Press Limited.

Commissioning Editor: Deb Aaronson
Project Editor: Sophie Hodgkin
Production Controllers: Nerissa Dominguez Vales and Sue Medlicott

Edited with Lana Petrusevych
Art Direction and Design: Eva Moreau Ikidbachian, Petronio Associates
Design Assistant: Kevin Rosa
Editorial assistants: Carolina Queirós and Emmaline Saito
Copy Editors: Peter Petronio and Reine Marie Melvin
Engraving: Mandarine

Still Life Photography: Mathieu Boutang and Philippe Lacombe

Every reasonable effort has been made to acknowledge the ownership of copyright for photographs included in this volume. Any errors are inadvertent and will be corrected in subsequent editions provided notification is sent in writing to the publisher.

Printed in China